MILLENNIUM

Apocalypse and Antichrist and
Old English Monsters c. 1000 A. D.

MILLENNIUM

Apocalypse and Antichrist and Old English Monsters c. 1000 A. D.

Contraria sunt complementaria

"Now, therefore, it is meet to sing of endings, of what was, and
may be no longer. ... A last sigh for a lost world, a tear for its
passing. Also, however, a last hurrah."—Salman Rushdie,
The Moor's Last Sigh.

Zacharias P. Thundy
Northern Michigan University

Cross Cultural Publications, Inc.

CrossRoads Books

Cross Cultural Publicaations, Inc.
Cross Roads Books
Post Office Box 506
Notre Dame, Indiana 46556
U S A
Phone: (219) 273-6526, 1-800-561-6526
Fax: (219) 273-5973

First Cross Cultural Publication Edition 1998
Manufactured in the U S A
Set in Bembo True Type

ISBN: 0-940121-51-4

Library of Congress Catalog-in-Publication Data

Thundy, Zacharias P.
Millennium: Apocalypse, Antichrist, and Old English Monsters c. 1000
Includes bibliography and index
History—Religion—Literature—Hinduism—Buddhism—Christianity—Islam
2. Anglo-Saxon History—Old English Poetry—Old English Literature
3. Apocalypse—Origins—Development in East and West
4. Antichrist—Origins—development in East and West
98-73773

CONTENTS

APOCALYPSE AND ANTICHRIST IN THE FIRST MILLENNIUM

APOCALYPTIC TRADITION OF
EARLY ENGLAND

Preface

I live on two locations in the Midwest, commuting between Marquette, Michigan, and South Bend, Indiana. I notice the very same phenomenon repeating itself in both cities. In Marquette, the "Beef-A-Roo" restaurant that I used to drive past every day is now Mandarin Garden, a Chinese restaurant; in South Bend, the Kentucky Fried Chicken restaurant that my son was fond of eating at is now "The Malabar, Cuisine of India." Thirty-five percent of the student population of California is Asian. On account of the large number of Asian students at MIT, some people say that *MIT* stands for "Made in Taiwan"!—one MIT graduate recently corrected me, "*MIT* stands for 'Millionaires in Training'." These are examples—by no means isolated but replicated all over Europe as well—of the counter-colonization of the West by the East. East continues to leak into the West across porous borders as in the past. One of the intentions of this book is to show that the convenient and comfortable division between East and West in the world of culture and literature is a very artificial one and that the boundary lines between the two are so fuzzy that often one is not easily distinguishable from the other. I shall develop this theory in the concluding chapter, "Fuzzy Literature," according to the principles of fuzzy logic.

Not only culinary art but also modern culture and economy have gone global during the last few decades. Internet and telecommunication technology are bringing worlds that were once far apart together—and doing it faster now than ever before. What happens on the Pacific rim has its reverberations on the Atlantic rim. The volatility of the stock markets is an excellent case in point: the ups and downs on the stock markets in Hong Kong, Seoul, and Jakarta have immediate impact on the stock markets of London, New York, and Paris the very same day.

Indeed, lately the world has gone topsy-turvy. The Atlantic colonization of the last millennium has been replaced by the counter-colonization of the West of the Atlantic rim by the East of the Pacific rim. Up until the

1950s America looked westward across the Atlantic to Europe. The fact that now twice as many planes and ships fly and ply across the Pacific as across the Atlantic plainly indicates that there is more commercial and cultural intercourse between the East and the United States than ever before. The recent study *Millennium:A History of the Last Thousand Years* (1995) by Felipé Fernandez-Armesto is a fascinating analysis of the fate of civilizations in which "'western supremacy' is presented as imperfect, precarious, and short-lived" (18). He writes:

> As the end of the millennium draws on, it is already apparent that the preponderance of Atlantic civilization is over and that the initiative has shifted again, this time to some highly "developed," technically proficient communities of the Pacific seaboard, typified by California and Japan". (18)

The Pacific challenge, mainly from China, Japan, the Indian Peninsula, and the rest of the Pacific rim represented by California, leads "back to a world balance similar to that of a thousand years ago, when initiative in human affairs belonged on Pacific coasts" (14). In fact, the rise of Atlantic hegemony itself began with the absorption of Oriental influences in arts, sciences, and technology by the West: "Throughout the first-half of our millennium, and for a thousand years before that, all fruitful initiatives in scientific ideas, all powerful innovations in technology, came from China" (707). Ironically, the three inventions that helped establish Western hegemony—the magnetic compass, gunpowder, and the printing press—existed in China for centuries before they were introduced into Europe. Joseph Needham's classical series Science *and Civilization in China* (1954 -) lists several other inventions the West borrowed from China between the first and the eighteenth centuries: the efficient harness, the suspension bridge, the cross bow, water-powered metallurgical bowing machines, the sternport rudder, canal lock-gates, the iron-chain suspension bridge, cast iron, the first cybernetic machine, the man-lifting kite, paper, porcelain, and the parachute. The newest and most surprising revelation is that of the mechanical clockwork, which China had been using for six centuries, long before the clocks of fourteenth-century Europe. "Important inventions in hydraulic engineering traveled westwards; and despite the supposed conservatism of sailors, there was hardly any Western century which did not see the adoption of some nautical technique from the East" (IV: xlviii). Of course, the West returned the favor by bestowing on China the crankshaft, trepanning, water clocks, and force-pumping for liquids. Already before the end of the first millennium, China and India had created a numerical system with a symbol for zero while Europe was still struggling with the Roman numeral system. By the twelfth century, the Arabs borrowed the

Indian mathematical system and popularized it in Europe during the Arab
dominance of Spain and Sicily.

Today the West is re-seeking Eastern technology and expertise, and Eastern technological products overflow our hi-tech stores and parking lots.
We are also rediscovering Tao and Zen, Yoga and the *Gita*, martial arts and
alternate health-care products perhaps more eagerly than before. No one
seems to think any longer that such cultural exchange is a "waste of Christian kisses on a heathen idol's foot," as Kipling would put it. This book will
reveal that the Europeans of the first millennium also did what their children are doing in the second millennium and will continue to do in the
third millennium by acquiring the Oriental taste not only in culinary art
but also in apocalyptic thinking and literary art—from the Persians, Indians, Chinese, and Arabs.

The idea of the end has always fascinated us. Not only are we interested
in our own death but also in the possible end of the domination of a political party like the Democrats and the Republicans in government and politics, in the death of languages, in the disappearance of biological species, in
the decline and fall of empires like the Roman, German, British, and Soviet
empires, and in the rise of a superpower like the United States in the West
and of China in the East. Thus the twin poles of rise and fall, birth and
death, and East and West seem to continually attract and repel each other in
our thinking. This idea is particularly interesting during these last few years
of the second millennium of the Christian Era, even in countries that are
not professedly Christian.

At this juncture in our cultural history when we are intrigued by the
prospects of the end of the second millennium and the birth of the third
millennium, it is useful to look back to the time when our ancestors mulled
over the end of the first millennium. Their thinking was characterized by
the twin notions of Apocalypse and Antichrist. For them Apocalypse sig-
naled the end of the universe brought about in cataclysmic fashion with
the appearance of the demonic figure of Antichrist, who would battle the
benevolent power of Christ, the establisher of a new era and a new earth.

The general public is fascinated during the last years of the millennium
by the idea of the Apocalypse and the specter of Antichrist; for example,
Fox's TV thriller "Millennium" on Friday nights, with its images of Armageddon, is a very popular show. In bookstores around the country, prophecies of Nostradamus, *The Bible Code*, and a number of American Indian
and New Age books are best sellers; people are not tired of watching mov-
ies like *Contact* and *The Seventh Seal*. According to a recent *US News*
poll, sixty-six percent of Americans say they believe that Jesus Christ will

return to earth some day—an increase from the sixty-one percent who
believed in the Second Coming three years ago. Of course, America's fascination with apocalypticism began with Christopher Columbus, who
believed the world would end in 1650, and with the early Puritans who
thought that their New England settlements were the outposts of the kingdom Jesus Christ would establish at his Second Coming.

I have divided this book about the religious history of the Apocalypse,
Antichrist during the first Christian millennium into two parts: macro history and micro history. The first part is a historical overview of Apocalypse
and Antichrist in the literature of the Eastern world and the Western world
during the first millennium and before, stretching all the way from the frontiers of India to the wide world of Mediterranean culture. It is presented
more or less in summary fashion. The second part shows how complex are
the notions of the Apocalypse and Antichrist toward the end of the first
millennium for the people of England known as the Anglo-Saxons.

The introductory essay shows that our abiding interest in the importance of the end of a millennium is an exercise both in wisdom and
folly. Though the year 2000 is an arbitrary year in the computation of
the Christian calendar, its imminent arrival could turn into a nightmare
on account of the computer crisis it may bring about. The anticipated
computer crash across the world could very well create an economic
meltdown. Nonetheless, the end of a millennium is also a call for renewal. Unfortunately, history shows that calls for apocalyptic asceticism
have created not only renewal and hope but chaos and tragedy.

Part one, chapter one, traces the history of the formation of the idea of
the Apocalypse from various cultural traditions such as Jewish and Islamic
besides Christian. Chapter two dwells at length on the crystallization of
this tradition in the last book of the Christian Bible called the Apocalypse
and provides an analysis of the literary genre of the apocalypse. Chapter
three shows how this literary tradition developed differently but in close
proximity and association with the cultural worlds known today as the
Christian East and Christian West—Rome and Byzantium—with the world
of Islam emerging phoenix-like from the ashes of the Eastern Roman
Empire. Chapter four tells the story of the evolution of Antichrist in the
East and his migration from the East to the West.

Part two is an attempt to locate the idea of both the Apocalypse and
Antichrist in Britain among the early English people, who are traditionally
known as "Anglo-Saxons" in history. After identifying the ethnic origins—
albeit controversially—of the English people in chapter five, I shall discuss
in chapter six the cultural heritage of the English or Anglo-Saxons as bor-

dering on the Eastern world. Chapter seven shows rather briefly and derivatively how the preachers and poets of Anglo-Saxon England developed a literary culture on the Apocalypse and Antichrist. Chapter eight is an attempt to summarily present the Christianized pagan view of the apocalyptic tradition as found in the Germanic tradition of Iceland. Chapter nine, the longest chapter in the book, shows how an English poet fused Western Christian, Eastern Christian, and Germanic apocalyptic traditions imaginatively and created the national epic *Beowulf.* The Appendix gives modern English translations of three sermons on the end of the world and Antichrist by Archbishop Wulfstan of England, who lived at the end of the first millennium and the beginning of the second millennium.

In the conclusion I present my theoretical reflections on the nature of literature—I call all literature "fuzzy literature"—as a forum of various belongings, as a preserve of fault lines, as a presence of noted absences, and as a reflection of reality in the elusive terms of "East" and "West." Indeed, this book is all about the fuzzy relationship that exists between East and West, between Eastern literature and Western literature on the subject of Apocalypse and Antichrist during the first millennium of the Common Era/Christian Era. The biblical literary genre of the apocalypse as well as the Christian idea of Antichrist is an essential centerpiece of Western Christianity; however, my study will show that biblical and European apocalypse and Antichrist are as much Eastern as well. As the Anglo-Saxon world of the first millennium is Eastern in many ways, so also the classic *Beowulf* is an Eastern text. That means, contraries like non-Christian and Christian apocalypses, historical and transcendental antichrists, Eastern thought and its Western adaptations coexisted as complementaries in the England of the first millennium. And they still do.

Finally, I wish to record my gratitude to Northern Michigan university and its administration for providing me time and other assistance during the preparation of this book. The University of Notre Dame was my home during the time I wrote this book. My good friend Jim Jones carefully read the manuscript and made several suggestions for revision. Karen Wallingford helped in the final preparation of this manuscript and its index. My professional colleagues all over the world on the Internet have been terrific intellectual resources for the development of ideas. My sincere thanks to you all. As always, my wife Gina and sons Zach and Tonio continue to support me with love and care unmatched in this world. I dedicate this book to my family with all my affection.

Millennium—Wisdom and Folly

And it shall come to pass afterwards: your sons and your daughters shall prophesy and the old among you shall dream dreams and your young shall see visions. (Joel 2: 28)

India's explosion of five nuclear devices on May 11 and May 13, 1998, dramatized once again the specter of the nuclear danger lurking in the wings. The meltdown of the Chernobyl atomic reactor, the radiation leak at the Three Mile Island site, and the presence of thousands of operational nuclear warheads in the weapons arsenals of Russia, the U.S., France, China, Britain, Israel, and India are also grim reminders of a pending, unforeseen, unpredictable nuclear holocaust that our generation may face any time in the future, even in 2000. What was particularly surprising about India's blasts was that the intelligence corps of all the nations, especially the CIA, were caught flat-footed—not once but twice—reminding us of the possibility of an unexpected nuclear catastrophe, like the sudden appearance of the legendary Antichrist and his short but disastrous reign, the harbinger of imminent end. India's military strategy makes sense: it is flanked on two sides by hostile nations, Pakistan and China; it had fought three wars with Pakistan during the last fifty years; China is a military colossus which invaded India suddenly and successfully in 1962. Like India, more nations, living in tough neighborhoods, may soon arm themselves with the bomb, possibly ushering in an apocalyptic scenario, similar to what the world saw in August 1914 when the nations of Europe armed themselves to the teeth, only with less formidable weapons of mass destruction. How do we keep the nuclear genie bottled up in order to prevent the end of the world, we ask ourselves.

Indeed, the idea of the end of the world had been with us from the very

beginning. Teleology, or preoccupation with ends and comfort in conclu-
sions, is one of our striking characteristics. As soon as the day dawns, we
look forward to the end of the working day; come Monday, immediately
we envision Friday and sigh with relief as the sun rises on Friday. We also
look forward to the dawning of a new day to put an end to the insanity of
darkness; likewise, we soon get tired of weekends and seek out the stress
and strain of the work week. Then, as we survive winter's chills, spring
cheers us up, and we long to resume the pilgrimage of life like Chaucer's
Canterbury pilgrims:

> When the sweet showers of April have pierced to the root the dryness of
> March, and bathed every vein in moisture whose quickening brings forth
> the flowers; when Zephyr also with his sweet breath has quickened the ten-
> der new shoots in holt and moor, and the young sun has run his half-course
> in the Ram, and little birds make melody and sleep all night with eyes open,
> so nature pricks them in their hearts; then folks long to go on pilgrimage to
> renowned shrines in sundry distant lands, and palmers to seek strange shores.
> And especially from every shire's end in England they go their way to Can-
> terbury, to seek the holy blessed martyr who helped them when they were
> sick. (lines 1-18)

We entertain a love-hate relationship toward all beginnings and ends.
We hate all beginnings, noting with sadness that they smell of mortality. All
the same we love endings because we know that there is no new beginning
without end, no construction without destruction: "Unless the grain of
wheat falls and dies, it will remain the same, but if it dies it will bear abun-
dant fruit, reminds the Gospel (John 12:24). We can't have one without the
other. We console ourselves: "For everything there is a season, and a time
for every matter under heaven: a time to be born and a time to die...a time
for war and a time for peace" (Ecclesiastes 3: 1-8).

Most of us do not expect to see our one-hundredth birthday; we are
often more than satisfied with our biblically allotted age of three-score-
and-ten. As for infancy, we celebrate the completions of days, weeks, and
months till the child is a one-year old. After that critical date we limit the
calibration of celebration to annual birthdays. After Baptism, come Communion and Confirmation for Christians. After celebrating the rites of
puberty and nuptials, we count time in chunks of twenty-five and tens—
silver jubilee, golden jubilee, and diamond jubilee, septuagenerianhood,
octogenerianhood, nonagenarian status, and the century mark. If we die
before we reach the milestones of silver, gold, and diamond, we console
ourselves, saying, "Who the gods love die young"; indeed, the end of life on
earth is the beginning of the life with the gods; life is not ended; it has only
changed. We concur with Virgil: "Tempora mutantur et nos mutamur in

illis" (Times change and we change with them).

As for the life of nations, normally we establish eras—from or before the foundation of Rome, from or before the birth of Christ, from and before the Hegira (the Prophet's flight from Mecca to Medina). We celebrate the milestones of the eras in hundreds because usually a dynasty or a certain nation tends to last only a few hundred years. That makes sense. The Roman Empire probably lasted the longest; even on the invincible British Empire the sun set after two hundred years; the ideal world of the classless society envisaged by the Soviet Empire lasted less than a hundred years. Of course, reaching the century mark is a significant achievement in the game of cricket as in the life of a nation; in American football one-hundred yards of rushing during one game and a thousand yards during the regular season are considered important achievements.

Calendrics and Convenience

Computation is arbitrary when we calculate the end and the beginning of an age in the life of nations. The dates of the birth of the Roman Empire and of the British Empire are quite arbitrary. Conveniently we fix a date and then count backwards and forwards. In fact, there is no intrinsic value in mathematics for the number 1000. Decimality is not sacred with all cultures; for example, the Mayans in Central America and the Mundas in India preferred vigesimal mathematics based on twenty. In the Christian West we have preferred to go with decimal mathematics learned from the Middle East and to embrace the Mediterranean myth of the thousand-year reign of the Jesus of the Christian book of Apocalypse—an arbitrary choice fraught with important calendric consequences.

The choice of 1000 as a milestone for formulating end in different configurations like 2000, 3000, 5000, and so on holds also a thoroughly limiting factor for the peoples of the Bible (Hebrews, Christians, and Muslims), which interpretatively calculates the age of the human race to a few thousand years. Literal interpreters of the Bible have failed to recognize that humankind, the universe, and the gods are much older. Further, the peoples of the Book operate within a closed universe, the world of the solar system. On the other hand, in Indian mythology, 366 years (a human year is a day for the gods) make a divine year, and 12,000 divine years make an eon (*caturyuga*). One thousand eons make a day of Brahma (*kalpa*), and the same number makes his night. In each *kalpa*, fourteen Manus (Adam-like ancestors of the human race) appear one after another spawning different human races, each one living for a period of 852,000 years! We live currently during the reign of the seventh Manu. We still have a long way to go, many more millennia to go!

The Christian preoccupation with the end of the world at the end of a millennium, on the contrary, takes a limited perspective on the duration of the present universe. If the end must come, it must come soon, trumpets the classical Christian view. Stephen Jay Gould in his *Questioning the Millennium* argues that the basic concept of the millennium in Western culture arose from our mental effort "to wrest order and meaning from a recalcitrant world" (97). Feeling that we can't afford to wait interminably for the inevitable end to come, we are tempted to act hastily and shortsightedly in order to make the best of both worlds. We want to usher in the new world order, the new year, the new glorious age of the triumphant reign of Christ and his saints for a thousand years with more "terminal nuttiness" than profound insight (36). We pray with confidence, "Thy Kingdom come,...for thine is the kingdom, the power, and glory for ever and ever." Of course, Christ cannot start his reign until Antichrist appears. Indeed, some people might even suggest that Antichrist has already appeared in the horizon with the computer revolution.

Computronics and Catastrophe

Computer non-cognoscenti have suddenly arrived at the cognizance that the year 2000 is not an easy-to-fix computer bug and that we are in a state of future shock for the simple reason that most computers use two numbers to represent years and, therefore, can't distinguish between 1900 and 2000 since the computer codes can't comprehend dates beyond 1999. This problem could cause computers around the world to crash on January 1, 2000. The Y2K bug is projected to have a terrible impact on the nation's economy with a possible growth rate of only 0.3 percentage points for the year 1999, according to a Standard & Poor's report prepared for *Business Week* magazine; the cut would be half-a-percentage point off growth in 2000 and 2001.[1] The computer problem will slow down the economy to the turn of a loss of $119 billion in the year 2000.

The blame for this potential tragedy can be squarely laid at the door of the computer industry, which controls our economy and which knew of the enormity of the problem for years. Instead of diverting resources for forging ahead with new productive programs, we will be diverting our energy for fixing old programs. C. Jones, head of Software Productivity Research, says that finding and fixing all Y2K-affected software would require over 700,000 person-years (93). There is truth in the rumor that the year 2000 is to bring in many computer failures which could send the economy into a tail spin. The Federal Reserve policymaker and Central Bank Governor, Susan Phillips, said in an interview on May 5, 1998, that the diversion resources will indeed lead to slower productivity growth and possibly higher inflation: "It is at least something that will be a minor disruption. If it's not done well, it could have more of an impact" (*USA Today*, May 6, 1988, B-1). According to some economists, the projected disaster could be mind-boggling:

> There are 40 years of software "out there," made up of billions of lines of code spread over different programming languages, operating systems, databases, and hardware platforms. It isn't enough for a corporation to debug its own software. It must synchronize with all its vendors, suppliers, and customers in every town and village in every country around the world. Not only must the changes be made, they must be made in exactly the same way. Or computers will crash. If a small regional German *Landesbank*, for example, chooses a different method to solve its Y2K problem than, say, Citibank, their computer systems could corrupt each other as the banks trade currencies. Ditto for a Taiwanese motherboard manufacturer that supplies Dell Computer or Compaq Computer. (154)

One disastrous scenario is that the IRS and Medicare payment systems could experience severe disruptions, stopping the delivery of refunds and reimbursement checks. In fact, some sixty senior corporate executives—from companies like Texas Instruments, Unilever, Ford, Bombardier, and Lloyds TSB Banking—recently warned the leaders of USA, Canada, and Britain that government failure to solve Y2K problems could produce delays in welfare payments, breakdown in revenue-collections and debt-management, disruption of telephone communications systems software, malfunctions in air-traffic control, and serious glitches in defense systems (154). The financial picture is bleak for many major companies and institutions. It has been estimated that the Columbus (Ohio) school system with 65,000 students may have to come up with $8 million to fix its own computers.

What is significant about the computronic catastrophe is that it arrives on the world scene and in popular imagination, like Antichrist, on schedule, in the year 2000 as an unprecedented economic event with a severe jolt to the economy. We may be unwilling and unready to face Antichrist in 2000, but we are getting ready to face the computronic catastrophe of Y2K. The positive outcome of a potential solution to the problem of Y2K is that just as we may be able to avert a computer catastrophe and economic meltdown in the year 2000, we may as well be able to postpone the inevitable advent of Antichrist for an unforeseeable future.

Apocalypse and Crisis Management

The proclamation that apocalypse is at hand is at the heart of the moral teaching and reform-oriented preaching of the masters of religion like Prophet Joel, Tathagata Buddha, John the Baptist, and Jesus the Nazorean. The end is fast approaching and therefore change your ways which are evil and ungodly, they warn almost in unison. All the major religions of the world, as we shall see in the following chapters, thrive on apocalyptic ideology. In particular, apocalypticism is the birthmark and benchmark of Judeo-Christian religious thinking. For example, Prophet Joel spoke to the people of Israel facing exile in Babylon:

> Blow the trumpet in Zion;
> Sound the alarm on my holy mountain!
> Let all the inhabitants of the land tremble,
> For the day of the Lord is coming; it is near,
> A day of darkness and gloom,
> A day of clouds and thick darkness. (12;1-2)

As the beleaguered people of Israel prayed to Yahweh, the Lord felt compassion for them and averted catastrophe and promised an era of peace and prosperity: "Behold, I am sending to you grain, wine, and oil, and you will be satisfied, and I will no more make you a reproach among the nations" (2:19).

A few hundred years later, John the Baptist preached repentance and reform of life and forgiveness of sins:

> Repent, for the kingdom of God is at hand....You brood of vipers! Who warned you to flee from the wrath to come? Bear fruits that befit repentance, and do not begin to say to yourselves, "We have Abraham as our father"; for I tell you, God is able from these stones to raise up children to Abraham. Even now the ax is laid to the root of the trees; every tree therefore that does not bear good fruit is cut down and thrown into the fire." And the multitudes asked him, "What then shall we do?" And he answered them, "He who has two coats, let him share with him who has none; and he who has food, let him do likewise." Tax collectors also came to be baptized, and said to him, "Teacher, what shall we do?" And he said to them, "Collect no more than is appointed you." Soldiers also asked him, "And we, what shall we do?" And he said to them, "Rob no one by violence or by false accusation and be content with your wages". (Luke 3: 7-14)

Jesus, true to the spirit of the meaning of his surname "Nazorean" (rebel and reformer) and echoing the teaching of Buddha, followed the footsteps of his fellow reformer and Cousin John and preached the theme of conversion and urged on his hearers the importance of renunciation of pomp and glory and the adoption of a simple life style as Buddha and the Baptist had done before:

> If any man would come after me, let him deny himself and take up his cross and follow me. For whoever would save his life will lose it, and whoever loses his life for my sake will find it. For what will it profit a man, if he gains the whole world and forfeits his life? Or what shall a man give in return for his life? For the Son of Man is to come with his angels in the glory of his Father, and then he will repay every man for what he has done. (Matt. 16:24-28)

The followers of Jesus continued the same tradition. For instance, the Jesus of the Apocalypse, according to the author of that magnificent literary masterpiece, also threatens the people with dire punishment for those who refuse to change:

> The time is near. Let the evildoer still do evil, and filthy still be filthy, and the righteous do right, and the holy still be holy. Behold, I am coming soon, bringing my recompense, to repay everyone for what he has done. I am the Alpha and the Omega, the first and the last, the beginning and the end. Blessed are those who wash their robes, that they may have the right to the tree of life and that they may enter the city by the gates. Outside are the dogs and sorcerers and fornicators and murderers and idolaters, and everyone who loves and practices falsehood. (Apoc. 22: 10-15)

The rest of this book will show that the apocalyptic spirit of reform and the call to repentance with the promise of good times for the virtuous and bad times for the wicked continued throughout the tumultuous history of Eastern and Western Christianity during the first millennium. The persecuted, wretched, downtrodden, dispossessed, disenfranchised Christians continued to seek comfort and refuge in apocalypticism and in the ideology of the millennial reign of the saints, while the prosperous and empowered believers spiritualized and personalized the notion of the end as pertaining rather to their own certain personal deaths, potential reward in Heaven, possible punishment in Hell, or probable period of purification in Purgatory than to the cosmos. The established Church from the fourth century officially taught that the millennium of the reign of saints had already arrived with the establishment of the triumphant Church since the days of Emperor Constantine and even earlier with the founding of the Church at Pentecost with the Descent of the Holy Ghost after the Ascension of Christ to the right hand of the Father, as St. Augustine would argue in his *City of God.* Thus the idea of a catastrophic millennial end of the world and an impending millennial reign of the saints gradually receded from the official teaching of Church authorities, but the ream just refused to die in the religious and political imagination of the ank and file of the believers, as subsequent chapters in this book will ￼ .ow for the first one thousand years.

Apocalypse and Insanity?

In the twelfth century, the Calabrian abbot Joachim of Fiore, claiming a special Easter revelation, reintroduced the historical reading of the Apocalypse and millenarism into Christianity and forecast the dawning of the third age of the Holy Spirit and of the reformed monastic Church to be ushered in after the defeat of Antichrist. The followers of Joachim saw a role for papacy in the coming crisis leading to a better society. They saw bad popes as precursors or incarnations of Antichrist the false teacher and good popes as agents of Christ in the restoration of God's rule on earth. The fourteenth-century Lollards in England and Hussites in Bohemia identified the Papacy with the evil figures of the Apocalypse. Reformation theologians continued their polemics against the Catholic Church in the same vein and concluded that the Papacy was the institutional avatar of Antichrist. Luther, for example, saw in the three woes pronounced by the eagle in Apocalypse 8:13 as the Heretic Arius, Islam, and the papal empire; however, Luther viewed the biblical millennium as the thousand years that had already begun at the time of the prophecy made in the Apocalypse.

Puritan reformation thought, on the other hand, reversed the European Reformation view of the papacy as the apocalyptic Babylon and preached that the Established Anglican Church was the Babylon in England. John Bale saw in the Apocalypse a record of the struggle of the evangelical Church with the Babylonish Church throughout time as Augustine viewed the history of humankind as an ongoing conflict between the City of God and the City of Man. John Napier, the Scottish mathematician, saw the defeat of the Spanish Armada in 1586 as a triumph over Antichrist and predicted that the last age of history had begun in 1541 and would last until 1786. Newton carried over the mathematical approach to record prophetic history with precise dating to the dismay of Voltaire. Earlier, Joseph Mede of Cambridge had calculated that Christ's Second Coming would take place between 1625 and 1716, bringing about a millennium of peace and prosperity. Since Christ did not return during the proposed period, Daniel Whitby favored a post-millennial coming of Christ, a view favored by the first great American commentator of the Apocalypse, Jonathan Edwards, in the eighteenth century. John Nelson Darby, the founder of the Plymouth Brethren and the precursor of American fundamentalism continued the Puritan apocalyptic tradition of historicizing the Apocalypse.

The Puritan tradition bequeathed the cherished view that America is the elect nation of the Apocalypse, the holy city on the hill, along with the belief in the imminent coming of Christ at the end of the world. In the 1840s William Miller predicted that the world would end in a fiery conflagration sometime between March 21, 1843, and March 21, 1844. When the predicted event did not take place, he changed the date to October 22, 1844. The failure of the fulfillment of the "prophecy" led to a conference of the Millerites in 1845 with the conclusion that Miller misread the prophecies of Daniel and the Apocalypse, but many disillusioned followers left the fold. The remaining faithful stuck to the observance of the Sabbath, the seventh day of the week, leading to the eventual formation of the group the Seventh Day Adventists. The Jehova's Witnesses, an offshoot of millenarist movements, believe that the devil is in control now but will face Christ in the battle of Armageddon, which will lead to the reign of Christ. Charles Taze Russell (1852-1916), the founder of the movement, talked about Christ's invisible return in 1874 and the visible return in 1914. Russell was right about the Armageddon of World War I, but that war was eclipsed by World War II in 1939 in brutality and destruction.

The massive massacre of the Indians at Wounded Knee by the United States soldiers was a sad event arising from millenarian beliefs. The Northern Paiute Wovoka (1856-1932), renamed Jack Wilson by his white foster parents, became inspired by apocalyptic beliefs and developed the rite of the Ghost Dance to hasten the millennium. He preached to his fellow Indians that if they separated themselves from the world of the whites, practiced pacifism, and performed the Ghost Dance at regular intervals, a millennial renewal would occur: the buffalo would return; the white man would disappear; the land would become fertile and prosperous. The Ghost Dance practice spread from Texas to Manitoba. The ecstatic religion found its way also to the Ogala Sioux community of Wounded Knee in South Dakota. Many Sioux were led to believe that the special Ghost shirts they wore protected them against the white man's bullets. Chief Sitting Bull supported the movement. The local government agent, alarmed by the popular support of the Ghost Dance movement, wrote to the commissioner:

> I feel it my duty to report the present "craze" and nature of the excitement existing among the Sitting Bull faction of Indians over the expected Indian millennium, the annihilation of the white man and the supremacy of the Indian, which is looked for in the near future and promised by the Indian medicine men as not later than next spring. (cited by Gould 59)

The commissioner's decision to arrest Sitting Bull led to the deaths of Sitting Bull and eight followers including the deaths of six police officers. The nervous government officials decided to forestall any further damage by arresting Chief Big Foot of the Lakota Sioux and by bringing the band to a reservation. On the morning of December 29, 1890, government soldiers fired at crowds of panic-stricken Indians, leaving 84 Indian men, 62 women and children dead; 30 white soldiers also died in the melee. Thus ended another chapter of apocalyptic irrationality in America.

David Koresh started a new chapter of similar apocalyptic tragedy in 1994 at Waco, Texas, leaving tens of men, women, and children dead in flames. The Oklahoma City bombing of the federal building on the anniversary of the Waco tragedy on April 19, 1995, closed the Koresh chapter by renewing carnage resulting in the death of some 168 and the wounding another hundred innocent bystanders. A similar apocalyptic cult resulted in the tragic suicide of thirty-nine people of the Heaven's Gate in San Diego; their official statement, made before the mass suicide, said:

> We came from the Level Above Human in distant space and we have now exited the bodies that we were wearing for our earthly task, to return to the world from whence we came—task completed. The distant space we refer to is what your religious literature would call the Kingdom of Heaven or the Kingdom of God. We came for the purpose of offering a doorway to the Kingdom of God at the end of this civilization, the end of this millennium. (Gould 53)

If the recent surge in apocalyptic activities is any indication, the propensity for apocalyptic excess will continue, and more tragic events are likely to happen before the ball drops on Time Square on New Year's eve in the year 2000. Nonetheless, there is a silver lining even to the darkest cloud. According to some historians, a period of warmth during the year 1000 brought not disaster but prosperity to Europe. The current economic boom and low unemployment rates and technological revolution could also be viewed as a harbinger of better things to come during the third millennium of the common era, as a postponement of the end of the world into the distant future.

NOTES

1. Michael J. Mandel et al., "Zap! How the year 2000 Bug Will Hurt the Economy," *Business Week*, March 2, 1998: 93.

PART I

APOCALYPSE AND
ANTICHRIST IN THE FIRST
MILLENNIUM

CHAPTER ONE

Apocalyptic Tradition

"Natura abhorret a vacuo" (Nature abhors the vacuum), said Descartes; that is, nothing comes out of nothing, and no idea is born fully grown, like the sweet-sixteen adult Athena from Jupiter's forehead. Or, as Salman Rushdie would put it through the mouth of Haroun, "Everything comes from somewhere..., so these stories can't simply come out of thin air."[1] Indeed, a conceptual tradition is not born fully grown but transformed constantly like Heracleitus's river into which we can't even descend once because the river is in constant motion. The apocalyptic idea is a similar notion in constant motion.

Though the Book of Apocalypse is popularly known as a revealed book of the Christian Bible, the apocalyptic concept is neither exclusively nor proprietarily Christian. Since the concept of apocalypticism is not exclusively Christian and since Christianity is a descendant of Judaism, one would suggest that we should look for apocalypticism's antecedents in Judaism. Of course, Jewish literature abounds in the use of apocalyptic types and legends. Interestingly, Judaism is not the only player in the apocalyptic field, nor is Jewish apocalypticism an Athena-like figure conceived and born immaculately. In fact, there are numerous non-Semitic apocalyptic ideas found in the Hebrew tradition, which necessitate the recognition of non-Jewish apocalyptic literary traditions including Islamic traditions which vied for notice at least as objects of intellectual curiosity during the first millennium as is the case with us today toward the end of the second millennium of the Common/Christian Era. So it is necessary to give non-biblical, particularly Eastern, literary traditions their due as we discuss the Western apocalyptic traditions of the first thousand years.

Apocalypse

The Greek term *apocalypse* means "revelation." Traditionally, the word is associated in the English-speaking world with the Catholic titling of the last book of the Christian Bible, which in the King James Version as well as in later English non-Catholic versions is called "The Book of Revelation" or "Revelation to John" as in the Revised Standard Version. Currently, the word *apocalyptic* (from the German *Apokalyptik*) is used to represent the identifiable literary genre of apocalypse and the eschatological doctrine of the last things (death, the end of the world, judgment, hell, purgatory, and heaven) known in literature as apocalypticism. From a historical perspective there seems to be a connection between apocalypse and apocalypticism. The apocalyptic form is usually the literary vehicle for eschatological thought.[2]

Apocalypse as Literary Genre

Though Gerhard von Rad refused to consider the apocalyptic as a distinct literary type, modern scholars tend to view it as a genre with subgenres.[3] For example, John Collins, who edited the *Semeia* volume on the genre issue, writes:

> "Apocalypse" is a genre of revelatory literature with a narrative framework, in which a revelation is mediated by an otherworldly being to a human recipient, disclosing a transcendent reality which is both temporal, insofar as it envisages eschatological salvation, and spatial, insofar as it involves another supernatural world.[4]

The genre of apocalypse, understood thus, certainly accommodates the Jewish books of Daniel (chs. 7-12), 1 Enoch, 4 Ezra, 2 Baruch, and the Christian book of Apocalypse/Revelation ascribed to Evangelist John.

The master-paradigm of the genre, according to Collins, entails the framework of revelation and its content. Within the framework, a medium—God, angel(s), vision or a combination of all three—conveys the revelation (epiphany) to the visionary or recipient. Discourse, dialogue, otherworldly journey, and human recipient are part of this framework. The content of the revelation could be cosmic history, cosmogony, theogony, and/or eschatology—personal, national, and/or cosmic.

Collins distinguishes two major types of apocalypses: (1) those with other-worldly journeys and (2) those without. The eschatological contents of these two types differ in the following ways:

1. Historical apocalypses contain historical references and allusions as well as eschatological crises; Daniel (7-12) belongs to this category.

2. Cosmic and political apocalypses contain both cosmic and political eschatology; for example, the Apocalypse of John.

3. Personal apocalypses deal with the destinies of individuals rather than those of nations and the universe; for example, the Gnostic apocalypses of Adam, of James, and of Peter.

These generic divisions are often of academic interest only simply because a given apocalypse may cut across all the various subgenres as does the Johannine Apocalypse. What is important to note here is the common denominator found in all these apocalypses: eschatology, be it cosmic, historico-political, and/or personal. Furthermore, apocalyptic writings are not uniquely Jewish and Christian; rather, apocalypticism is a universal phenomenon (for example, Indo-European), biblical (Hebrew and Christian), and para-biblical (Islamic, for instance). All three of these different types of apocalypse have left their indelible marks on the Western apocalypticism of the first millennium.

Eschatology as Apocalypse

For the practical purposes of this book, apocalypticism means eschatology, "the science or teachings concerning the last things (*ta eschata*)," whether eschatological knowledge is mediated through a vision by an otherworldly figure or not. Though the Greek term *eschatology* was introduced into English only in the nineteenth century, eschatological ideas are much more ancient. In fact, all cultures not only entertain ideas of the beginning—of gods, of the universe, and of humankind—but also discuss ideas of death and the end of all things including gods and mystify the future with colorful stories and images. Often the notion of end is not a return to absolute chaos or absolute order. As for humans, rebirth and resurrection are possibilities, entailing the process of purification after death through purgatory or a cycle of rebirths. Similarly, the universe could also undergo the process of recycling or expect the appearance of a new heaven and a new earth. The doctrinal option is whether the end of this age is followed by eternity or by a golden age or by a millennium or by a series of ages or cycles. Different religions teach different eschatological doctrines.

A. Pre-Christian

Apocalypticism found in the Hebrew and Christian scriptures owes a great deal to non-Jewish religions which directly and indirectly influenced the biblical traditions. The pagan Anglo-Saxons, on their part, not only adopted Roman Christianity but in turn paganized or Germanized Christianity and Christian apocalypticism.[5] It is perhaps this Germanizing movement in the history of European Christianity between 400 and 1000 that eventually culminated in Hilaire Belloc's classical statement: "The Faith is Europe. And Europe is the Faith," leading the way to Christianity's Eurocentrism. Avery Dulles writes:

> Originally centered in the Mediterranean countries, Catholic Christianity later found its primary home in Europe.... As a plea to Europeans to recover the religious roots of their former unity, this slogan could be defended. Christianity was in possession as the religion of the Europeans, and the Christianity that had united Europe was Catholic. The Ottoman emperors helped Germanize Christianity throughout Western Europe during the tenth and eleventh centuries, while the Gregorian, Cistercian, and Franciscan movements seemed to have been de-Germanizing movements.[6]

It is true that post-colonial Christianity is trying to shed its predominantly European, Germanic image. As James Russell points out, this transformation can be witnessed "in the Church's ecumenical relationships with representatives of non-European Christianity and non-Christian religions, its appointment of more non-European prelates, in its canonization of more non-European saints, and in its virtual elimination of Germanic elements from liturgical rites."[7] This de-Germanicization of the Church or the divesting of the aristocratic character of the Germanized European Church is conceived of as a return to the *sitz-im-Leben* of the early Church.[8] Characteristically, the pre-Germanic Church was an Eastern Church, taking its orientation, inspiration, and theology from the East. Therefore, submerged under the Germanic veneer of the Mediterranean Christianity we should expect to find traces of Eastern apocalyptic thought. Interestingly, the Anglo-Saxon and Germanic kings and churchmen also had extensive contact with Byzantium and the East, which means that the medieval Germanic thinkers and writers were not altogether xenophobic or strangers to Eastern Christian and non-Christian thought.

Non-Jewish Apocalypse

Undoubtedly, Jewish apocalypses have been the most influential factors in the development of Christian apocalypticism.[9] Though most scholars tend to argue for pure Israelite and Canaanite sources for the study of the Jewish apocalyptic,[10] some see the origins of this phenomenon in non-Jewish, Oriental traditions.[11]

The Oriental influence on Western apocalypticism should be seen in the broader meaning of intertextuality, which is based upon the propositions that "every text builds itself as a mosaic of quotations, every text is absorption and transformation of another text."[12] In its narrowest sense, intertextuality is limited to source, allusion, parody, or source criticism. In the larger sense, intertextuality also refers to generic resemblances found in common sets of plots, characters, images, and conventions. Following Julia Kristeva's lead, we can define a "text" as a system of signs and intertextuality as the transposition of one or several systems of signs into another. In this sense, intertextuality can be described as repeating a previously heard story reshaped by our consciousness.[13] It is the oral-aural intertextuality that was at work in ancient apocalyptic traditions. Only in this sense, in the absence of datable literary manuscripts, I discuss the presence of Oriental sub-texts in Anglo-Saxon and European apocalyptic texts.

It is customary to talk about the presence of Western travelers and traders like Marco Polo in the East during the Middle Ages but not about the presence of Eastern travelers in the West. The narrative of the eighth-century Arab traveler Ibn Fadlan in Europe, the discovery of over 200,000 Arabic coins in Sweden alone during the Viking Age, and the presence of the Buddha-statue in Scandinavia from the Viking Age and of the Chinese cup from Gotland all suggest the presence of the Orient in Europe. In the fifth century we hear of Britons in Syria; we hear of the British Pelagius in Rome during the time of St. Augustine; in the sixth-century Procopius could give news on Britain; in seventh-century Egypt there are references of contact with Cornwall.[14] While Procopius complained of Justinian's attempts to make diplomatic contacts with Britain (*Anekdota*, xix. 13), Spain entertained a Byzantine colony at Merida with a diplomatic mission while another existed at Bordeaux.[15] Sture Bolin who studied the Viking hoard of Arabic coins in Scandinavia and Russia argues for close commercial connections between Frankish and Arab worlds.[16] Bolin also points out that Charlemagne's coin reforms were based on an Islamic model. Maurice Lombard even maintains that it was the economic relationship between Islam and Europe that brought about the economic revival of the West.[17] Indeed, these mercantile, economic, and diplomatic exchanges suggest the presence of oral-aural intertextuality in the transmission of cultural traditions. There is every likelihood, therefore, that Eastern apocalyptic thought also penetrated the West at various times in various stages—more about the East-West contact in the section on Byzantine apocalypses.

Asian Apocalypses

Undoubtedly, different peoples of the world shared similar apocalyptic views through cultural interaction, which took place primarily on the oral-aural level rather through the transmission and study of literary texts in

Sanskrit, Pali, or Pahlavi. We cannot discount the fact that there were so many wandering scholars in ancient antiquity as there are today; these wandering scholars went to libraries and masters and studied original texts, but often most teachers learned more through word of mouth than from written texts then as now.

Ancient Eastern eschatology is both personal and cosmic, but not historical and political. For pragmatic and comparative purposes, I am forced to simplify the Asian apocalyptic systems, which are very complex compared to the later Jewish and Christian systems found in the written Bible. The following discussion is limited to personal and cosmic apocalypticism in terms of the Ages of the World.

Hinduism

In Hinduism personal eschatology means that after death the souls of the good go to heaven while the wicked souls suffer in hell or are reborn in punishment for sins committed in the previous life. The sinful soul must pass through endless existences on earth, in hell, and even heaven, depending on the seriousness of its sins, in order to obtain liberation (*moksha*), according to the judgment of Lord Yama or Dharma or Karma. The universe endures through four Ages (*yugas*), roughly corresponding to the Gold, Silver, Bronze, and Iron Ages of Greek mythology, which adapted the earlier Indian notion of the Four Ages. In India these chronological Ages are called *krta, dvapara, treta,* and *kali,* after the four sides of the dice. *Krta* is the most perfect Age, marked by four dots; *treta* is less perfect and is marked by three dots; in *dvapara* Age virtue diminishes by two quarters (two dots); in the *kaliyuga* only one quarter (one dot) of virtue remains.

The length of the Age marks the proportion of the decline of moral virtue. *Krtayuga* lasts 4,000 years with a dawn and twilight of 400 years each attached to it; *tretayuga* lasts 3,000 years plus 300 years each of dawn and twilight; *dvaparayuga* lasts 2,000 years plus 400 years of dawn and twilight; *kaliyuga,* the last Age, is limited to 1,000 years with and additional 200 years to account for its ushering in and fading out. The total length of the fourfold *yuga,* which is called *mahayuga* or *chaturyuga,* is 12,000 years. When the years are conveniently calculated as divine years—one divine year equals 360 human years—we get 4,320,000 years in each *mahayuga.* One thousand *mahayugas* form a *kalpa,* the actual duration from creation to the destruction of the universe. At the end of the *kaliyuga* of a *kalpa,* the universe is destroyed by fire and flood. Creator Brahma absorbs the heaven with the gods and the good ones in it into himself. Then follows the Age-long sleep of Brahma for a *kalpa,* after which he recreates the universe.

Thus the process of birth and rebirth starts all over again except for those who have already been absorbed by Brahma.[18]

Buddhism

Buddhism, being an offshoot of Hinduism, logically speaking, holds apocalyptic views similar to those of mainline Hinduism.

According to the law of *karma* or the principle of judgment, a person upon death, depending upon good deeds and bad deeds performed in the present life, reenters one of the six forms (*skandha*) of existence: god, human, asura, animal, plant, ghost (hell-dweller). The shortest period of stay in hell is 500 years, after which the damned ones move on to a higher state of existence. There is no finality attached to heavenly life; life in heaven may be followed again by life on earth or even in hell. *Nirvana,* or extinction of all attachments, including selfhood, is the ultimate goal of existence.

The Buddhist views on the Ages of the world are much like the Hindu views of the same; there is an endless succession of the worlds (*yugas* or *kalpas*) with no ultimate consummation or the end of the worlds to be followed by eternity except for souls reaching *nirvana.*

The four *yugas* have the same names except that the order of succession is reversed as *kali, dvapara, treta,* and *krta* to be followed by *kaliyuga* again. In lieu of the Hindu *mahayuga* of four ages, the Buddhist sages propose an *antharakalpa* of eight Ages lasting to 1,680,000 years. Twenty *antharakalpas* form an *asankhyeyakalpa,* and four of the latter constitute a *mahakalpa.* During an *asankhyeyakalpa,* fire, water, or wind brings about the world's destruction, followed by periods of void, recreation, and existence. During the existence phase, the perfect Age is followed by gradual deterioration of morals spread over long periods or *kalpas.* A hundred thousand years before the end of the *mahakalpa,* a god appears on earth to warn humankind of impending destruction by fire, wind, or water. In later ages, five Buddhas will appear; four of these enlightened ones (Krakuchanda, Kanakamuni, Kasyapa, and Gautama) have already appeared. The fifth Buddha, Maitreya, has yet to come.[19]

Zoroastrianism

From late Pahlavi (Persian) books, whose origins go back to the Jewish pre-exilic times (seventh century BCE),[20] it is possible to sum up Zoroastrian teachings, which in all likelihood influenced Hebrew thought.[21]

After the death of the righteous individual, the departing soul of the deceased meets with its alter ego (*daena*) in the shape of a beautiful maiden, tall and straight, who tells the soul of the deceased (in male form) how his good thoughts, words, and deeds have made her very attractive and beautiful. This beautiful maiden, who is the personification of good thoughts, words, and deeds of the soul, is the better half of the soul which remains in the invisible regions while the other part resides, endowed with a body, on earth. She is to guide him on the dangerous road toward the realm of lights, where the soul will find its place with Vohu Manah and will pass before Ahura Mazda, the Supreme Principle of good. In the Persian tradition, the maiden will lead the soul across a bridge over the river (*chinvat paratush*).[22] In the case of the wicked person, the *daena* appears as a hideous woman, the unseemly personification of evil thoughts, evil words, and evil deeds. The bridge is sword-like on one surface, over which the evil soul should tread and eventually fall headlong into the abyss below, whereas the blessed soul walks over the broad surface of the bridge toward Ahura Mazda and to the blissful realm.

According to Zoroastrian cosmology, there are four world Ages of 3000 years each. Zarathustra's birth took place at the beginning of the billennium of the Third Age. At various stages of this era, virtue wanes and waxes. With the birth of the savior-figure Saoshyant, a new order or Golden Age will dawn. The negative power of Ahriman (Supreme Principle of evil) and of his angels will be destroyed in the final conflagration with the ultimate triumph of Ahura Mazda (Hormuzd). Then the Last Juidgment of the dead will take place with the separation of the just from the unjust. The righteous will pass through fire unscathed to heaven and the wicked will wade through molten metal to suffer punishment in hell for three years. After the period of punishment is over, hell itself will be purified and earth will be restored to its pristine stage and both will be united to heaven.

Biblical Apocalypses

Jewish Thinking

Modern scholarship, on the basis of a historical analysis of the extant biblical texts, has concluded that retributive judgment after death is a late development in Jewish thought. The older Jewish tradition supposedly taught that after death the soul went to sheol while retribution or reward for good deeds and punishment for sin, is limited to this life. The emphasis seems to have been on the nation rather than on the individual; the nation is the recipient of Yahweh's wrath and good will. He blesses or punishes the nation according to its obedience and disobedience to the Covenant. Though this is the orthodox view, scattered evidence throughout the Hebrew Bible seems to suggest that there were unofficial popular forms of

Judaism that held beliefs in heaven, hell, and resurrection—if the New Testament reference to the thoughts of the sages (rabbis like Jesus and Pharisees) on angels and resurrection are reliable historical records of the early Christian or late Jewish times.

The Jewish nation suffered a series of misfortunes following the catastrophes of the seventh century and after: the fall of Jerusalem and the destruction of Solomon's Temple (587/6 BCE), the subsequent Babylonian Exile, the failure of the "return to Zion" prophesied by 2 Isaiah, Seleucid persecutions reflected in the Book of Daniel, the disappointments of the Hasmonean kings, the oppressive Roman rule, and the destruction of the Herodian Temple in 70 CE followed by the dispersion of the Jews in the Diaspora.

During this long period of disappointments and disillusions, apocalyptic ideas flourished in Jewish communities under Persian and Hellenistic auspices. As a result, there exist a large number of apocalyptic works, some even espousing mutually exclusive ideas.[23]

The most prominent and influential Jewish apocalypse on the Ages of the World is the historicized sequence found in the Book of Daniel (second or third century BCE). Daniel's vision of the four empires followed by a divine kingdom and symbolized by metals and beasts (Daniel 2 and 7) is an adaptation of Persian thought. Daniel's four metals and four beasts seem to be based on the classical divisions of the Gold, Silver, Bronze, and Iron Ages; the four beasts stand perhaps for four empires. The author of the Book of Daniel prefers the seventy-week conception of Jeremiah 25:12 and 29:13 rather than the Babylonian year of seventy-two weeks of five days each. Daniel 9 divides history from the Babylonian Exile to the end into seventy heptads. There are also other paradigms in Jewish tradition that divide the history of the world into seven ages of a thousand years each (Testament of Abraham 19) and six ages of a thousand years along with a restful millennium (2 Enoch 33:1-2)—probably this tradition has found its way into the Johannine Apocalypse (ch. 20), where the messianic interregnum will last a thousand years; in Ezrah (7:28), however, the messianic period lasts only four hundred years, followed by Christ's second coming and the general resurrection. Remarkably, one basic distinction sustained in all the various schemata of the World Ages is that between this world and the world to come.

Christian Thinking

Christianity started out as an apocalyptic movement. From the first century to the twentieth century it has produced a vast array of apocalyptic literature. It does so by Christianizing Jewish and non-Jewish apocalypses; for example, Jude 9 and 14 use apocryphal quotations.

Some scholars think that Christian apocalypticism is a purely Jewish phenomenon, a flowering of the Jewish tradition of prophecy. Philip Vielhauer states:

> It is a Jewish reaction to the advancing Hellenistic culture, and seeks by harking back to wisdom and revelation to strengthen the self-consciousness of Judaism. Although itself a syncretistic phenomenon, it is an act of Jewish self-affirmation, directed against syncretistic dissolution of Judaism such as was making headway in some circles of Judaism at the beginning of the second century before Christ.[24]

On the other hand, Martin Buber and Gerhard von Rad argue for significant contributions from Iranian dualism to Jewish-Christian apocalyptic:

> The prophetic belief in the End is in all essentials autochthonous, whereas the apocalyptic is really built up from elements of Iranian dualism. Accordingly, the former predicts a completion of creation, the latter its dissolution, its replacement by another world of completely different kind; the former allows the now aimless powers, "evil," to find their way to God and change to good, the latter sees good and evil finally separated at the end of days, the one redeemed, the other unredeemed for ever; the former believes in the sanctification of the earth, the latter despairs of it as hopelessly ruined; the former allows the original creative will of God to be fulfilled without remainder, the latter makes the faithless creation powerful over the Creator, in that it compels him to surrender nature....
>
> The apocalyptic writers wish to assume an irrevocably fixed future event; therefore, they are rooted in Iranian ideas which divided history into equal thousand-year cycles and fixed, with numerical accuracy, the end of the world, the final triumph of good over evil. It was otherwise with the prophets of Israel: they prophesied "to the converted"; that is to say, they did not state something which would happen in any event but something which would happen, if those summoned to conversion were not converted.[25]

Though von Rad finds apocalypticism irreconcilable with prophecy, Hanson sees prophecy as the starting point of apocalyptic thought (557).

Undoubtedly, Christian writers took over Jewish apocalyptic material (ideas, images, and schemata of the genre). But they also relied heavily on much non-Jewish, parabiblical material especially for the development of the notions of *parousia* (the second coming of Christ) and Antichrist.

The *parousia* of Christ takes place suddenly and unexpectedly; hence believers should be constantly prepared to meet the Lord (Matt. 24:26 ff.), who will judge according to the *ius talionis* (Mark 8:38; Luke 12:8). The faithful, however, will be resurrected at the *parousia* (Mark; 13:24-27; 2

Thess. 1: 5-10). In 1 Cor. 15: 23-28, a messianic interregnum is expected to precede the *parousia*:"Full completion comes after that when Christ places kingship in the hands of God, his Father, having first dispossessed every other sort of rule...; his reign...must continue until he has put all his enemies under his feet." (1 Cor. 15: 24-27)—this idea, as we shall see later, will be developed into the myth of the last emperor. These are the signs of the times: persecutions, wars, famine, ruin of families, and the appearance of the last great adversary; these signs are designed to warn the believers of the impending doom and to exhort them to be vigilant and be prepared for the *parousia* of Christ (1 Thess. 5: 1 ff.)

The problem that seems to have vexed the early Christians was whether the *parousia* was imminent as shown in 2 Thess. 2: 1-12. The author of the epistle claims that the great apostasy (Daniel 11:31; Jubilees 23: 14-23; Enoch 91: 7) must come first and Antichrist appear before the coming of Christ. Though the mystery of lawlessness is at work, the appearance of Antichrist is delayed by a restraining power (*to katechon* of 2 Thess. 2: 6-7). The Fathers of the Church for a while identified the *katechon* with the Roman Empire (*imperium romanum*), as will be explained below.

The eschatological opponent of God is called Antichrist. He is the mythological monster, the Serpent Adversary of God in the Garden of Eden; even though discomfited once, he will reappear at the end as the dragon-Satan and then be finally defeated.

In the New Testament, the title of "Antichrist" appears only in 2 John 7, 1 John 2: 18, 22; 4:3—*anti* meaning "in the place of" and "hostile to." The figure of Antichrist, however, appears in several other places in the New Testament as in Mark 13: 22; 2 Thess. 2: 9 ff.; 1 John 2: 18, 23; 4: 1-3; 2 John 7; Apoc. 13: 11-18, 16: 13, 19: 20, 20: 10. Antichrist is also an eschatological world-ruler as in Mark 13: 9-13 (along with Daniel 7: 25) and 8: 10, 24. The Seleucid Empire of Daniel becomes the Roman Empire or Antichrist in the New Testament.

We should distinguish between the Synoptic apocalypse and Johannine apocalypse. In this chapter I shall briefly touch upon the Synoptic apocalyptic tradition and treat the Johannine apocalypse separately in the next chapter.

Synoptic Vision

The synoptic apocalypse (Mark, Matthew, and Luke) gives a summary of the events of the End.

Mark (ch. 13) presents this eschatology as Jesus' secret teaching to four close friends who raise the question, "When will the end happen?" Jesus

answers the question by visualizing a picture of the future: many false leaders will come and parade themselves as Christ; there will be wars, earthquakes, and famines; Jewish and Roman courts will persecute the disciples;
the greatest affliction will be the profanation of the Temple—Emperor
Caligula demanded that his statue be set up in the Temple—and flight to
the mountains and the appearance of false prophets and messiahs; finally,
the Son of Man will appear and gather the elect. Jesus concludes the sermon urging the disciples to be in a state of readiness since the date of the
end is unknown though it is near.

The main difference between Mark and the other two Synoptics is that
the latter two change the private teaching of Jesus into public teaching and
place stress on the delay of the *parousia*. In contrast to Mark 13:4, where
the destruction of the Temple is spoken of in the same breath as the end of
the world, Matthew distinguishes between the destruction of the Temple
(24: 1-2), which he assumes as a past event (22:7) and the *parousia* which
will take place at the end of the world (24:3). In Matthew (24), apocalyptic
calamities take on a future character, whereas in Mark "the beginning of
the woes" (24;8) relates to the present. Luke (21: 5-36), on his part, seems
to postpone *parousia* farther down the road. He (21: 8-11) advances the
persecution of the Church to the beginning of the events which are described in Mark 13: 5-8 and locates it long before the *parousia*; also, for him
the destruction of Jerusalem is just an event in past history and not necessarily an eschatological event. On the other hand, Luke does not engage in
any polemics against the imminent expectation of the *parousia*, nor does
he renounce it. His emphasis is on constant preparedness.[26]

Parabiblical Eschatology

Medieval apocalypticism inherited its ethos not only from the biblical
apocalypticism of later Judaism and Christian antiquity but also from post-
biblical apocalyptic thought. The two prominent post-biblical apocalyptic
traditions are found in Manichean and Islamic thought.

Manichean Apocalypse

Western eschatological thought and preaching was shaped to a great
extent by St. Augustine, a former adherent of Manicheism, an important
religious movement in the Mediterranean world during the early stages
(350-1000) of the Christian religion. As for the enduring impact of
Manicheism, it may be pointed out that Augustine's views of the two cities
seem to have been shaped by Manichean dualism.[27]

Mani (third century CE) preached that there are two eternal principles,

Light and Dark, that this visible universe came into existence through the admixture of Dark with light and that the children of Light should strive not to save this corrupt world but to separate particles of light from the Dark substance. There are three true periods in the evolution and devolution of the universe: (1) The Early Period is before the attack by the agents of the Dark (demons), when the kingdoms of the gods and demons coexisted in strict separation; (2) The Middle Period is the time from the beginning of the attack by the demons and the intermingling of Light and Dark elements till the end of the world; (3) The Third and Last Period coincides with the restoration of the divine kingdoms and the destruction of the kingdoms of the demons and the eternal imprisonment of the demons.[28] St.Augustine attacks the *duo principia* or *duae naturae* and the three stages of their conflict, which he calls *initium, medium*, and *finis*.[29] At one point, Augustine disparages Manichean timings as "the battle of God, the defilement of God, and the condemnation of God"; in this report, Augustine misrepresents the last time phase which in Manichean thought is imprisonment of matter and triumph of light.[30]

The Third Period is marked by a series of five wars waged by the Good Empire against the Evil Empire according to Mani's *Kephalaia*[31] The Third Period is a time of disasters and moral decline, accompanied by slavery, rapes, robberies, wars, and bloodshed. It is during this time that the Saviors—Zarathustra, Jesus, and Mani—wage wars against error. Mani is the last of the Saviors, and the Manicheans will be persecuted relentlessly by their enemies until the great war. A great king will emerge victorious at the end of this war and he will commence his peaceful reign. At this time sinners will repent, the evil-doers will be burnt, the holy books will survive, and the Manichean Church will flourish. Yet, within the life-time of Mani's own generation Antichrist will come. He will, however, be quickly defeated, paving the way for the coming of Jesus the Light and the Last Judgment as described in the synoptic gospels. As the rule of Jesus will usher in a new golden age, gods, angels, and elect will live together in peace and all evil will be removed from the world. Then people will shed their body like a cloak and ascend to heaven. Then follow the dissolution and destruction of the world as all the remaining particles of light will be set free in the final conflagration. The dark substance, the *bolos*, will become the prison of the demons, while the saved will sit on thrones of light with Jesus' Apostles. The *bolos* will be surrounded by the New World (*aion*) and Paradise, as atmosphere and orbits of the planets surround the earth.

Manichean apocalyptic ideas, as the foregone survey shows, are developed from Christian as well as Jewish, Gnostic, Indian, and Zoroastrian resources. As in Zoroastrian thought, there are three periods of renewals by prophets—Zoroaster, Christ, and Mani.[32] Mani's followers viewed Mani as the fulfillment of salvation and as the last preparation for the fast approaching war between Light and Dark and for the end of the world. Western Christian apocalyptic thought seems to run on parallel tracks with Manicheism.[33] Though Mani himself uses Matthew 24 and 25 as the basis of his eschatology, he employs Persian names and terms; for example, the judge Xradeshahryazd, the god of world of wisdom, is none other than Jesus Christ.[34] Mani relates biblical images to the mythology of Persia and to the languages of the East, assuring that his religion incorporated the wisdom of all nations and religions. In a parable taken from Buddhism, Mani likens his religion to the ocean into which all religious traditions flow (Klimkeit 7). The upshot of the parable is simply that the Manichean missionary can employ legitimately the symbols, myths, and traditions of all other religions. One wonders whether the former Manichean Augustine's own parable of the angel-child trying to draw the sea into a hole on the beach is a veiled tribute to the unfathomable richness of the Manichean tradition. It is important to note that in Eastern Manicheism the Buddhas appear as Messengers of Light and Jesus himself is referred to in a document as "Christ-Buddha" (Klimkeit 5).

Finally, the dissemination of Manichean ideas by Manichean missionaries in the Mediterranean world during the time of Augustine and after seems to indicate that perhaps Manichean apocalyptic thought may have made a significant impact on Western apocalyptic thought especially through the writings of Augustine.

Islamic Apocalypse

There is some agreement today that the medieval eschatology of Dante's *Divine Comedy* bears the distinctive stamp of Islamic theories of life after death.[35] Cultural and intellectual interchange between medieval Christian and Islamic literature in and through Arab Spain from the ninth century is increasingly being recognized by scholars.[36] This means that Islam had a significant presence in medieval Christianity, which absorbed much from the Islamic cultures of Spain, Sicily, and Baghdad.

The Qur'an is fundamentally an eschatological scripture, where Allah is both creator and judge. In the Holy Book, "the day of judgment," "the day of resurrection," "the day," "the hour," "the inevitable," are repeatedly referred to. On the day of final resurrection, Allah will resurrect all humans, body and soul, and judge them according to their acceptance or rejection of his messengers. He will then consign them to punishment in hell

(*Jahannam*) or paradise (*Jannah*); the former is hot and dry and its inhabitants always thirsty; the latter, on the other hand, is cool and moist and its inhabitants always happy and content. Though the end of the world is presented in the Qur'an as imminent, there is no indication of its precise time as in the Christian Bible. Originally, it seems, the early Muslims were convinced that the end would come one hundred years after the *hijra* (622— the year of Mohammed's move from Mecca to Medina); that is, in 722, when Constantinople would be taken. But we know that the two important Arab attempts to capture Constantinople in 674-677 (during the reign of Emperor Constantine IV and Ummayad Caliph Muawiyah I) and in 717-718 (during the time of Emperor Leo III and Caliph Sulayman) were unsuccessful. Since Constantinople was not captured, preachers postponed the "final hour" indefinitely. The Muslim hadiths continued to proclaim that the end of the world would be preceded by the fall of Constantinople. One hadith reads: "If the world had only one day to live, God would lengthen it to permit one man of my family to bring under subjection the mountains of Daylam and Constantinople."[37] According to some hadiths, seven years must pass before the appearance of the Antichrist figure, al-Dajjal (Vasiliev 474).

Details of the last days receive more attention in post-Qur'anic thought. For example, the enemy of God, al-Dajjal, will emerge toward the end of time after a long period of social and natural decline and will conquer the earth until killed by Jesus or a Mahdi. The Mahdi, a non-Qur'anic figure, will be a member of the Prophet's family and will be sent to restore peace and justice on earth as interpreter of revelation and restorer of the Islamic law.

According to Qur'anic commentaries, the Archangel Israfil will announce the Judgment Day with two blasts from his trumpet. Thereupon the souls will arise and be reunited with their bodies. Their deeds will be read from the Book of Life and weighed on scales. As the souls cross over the bridge of fire, the sinful believers will fall into the fire temporarily while sinful unbelievers will remain in the fire for ever. The saved ones will cross safely over to Paradise to enjoy Allah's vision.

The Shia Muslims emphasize the role of the biological descendants of the Prophet through his daughter Fatimah and cousin 'Ali. The twelfth and last of the Imams, al-'Qaim, will return as Mahdi before the Final Day and engage al-Dajjal, Antichrist, in combat. The Mahdi will kill al-Dajjal and all the enemies of the family of the Prophet. Then Jesus, too, will descend in Damascus and rule for a period of time. After that the Mahdi himself will rule the world in peace and justice for some time. Only then will the end of the universe take place.

Folk tradition in many Islamic countries accord special importance to century years as those during which a "renewer" will appear to purify faith. The year 1400, which happened to be the year 1979 of the Common Era was one of those of years because by the lunar Muslim calendar after the *hijra*, the year 1400 began in November of 1979. That year a group of messianic Sunni Muslim zealots seized the Great Mosque in Mecca and proclaimed that the Mahdi had appeared; no doubt, the successful revolution in Iran earlier that year (1979) helped ignite the speculation. The Saudi troops recaptured the Mosque in a few days.[38]

In the Islamic sufi tradition, as in the spiritualized Augustinian apocalyptic thought, the early ascetics like Hasan al-Basri (d. 728) cherished a more spiritual outlook. They sought God because they rejected the joys and temptations of this world. Love for God made the sufi mystic Rabi'ah al-Adawiyah (d. 801) even to forget heaven and hell; burning love for God and trust in God replace hope for reward and fear of punishment in sufi mystic thought. The sufis emphasize vision and experience of God over the sensuous joys of traditional paradise.[39]

In short, as the Western medieval Christians continued to encounter the wider world of Eastern culture, they learned a great deal from the East and discovered that the East shared many eschatological views in common with their own faith. This intercultural encounter also contributed fuzziness, pluralism, and heterogeneity to the Western Christians' own visions of the end.

NOTES

1. Salman Rushdie, *Haroun and the Sea of Stories* (New York, 1990), p.17.; Rushdie would also add:"Oh...that's too much too Complicated to Explain" (p.17).

2. Klaus Koch, *The Rediscovery of Apocalyptic* (Naperville, 1972); Paul D. Hanson,"Prolegomena to the Study of Jewish Apocalyptic," in *Magnalia Dei:The Mighty Acts of God*, edited by F. M. Cross et al (Philadelphia, 1976), pp. 29-30. For a good introduction to the topic, see Bernard McGinn, *Apocalypticism in the Western Tradition* (Brookfield, 1994), pp. 1-39 and Robert W. Funk, ed., *Apocalypticism* (New York, 1969).

3. Gerhard von Rad, *Theologie des alten Testaments* (Munich, 1965), II: 330; *Semeia* 14 (1979): *Apocalypse:The Morphology of a Genre*, passim.

4. *Semeia*, 9; see also D. S. Russell, *The Method and Message of Jewish Apocalyptic* (Philadelphia, 1964), ch. 4; K. Koch, *The Rediscovery of the Apocalyptic*, passim.

5. See the important work of James C. Russell, *The Germanization of Early Medieval Christianity* (Oxford, 1994).

6. Avery Dulles, *The Catholicity of the Church* (Oxford, 1985), p. 75.

7. Russell, viii; see also Avery Dulles, "The Emerging World Church: A Theological Reflection," *Proceedings of the Catholic Theological Society of America* 39 (1984): 1-12.

8. Ironically, much of the impetus for the de-Germanicization of the Catholic Church at the Second Vatican Council came from Germanic bishops and Germanic theologians like Döpfner, Frings, König, Rahner, Küng, Semmelroth, and Schillebeeckx.

9. See John J. Collins, "The Jewish Apocalypses," *Semeia* 14 (1979): 21-59 for a list and summary of extant Jewish apocalypses.

10. P. D. Hanson, "Prolegomena," pp. 27-34.

11. Wilhelm Bousset, *Die Religion des Judentums im späthellenistichen Zeitalter* (Tübingen, 1926); H. D. Betz, "On the Problem of the Religio-Historical Understanding of Apocalypticism," *JTC* 6 (1969): 134-156.

12. Julia Kristeva, *Semiotike, recherches pour une semanalyse* (Paris, 1969), p. 146.

13. See Judie Newman, *The Ballistic Bard: Post-colonial Fictions* (London, 1995), pp. 2-3.

14. E. A. Thompson, "Procopius on Britain and Brittania," *Classical Quarterly* 30 (1980): 498-507; M. G. Fuford, "Byzantium and Britain: A Mediterranean Perspective on Post-Roman Mediterranean Imports in Western Britain and Ireland, *"Medieval Archaelogy* 33 (1989): 1-6.

15. J. M. Wooding, "Cargoes in Trade along the Western Seaboard," cited by K. R. Dark, *Civitas to Kingdom: British Political Continuity 300-800* (Leicester, 1994), p. 211.

16. Sture Bolin, "Mohammed, Charlemagne, and Ruric," *Scandinavian Economic History Review* 1 (1952).

17. See "Mahomet et Charlemagne. Le Problème economique," *Annales* ESC 3 (1948): 188-89; cited by Richard Hodges and David Whitehouse, *Mohammed, Charlemagne, and the Origins of Europe* (Ithaca, 1983): 7-8.

18. The Indian system of the Ages of the universe is found in the epics and the puranas with many variations.

19. The Jaina view about the Ages of the world are very similar to the Hindu-Buddhist views. Even at this point, we can see strong similarities between the Christian views of Jesus preaching eschatology and of a paraclete yet to come and the Buddhist views of the Buddhas.

20. During the exile (sixth century BCE) the Jewish people lived in the Babylonian/Persian Empire.

21 oseph Ward Swain, "The Theory of the Four Monarchies," *Classical Philology* 35 (1940): 1-21.

22. See Mary Boyce, *A History of Zoroastrianism* I: *The Early Period* (Leiden: Brill, 1975): 116.

23. See the study by John Collins, "The Jewish Apocalypses," in *Semeia*, cited earlier.

24. P. Vielhauer and Georg Strecker, "Apocalypses and Related Subjects" in Hennecke and Schneemelcher, *New Testament Apocrypha* II (Westminster, 1989): 555.

25. Cited by Hennecke and Schneemelcher I: 556-7.

26. See Hennecke and Schneemelcher I: 579-82, especially for a good bibliography on synoptic apocalypticism.

27. The following passage from Augustine seems to accord a place for Manichean thought: "Sicut pictura cum colore nigro loco suo posito, ita universitas rerum (si quis possit intueri) etiam cum peccatoribus pulchra est, quamvis per seipsos consideratos sua deformitas turpet" *De Civitate Dei* , XI: 23). For nine years Augustine was a professing Manichee, and his conceptions of *Civitas Dei* and *Civitas Mundi* seem to be a reflection of the Manichean realms of Light and Dark. See F. C. Burkitt, *The Religion of the Manichees* (Cambridge, 1925), p. 11.

28. See A. Henrichs, "The Timing of Supernatural Events in Cologne Mani Codex," in *Codex Manichaicus Coloniensis*, Simposio Internat. Sept. 3-7, 1984, University of Calabria (Cosenza, 1986), 163-68; see also Ludwig Koenen, "How Dualistic is Mani's Dualism?" *Codex Manichaicus Coloniensis*, ed. Luigi Cirillo (Cosenza, 1990), p. 26.

29. See F. Decret, *L'Afrique manicheenne (ive-ve siècles)* (Paris, 1978), II: 229 ff. n. 160; Augustine, *Contra Faustum* 13: 6 (*CSEL* 25: 384).

30. See Henrichs, pp. 191-2; R. Strousma, "Aspects de l'eschatologie manicheenne," *Revue de l'histoire des religions* 198 (1981): 163-81. It is important to point out that syncretist Mani, like all masters, freely utilize Hindu, Jain, and Buddhist religious ideas also in the development of his own thought.

31. See H. J. Polotsky and A. Bohlig, *Kephalaia* (Stuttgart, 1940).

32. In the Pahlavi *Bundahisn*, the three periods of renewal last three thousand years apiece. Theopompos (fourth century BCE) refers to Ohrmazd's rule lasting 3,000 years, followed by Ahriman's rule of 3,000 years, which will end in a 3,000 years' war between Ohrmazd and Ahriman and the defeat of Ahriman.

33. See L. Koenen, "Manichaean Apocalypticism at the Crossroads of Iranian, Egyptian, Jewish, and Christian Thought," *Codex Manichaicus Coloniensis* (Cosenza, 1986), pp. 285-332; I am indebted to this article for the substance of the section on Mani.

34. See Hans-Joachim Klimkeit, *Gnosis on the Silk Road: Gnostic Texts from Central Asia* (San Francisco, 1992), pp. 241-9.

35. Asín Palacios, *La escatalogia musulmana en la Divina Commedia* (Madrid-Granada, 1943), pp. 493 ff.

36. Alice E. Lasater, *Spain to England: A Comparative Study of Arabic, European, and English Literature of the Middle Ages* (Jackson, 1974).

37. See M. Canard, "Les expéditions des Arabes contre Constantinople dans l'histoire et dans la légende," *Journal Asiatique*, 208 (1926): 108; cited by Vasiliev, pp. 473-4.

38. Michael Collins Dunn, "The Shiites of Saudi Arabia," *The Estimate*, 8, No. 23, 8 (November 1996): 5-8.

39. See James I. Smith and Yvonne Y. Haddad, *The Islamic Understanding of Death and Resurrection* (Albany, 1981); Fritz Meier, "The Ultimate Origin and the Hereafter in Islam," in *Studies in Honor of Gustav E. von Grunebaum*, ed. Girdhari L. Tikku (Urbana, 1971), pp. 96-112; Annemarie Schimmel, *Mystical Dimensions of Islam* (Chapel Hill, 1975); Bernard McGinn, *Antichrist* (San Francisco, 1994), pp. 111-3.

CHAPTER TWO

John's Apocalypse as Literature

The Synoptic and Pauline apocalyptic views find an alternate and more colorful version in the Book of Apocalypse ascribed to Apostle John. The Johannine epistles attributed to Presbyter John also contain several apocalyptic statements. The presbyter reminds his audience that Christ will reappear in the flesh to establish he messianic kingdom and warns against Antichrist who will preach the contrary. Presbyter John will develop the earlier apocalyptic views with plenty of details and defend them in the Book of Apocalypse, which is the only separate book of Christian apocalypse in the New Testament canon. This most remarkable book is not simply a rehashing or bashing of traditional Jewish apocalypses, even though it is closely related in genre to the Jewish tradition. On the contrary, it shows considerable affinity to Eastern apocalyptic thought as outlined in the previous chapter.

Title, Authorship, and Date

The oldest testimony as to the title of this book dates only from the fourth-century *Codex Sinaiticus*, which calls the book *apokalypsis ioannu* ("The Revelation of John"). The same title is also found in the *Codex Alexandrinus* and *Codex Ephraemi* of the fifth century. Other titles of the book have come to associate Apostle John with the work as in the Muratorian Canon of the early third century. Though modern critical scholarship shies away from ascribing the work to the authorship of Evangelist-Apostle John, the traditional authorship ascription to John gives the revelational content of the book authenticity and credibility in the eyes of the believer for the simple reason that official revelation, according to Church teaching, came to an end with the death of Apostle John. As for the date of the book's composition, the oldest tradition claims that the book was written in the last years of Emperor Domitian (90-96 CE), and this view is generally accepted today as orthodox.

Apocalypse and the Canon

Appropriately, the Apocalypse, the last book of the new Testament, was also one of the last books included officially in the biblical canon. Though the book was widely used in the West in the second century, its canonical status was challenged over and again. Marcion rejected the Apocalypse as authentically Christian on account of its strong ties to Jewish scriptures. Gaius of Rome (third century) suggested that the book was written by a certain Cerinthus. Also, Dionysius of Alexandria argued on literary grounds that Evangelist John could not have written the Apocalypse. In the fourth century, Cyril of Jerusalem even omitted the Apocalypse from the biblical canon. Historian Eusebius reported about the same time that while some considered the book genuine others viewed it as spurious.

In the East, canonical support for the Apocalypse was not universal. Athanasius accepted it as did Cyril of Alexandria, Gregory of Nazianzus, Basil the Great, and Gregory of Nyssa. The Syrian Church rejected it and refused to include it in the early Pshitta translation of the Bible. John of Damascus (eighth century), however, accepted the Apocalypse as Scripture. Eventually, the Eastern bishops came to include the Apocalypse in the biblical canon with the Trullian Synod of 692.

Western Church, on the contrary, continued to read the Apocalypse as Scripture and honored it with numerous commentaries, beginning with the first complete Latin commentary on it by Victorinus of Pettau (c. 303). Later, Eastern writers, like Oecumenius and Andreas, also wrote commentaries on the Apocalypse.

Apocalypse and Intertextuality

While Apocalypse chapter 11 sounds like a Jewish publication during the time of the Siege of Jerusalem, the vision of the Woman clothed with the sun, the moon, and the stars is an avatar of the Mother Goddess from the East, of the benevolent Indian Goddess Durga, and the image of the child with the dragon (chapter 12) appears like an image from Eastern mythology as well. The elements of the classical myth with the woman, dragon, child, his birth, and ascension are found in Babylon (Damkina, Marduk, and Tiamat), in Egypt (Hathor-Isis, Horus-Seth-Typhon), and in Greece (Leto-Apollo-Python). In the classical myth, a pregnant woman is pursued by the dragon for her child; she gives birth to the child who is taken up into heaven safely beyond the reach of the dragon-slayer (Vielhauer 585). While the work is redolent with references to Roman emperors and the Nero redivivus legend, the image of the prostitute is also evocative of blood-drinking Indian Goddess Kali. What is remarkable about this apocalyptic work is that the author worked over many literary and legendary traditions with different degrees of intensity and integration. Nonetheless, the author used the Hebrew Bible as the chief source, with numerous allusions and images, the main ones being the chariot vision of Ezekiel 1 and the Son of Man figure of Daniel 7.

The author does not copy his sources exactly; he reworks them, re-phrases them, and restates them. For example, the opening vision in Apoc. 1: 12-20 follows the text and outline of Daniel 10 and has two parts: a vision ("I saw") and an audience ("I heard"), but he modifies the text with details from Daniel 7 (the description of the hair of the Son of Man) and Exodus (the description of the robe and girdle) and from Ezekiel (the description of the feet and voice). On the other hand, the author seems to have invented the symbols of the seven lampstands (menorah?) and stars and their interpretation in 1:20.

Content

The editor/author of the Apocalypse announces the content of the book as revelation from Jesus Christ, as "what thou hast seen and what must happen soon"(1: 1) and the means whereby it is accomplished: "And he has sent his angel to disclose the pattern of it to his servant John" (1: 2), the visionary and witness of its truth.

The opening vision (1: 12-20) commissions the seer to record his vision and send it to the seven churches of Asia Minor. Chapters 2 and 3 contain the seven letters to the seven churches. The seer finds himself in the throne-room of heaven in chapters 4 and 5; the Lamb alone is found empowered to open the scroll with the seven seals. In chapter 6, the Lamb breaks the seven seals. As the seventh seal is broken in chapter 7, angels sound trumpets of God's wrath (8-9; 11: 14-19). In chapters 10 and 11, the seer receives two more commissionings, and two witnesses are introduced and dispatched. Chapter 12 describes a "great portent in heaven"—of the woman wearing the sun as her garment and of her child and of the menacing dragon. Two allies of the dragon—the beast from the sea and beast from the land—appear and rule the land in chapter 13. In chapter 14, the Lamb in the company of the 144,000 on Mount Zion announces the final judgment. Seven angels receive the commission to afflict the world with seven plagues with the libation of the seven vials of God's wrath (15-16). Chapters 17 and 18 describe the vision of the city of Babylon as a harlot sitting on a seven-headed beast and the fall of the city of Babylon. The victory song of chapter 19 is followed by Christ's coming as judge, the slaying of the two beasts (ch. 19), the binding and casting of the dragon into the abyss, and the beginning of the millennial reign of the Messiah (ch. 20). The visions reach their climax with the description of the new world and New Jerusalem (21:1 - 22:5). The epilogue (22:6-21) concludes the series of visions and auditions with warnings and threats against additions and deletions to the book and with the prayer "Come, Lord Jesus," reminiscent of the pre-Christian Buddhist prayer "Come, Maitreya [Buddha]," and the valediction (21: 21).

Two Revelations and Two Ecstasies

The apocalyptic dream vision is not haphazard as in a Joycean stream-of-consciousness narrative but rather symmetrical with two revelations and two ecstasies.[1] The two ecstasies break the Apocalypse into two similar divisions of unequal length. In the first ecstasy the voice bids the seer write what he is about to see (1: 10-11), and in the second ecstasy the voice invites him to come up into heaven (4: 1-2). The first ecstasy takes place on earth and is continued in heaven with the second one.

The First Ecstasy

In the first vision the seer faces a person resembling the Son of Man in the midst of seven golden candlesticks. The Son of Man gives John the command seven times to write epistles to the presiding angels of seven churches in Asia Minor. The seer explains that the seven candlesticks represent the seven churches and that their angels are represented by the seven stars that the Son of Man holds in his hand. Interestingly, the whole first part is composed of seven messages preceded by the preliminary section (1: 9-20 + 2: 1 - 3:22). The literary scheme is 1+7.

The Second Ecstasy

In the second vision the seer is in heaven, which is dominated by the throne of God, supported by the four living creatures and surrounded by the senate of the twenty-four ancients and angels of every kind (4-5). Here the seer, also one of the actors in the apocalyptic drama, observes a procession of visions projected as though on a screen.

What takes place next is an allegorical drama under the symbol of a sealed scroll. The breaking of the seven seals is accompanied by one or more passing visions. At the opening of the seventh seal, seven angels appear and receive seven trumpets. With the sounding of the seven trumpets, one or more visions occur. With the blowing of the seventh trumpet, the door of the temple of God opens to reveal the ark of the covenant. With the second opening of the heavenly temple, the glory of God is revealed, and seven angels come and pour out upon the world the seven vials of God's wrath. Babylon falls at the pouring out of the seventh vial. Seven voices ring out inviting the blessed to the wedding of the Lamb. A series of seven more visions follows, finally revealing heavenly Jerusalem.

Ring/Chiasmic Structure

In modern literary analysis, a literary work, like any physical object, is expected to be "scientifically" divided into chapters or clean divisions or sections (*section* comes from the Latin *secare*, meaning "to cut"). As a result of this literary policy dating from the later Middle Ages, we have systematically divided the books of ancients, including the Bible, conveniently and neatly into chapters and verses/sentences, whereas no such divisions existed in the works of the ancients, especially in the Bible, of which the Apocalypse is just a member. Now, as we examine the compositional structure of the Book of Apocalypse, what we find is that the author had conceived it not as chapters and verses but as seven series of seven, not dividing one seven from the other sevens but uniting one with the others almost like a labyrinth. This labyrinthine metaphor underlying artistic structure is indicated, for example, in the Greek myth of Daedalus and the Chaucerian poem *The House of Fame* as well as the modern *Portrait of the Artist as a Young Man* by James Joyce.

The author of the Apocalypse himself provides some clues to this architectonic structure of the work by the use of the metaphors of Temple and City with its walls, measuring rod, and stones. It is the totality that counts, but the totality itself is the end result of the dovetailing parts as in the case of the stones that dovetail to form the totality of the building. The structure of the whole and parts may also be compared to an onion which is made of several layers dovetailing into one another with precision.

This type of composition is based on the literary principle called *chiasmus*, employed by Greek and Latin classical writers including the writers of the Greek New Testament. Ward Tonsfeldt notes the same phenomenon in Greek and in Old English poetry and recognizes the articulation of "ring structure," as he calls it, to Aristarchus' observation that Homer tends to organize items in a series being repeated according to the principle *husteron proteron*, last first.[2] David R. Howlett calls this kind of versification rather as "biblical style" and lays down ten rules, of which "the first two—parallelism and chiasmus—are basic and most common.[3] Howlett finds this style employed not only in the Bible but also in Anglo-Irish writing. He writes:

> British-Latin writers such as Pelagius, Patrick, and Gildas, utterly distinct in every other way, all composed clearly and consistently in biblical style, as did later Anglo-Latin writers such as Aldhelm, the Monk of Whitby, Eddius Stephanus, Daniel bishop of Winchester, Bede, Boniface, Felix, Alcuin, and Aethelwulf. So also did the Old English compilers of Aethelberht's Law Code, Caedmon, the carvers of the Franks Casket and the Ruthwell Cross, the authors of "The Dream of the Rood," "The Leiden Riddle," "The Ruin," "The Rhyming Poem," and Cynewulf, and all the authors who belonged to the court of King Alfred the Great. (132)

Chiasmos in Greek designates the literary principle of the "placing crosswise" of words in a sentence. In rhetoric, the term denotes an inversion of the order of words or phrases which are repeated. The simplest application of the principle requires four lines. For example:

> A The sabbath
>
> B was made for man
>
> B′ And not man
>
> A′ for the sabbath.

The following example from St. Augustine is an excellent rhetorical example:

> A Ibi est *aurum*,
>
> B Ibi est *palea*,
>
> C Ibi *ignis* in angusto operatur.
>
> C′ *Ignis* ille non est diversus, et diversa agit,
>
> B′ *Paleam* in cinerem vertit,
>
> A′ *Auro* sordes tollet.[4]

Lund's study of the structure of the Apocalypse shows that the bibli-

cal author used the chiasmus-principle from the beginning to the end
of the book. The chiasmoi found in the construction of Apocalypse, as
Lund argues, "are not dislocations but are deliberate projections,
made...by the author himself in order to indicate to the reader the
proper sequence of the book" (327). The following general outline of
the Book of Apocalypse by Lund is a consistent application of the
chiasmus principle:

A   Prologue, 1: 1-20

    B   Seven Epistles, 2:1 - 5:14

        C   Seven Seals etc, 6:1-17; 7:1-17; 8:1-5

            D   Seven Trumpets, 8:13 - 11:19

                E   The Church's *Testimony in the Roman Empire*,
10:1-11

                F   The Church's *Testimony in Judaism*, 11:1-13

                F'   The Church *Persecuted* officially by Judaism,
12:1-17

                E'   The Church *Persecuted* officially by Judaism, 12:1-17

            D'   *Seven Bowls*, 16:1-17.

        C'   *Seven Angels*, etc, 14:6 - 15:4

    B'   *Seven Angels*, 17:1 - 22:9

A'   Epilogue, 22:10-21 (Lund 325-6)

Lund writes:

> In a book that follows such a literary pattern as this, in which the series of
> seven, and the passages in which they are framed, match one another like the
> stones in an arch, it is absolutely essential that the reader coming upon 7:1-17
> should somehow be made to look forward for its immediate counterpart in
> chapters 4 and 5 rather than backward to its more remote companion (14:1-5).
> (327)

Elisabeth Schüssler-Fiorenza, following the work of Loenertz, Lund,
and Giblin, also sees the Apocalypse-author's method as chiasmus or
intercalation (a break or interposition of a line, idea, or section) and
applies it to the entire work quite convincingly despite the subsequent
modifications made by Giblin.[5] She writes:

> Very important for the composition and structure of Rev. is the technique of
> intercalation of texts which makes diagramming of the successive sections of
> Rev. almost impossible. The author employs the method of intercalation in
> the following way: he narrates two formal units or two episodes (A and A')
> that essentially belong together. Between these two formal units of episodes
> he intercalates another form or scene (B) and thus requires the reader to see

the combined text as a whole. For instance, in structuring the introduction to the whole book the author intercalates the following formal units: superscription (A), prescript (B), and motto (A′). An example of intercalation of content units is the introduction to the trumpet septet. After the appearance of the seven angels with the seven trumpets in 8:2 (A′), there follows a heavenly liturgy 8:3-5 (B) and then the plagues begin at 8:6 (A′). (172)

Schüssler-Fiorenza gives the following surface structure of the Apocalypse:

A 1:1 - 8

B 1:9 - 3:22

C 4:1 - 9:21; 11:15-19

D 10:1 - 15:4

C′ 15:5 - 19:10

B′ 19:11 - 22:9

A′ 22:10 - 22:21

The preceding structural pattern indicates that, structurally speaking, the small prophetic scroll, (10:1 - 15:4) like the Psalmist's "corner stone," holds the central position. This concentric A B C D C′ B′ A′ pattern shows also the appropriateness of the epistolary framework of the Apocalypse. In this perspective, the book also can be seen as a Chinese box— the scroll within several boxes or envelopes or rings or the labyrinth or city with streets/rivers or the temple with the Holy of Holies and walls and passageways. Schüssler-Fiorenza writes:

> The structuralist analysis…of Rev. thus confirms the central position of the small prophetic scroll of the surface structure. Moreover, the seven letter visions do not form a separate unconnected part of Rev. but belong integrally to the book. Finally,…analysis…confirms the conclusion that the prophetic-apocalyptic judgment/salvation pattern is basic for Rev.

> In my analysis of the complex type…of Rev. I have maintained that this prophetic apocalyptic pattern is integrated into that of the prophetic-apostolic letter. If the epistolary framework defines the complex literary type of Rev., then the pattern of inclusion of symmetry has to be shown as the architectonic pattern of the whole work. That this is the case is indicated by the author's preference for the A B A′ pattern and the technique of intercalation. Since the two scroll visions and the three septets are decisive for the pattern of Rev. 4:1 - 19:10, this central unit of the book clearly exhibits the pattern A B A′. The letter septet, moreover, corresponds with the last section, 19:11 - 22:9. The introductory vision of this section 19:11 - 16 clearly resembles the inaugural vision and the seven letters (19:12; cf. 1:14 and 2:17; 19:15; cf.2:27 and especially the sword symbol in 19:15; cf. 1:16; 2:12). Moreover, the promises of the letters to the victorious one recur in 19:11 - 22:9. The first unit and last unit

of Rev. are thus related to each other as promise and fulfillment. (175)

The main function of the Apocalypse, then, would be in a sense the interpretation—metahistorical, i.e., an integrated, prophetic view of the Day of the Lord rather than the kind of historical count-down based on clock-and-calendar time line—of the scroll.

Schüssler-Fiorenza also shows the affinity of the chiasmic structure to the structure of the Greek drama in which the climax happens in the middle and the anticlimax or denouement at the end; the latter is tied up with the *in-medias-res* chiasmic beginning of the epics.[6] Scholars have also found the same structural pattern in the Hebrew Bible (176). We see the same concentric pattern in the visual art of the early Christian era. Two Romans coins of 35 - 36 CE, carrying the images of Augustus and Apollo exhibit the A B C D C′ B′ A′ structure.[7] Similarly, the golden candelabra of the Arch of Titus in Rome also exhibits the A B C D C′ B′ A′ pattern, which implies that the author of the Apocalypse may have had this candelabra or the menorah candle in mind for 11: 4 and for 1: 12-13, 20.

Numerical Structure

As mentioned earlier, the Apocalypse-author uses numbers and numerical structures as structural and thematic devices. The two basic numerical structures are the twofold revelations and ecstasies. Then there are seven septets—the seven letters, seven seals, seven trumpets, seven signs, seven bowls of wrath, seven stages in the fall of Babylon, and seven final scenes.[8] It is also possible to argue for six series of six, a symbol of incompleteness congruous with 666, the number of the Beast "expressing a lack of fulfillment" (Ford 48-49). Schüssler-Fiorenza views the narrative movement of the seven-sealed scroll as "a conical spiral moving from the vision of the Lamb's enthronement...to that of the Parousia" (171).

Interludes/Digressions

The forward movement—from a linear rather than an architectonic perspective—in the Apocalypse seems to be interrupted by the interludes. They are visions and hymns—7:1-17; 11:15-19; 12:10; 14:1-5; 15:2-4; 19:1-9; 20:4-6. The longest interlude is the prophetic messenger's speech in chapter 2-3, comprising the messages to the seven churches of Asia Minor. Through these visions and words, the author shows the relationship between the historical present and eschatological future.

The hymns and messages serve also as commentary and interpretation in the Apocalypse. Their role is similar to the function of the chorus in the Greek tragedy or to that of the songs of bards in Homer and the digressions in the Old English poem *Beowulf* (Schüssler-Fiorenza 171-2).

Images/Symbols

One fascinating feature of the Apocalypse that continues to baffle the interpretation of the book and challenge the imagination of its readers is the author's clever use of symbols and images. The main one—the image of the throne and the symbolism of the color white—are distributed over the whole book. The image of (eschatological) war (19:11 - 22:5) with the divine warrior is a powerful mythological motif, and it introduces the mythological beasts of the Behemoth, Leviathan, and the Dragon into the combat zone. The mythic image of the "woman with the eternal child (12: 1-5) is to be seen in the context of the Roman emperor cult. The emperor was conceived as the divine child, born of Goddess Roma, Queen of Heaven. Of course, in John's theology this child god is Christ Jesus, though the image could also stand for the messiah child of Mother Zion (Isaiah 66:7-9).[9] The author loves to play with the following symbols: animals, angels, seal, scroll, fire, water, plants, fruits, trees, precious stones, building, planets, plagues, and so on. All this shows that the biblical author works with various literary and religious traditions and opens up the possibility of further expanding almost unreachable horizons for the symbols and images of the Apocalypse.

Theology as Eschatology

The main concern of the Apocalypse is not salvation history as in the Hebrew Bible and the Gospels in general but eschatology, the destruction of the powers of evil and the establishment of God's Kingdom before the eschaton. That means history is subordinated to eschatology and the present receives its meaning from the future.[10] As almost all the commentaries of the Apocalypse make clear, the central purpose of the book is to strengthen the faith of the believers and encourage Christian communities persecuted by pagan Rome.

It is the eschatological preoccupation of the author that prevents him from providing a narrative of the continuous development of "historical" events from the beginning to the end as traditional Jewish apocalypses do. According to this apocalypticist, all past and present events climax in the eschatological event (6:12-17; 8:1; 11:15-19; 16:17-20; 14:6; 15:4) to which all history is subservient and subordinated.

The language of the Apocalypse emphasizes God's judgment in the end times. This judgment, however, unfolds in a dramatic series of events: the angry devil-dragon stalking the woman and her offspring (12:15-17), the destruction of God's enemies and the salvation of God's servants (11:18), the pouring out of God's wrath with the opening of the seven seals (ch. 6), the blasting of the last trumpet (11:15-18), the libation of the wine of wrath (14:10), the pouring out of the seven bowls of wrath (chapters. 15 and 16), the judgment of Babylon (16:19), and Christ's treading of the wine-press of God's fury (19:15). In the end all the nations of the earth and especially godless Babylon (14:8-18) will be overpowered and destroyed while the Christian community will be saved (7:1-8; 11:1-2); thus God will avenge the blood of his servants (19:2; 18:20).

The Apocalypse, in short, reveals God's plan for history by assuring the believers not only of the kairos of the end but also of Christ's coming. Thus the present time is the "short time" before the end. For the author both the end of the world and the coming of Christ are imminent at least as events of salvation history.

Apocalypse as Anti-Roman Scripture

One of the issues that troubled the minds of the Christian faithful in the early centuries was the Christian's attitude toward the Empire. While the Synoptic Gospels (Matt. 22:15-22; Mark 12:13-17; Luke 20:20-26) urged Christians to accept their obligations to the state such as paying Caesar his taxes, while St. Paul exhorted That Christians obey the earthly powers, which are ordained by God (Rom. 13:1-6), and while St. Paul himself expressed his pride in his Roman citizenship (Acts 21:39; 22; 25-28), the Apocalypse of John took a different view. For him Rome is the supreme enemy, the incarnation of evil, the satanic power, the great harlot, and the mother of all abominations, drunk with the blood of saints and martyrs (17: 5-6), doomed to be destroyed by God.

The reason for this condemnation of Rome was Caesar worship practised by the residents of the Roman Empire; Augustus, for example, was worshipped as the incarnate God in private and in public.[11] The first temple dedicated to the divine Caesar was built in 29 BCE at Pergamum.[12] Before the end of the first century of the common Era, Smyrna, Pergamum, Sardis, Philadelphia, and Laodicea—the recipient churches of the epistles of the seer and sage in the Apocalypse—all possessed such temples. Though Augustus discouraged emperor-worship, Caligula loved it. He ordered that Greek statues of gods be decapitated and his head replace the heads of Greek gods. He executed those who refused to swear by his godhead, according to Suetonius.[13] Caligula even proposed that his image be installed in the Holy of Holies of the Jerusalem Temple.[14] However, he died before his order was executed.

Caligula's successor, Claudius, had temples erected in his honor in Ephesus and Camulodonum in Britain; Boadicea led a revolt against this blasphemous act, against "the citadel of perpetual tyranny" (ix: 31). Nero also accepted divine honor as did Titus and Vespasian.

Caesar-worship involved addressing Caesar as "Lord" (*Kurios*), and offering sacrifices, for which a person received certification. For the Christian it was blasphemy to call Caesar "Lord" and offer him sacrifices. The choice was simple: Caesar or Christ? In fact, Rome persecuted Christians for failing to worship Caesar as god. For the author of the Apocalypse, the Roman Empire is the embodiment of satanic power, and emperor-worship is the supreme manifestation of that evil.

The seer of the Apocalypse perceives the beast rising from the sea, i.e., from the west for someone from Asia Minor. The seven heads and ten horns of the beast manifest its power. The seven heads point to the seven hills of Rome on which the great whore is seated. The seven heads seem to stand for the seven emperors Tiberius, Caligula, Claudius, Nero, Titus, Vespasian, and Domitian. The ten horns could stand for the governors of the ten dioceses/provinces of Rome.

In John's eyes the Roman Empire is the sum total of all evil that ever was and can be. The Dragon-Satan exercises his power through the beast, which is the Roman Empire. So, logically speaking, opposition to Satan involves opposition to Rome, and there is no room for compromise as long as Rome is the agent of Satan.

In chapter 13:18, John says that the number of the beast is 666. Though there is an alternate reading of 616 for the beast, the number 666 is almost universally accepted as correct. According to the principles of gematria, each letter in the name stands for a number and the total of the right name should be 666. Among the many candidates suggested for this dishonor, NERON KAISAR in Hebrew yields the right numbers: N = 50 + R = 200 + O = 6 + N = 50 + Q = 100 + S = 60 + R = 200 equal 666.

The author of the Apocalypse, briefly stated, sees satanic power at work in the Roman Empire and in emperor worship; Antichrist as Nero redivivus is a manifestation of the same evil imperialism, which can be embodied in the Roman Empire, or in other empires as in the vision of Daniel (chapter 7), as later interpreters of the Apocalypse would try to explicate. The following examples are worth noting here for future reference.

1. Ireneus suggests three names: (a). EUANTHAS, (b) TEITAN—referring possibly to Titus, (c) LATEINOS—a popular name that could stand for the Roman empire.

2. Primasius suggests the nonword ARNOUME with the possible meaning of "apostate."

3. Some reformers suggest the following: (a) ITALIKA EKLESIA, (b) HE KATINE BASILEIA, (c) PAPEISKOS, meaning the Roman Catholic Pope.

4. Some Catholic polemicists counter with the following: (a) LOUTHERANA, (b) SAXONEIOS, both suggesting Martin Luther.[15]

5. Muhammad as MAOMETIS yields the number 666. Pope Innocent III in 1213 called for a new crusade against Islam because he held that Muslim power was destined to last only 666 years.[16]

6. NA BONAPARTI (Napoleon Bonaparte) also yields the number 666!

7. HITLER can also be made to yield 666!

Ethics of Vengeance

In spite of the fact that St. Paul urges his followers not to avenge themselves (Rom. 12:19) as does Jesus' famous Sermon on the Mount, the Apocalypse "breathes a glowing hatred against all enemies and persecutors of Christianity."[17]

Basically, the Apocalypse espouses the view that God will execute vengeance. At the breaking of the fifth seal, the seer beholds beneath the altar the souls of those slaughtered for their faith in Christ; they cry in a loud voice: "Sovereign Lord,...how long now you will sit in judgment and exact vengeance for our blood from all those who dwell on earth?" (6:9-10). Bousset comments:

> One attempts in vain to weaken the strong attitude of vengeance found in this prayer. We must get accustomed to the fact that the Apocalyptist, as he views the martyr-ban, lives in stronger attitudes of hatred and of hope than we can condone.[18]

In fact, this prayer for revenge is fulfilled. The Angel of the waters responds:

> "Righteous are you, O Lord,...this is a just award...blood to drink for those

> who have shed the blood of your saints and prophets. They deserved it. As he
> said this, he heard the altar saying, "Yea, Lord, God Almighty, your judgments
> are true and just." (16:5-7)

Though vengeance is also acclaimed in the alleluia cry (19:12), the author praises God's justice as well. The heavenly throng is joyful as the
whore city of Babylon burns and the smoke rises up in everlasting
streams (19:3).

What is also noteworthy about vindication, justice, and victory for
the faithful is that it is all the result of both self-immolation and war.
The lamb alone is worthy to open the scroll because "you were slain
and by your blood you purchased for God men of every tribe and
language...and they shall reign upon the earth (5:5, 9-10). Victory comes
in the war against the beast and the dragon who wages war against the
believers and the Lamb (17: 14), but the followers of the Lamb will
participate in his victory. Yet, in chapter 19, the rider on the white horse
and the armies of heaven slay the unrighteous.

The Apocalypse, briefly stated, celebrates not only the victory of
Christian Church over pagan Rome, of Christ over Antichrist, and of
God over the devil but also the vindication of justice which implies the
justification of vengeance coming from God. Maybe the biblical author
is not at heart a pacifist; he does not condone unjust, unprovoked violence; in fact, he warns the unrighteous that God will punish them and
redeem his faithful in end times and thus transforms history into
eschatology. That is how the author of the Apocalypse comforts the
persecuted Christian community—with reference to the final and definitive reality of God's future kingdom, which has already come: "The
kingdom of world has become the kingdom of our Lord and of his
Christ, and he shall reign for ever and ever" (11:15).

NOTES

1. See Loenertz, *The Apocalypse of Saint John*, trans. H.J. Carpenter (London,
1947): ix-xixi.

2. H. Ward Tonsfeldt, "Ring Structure in *Beowulf*," *Neophilologus* 61 (1977): 44;
see also S. E. Bassett, *The Poetry of Homer* (Berkeley, 1938), pp. 119-28.

3. David R. Howlett, "Biblical Style in Early Insular Latin," in *Sources of Anglo-
Saxon Culture*, ed., Paul Szarmach (Kalamazoo, 1986), p. 131.

4. *Enarrationes in Ps. XXI* in Nils Wilhelm Lund, *Chiasmus in the New Testament: A Study in Formgeschichte* (Chapel Hill, 1942), p. 33.

5. Elisabeth Schüssler-Fiorenza, *The Book of Revelation: Justice and Judgment*
(Philadelphia, 1985); Charles H. Giblin, "Structural and Thematic Correlation in the

Theology of Revelation 16-22," *Biblica* 55 (1974): 487-505; see also Ugo Vanni, *La struttura litteraria dell'Apocalypse* (Roma, 1971).

6. See G. E. Duckworth, *Structural Patterns and Propositions in Virgil's Aeneid* (Ann Arbor, 1962); J. L. Myers, *Herodotus: Father of History* (Oxford, 1953); L. Richardson, *Poetical Theory in Republican Rome* (New Haven, 1944),; J. R. Donohue, *Are You the Christ?* (Missoula, 1973).

7. L. Richard, "The Temples of Apollo and Divus Augustus on Roman Coins," in *Essays and Studies Presented to William Ridgeway*, ed. E. C. Quiggan (Cambridge, 1913), pp. 198-212.

8. See Josephine M. Ford, *The Revelation of John*, Anchor Bible (New York, 1975), pp. 46-48.

9. Those familiar with Indian (Hindu) mythology will not fail to see the hovering presence of the myth of Lord Krishna and the Dragon Kaliya in this episode.

10. Rudolf Bultmann, *History and Eschatology: The Presence of Eternity* (New York, 1957).

11. See William Barclay, "Great Themes of the New Testament," *Expository Times* 70 (1958-59): 261.

12. Tacitus, *Annals*, iv: 37.

13. *Gaius Caligula*, 22, 27.

14. Josephus, *Antiquities of the Jews*, xvii: 7-8.

15. Perhaps the falling out of the name "Saxons" as referring to the inhabitants of England and the Scots' calling of the English as "Saxons" may have some suggestivity to Antichrist.

16. See Barclay, 292-6.

17. Walter Bauer, "Das Gebot der Fiendesliebe und die alten Christen," *Zeitschrift für Theologie und Kirche* 27 (1917): 10; cited by William Klassen, "Vengeance in the Apocalypse of John," *CBQ* 28 (1966): 301.

18. W. Bousset, *Die Offenbarung Johannes* (Göttingen 1906): 271; cited by Klassen, 303.

CHAPTER THREE

Apocalypse in Literature: East and West

The biblical invitation to open the scroll of the sevenfold seal served also as an invitation to interpret the riddled Apocalypse. In fact, like the legendary Pandora's box, the Apocalypse of John spawned a multitude of radical and moderate interpretations over a span of some eighteen hundred years. Since this study is restricted to early English apocalypticism (700-1000), I shall limit myself to a short survey of early Christian apocalypses and to patristic and early medieval interpretations of the Apocalypse in the East and the West, with which the Anglo-Saxons were familiar. I shall treat the Antichrist tradition in a separate chapter. This chapter is concerned only with Christian apocalypses inspired and influenced by John's Apocalypse.

Christian Apocalypses: A Common Tradition

According to Adela Y. Collins, there are twenty-four early Christian apocalypses that envisage eschatological salvation like John's Apocalypse; of these, fourteen are entire works.[1] They belong to two basic types according to the mode of revelation: (1) those in which the primary mode of revelation is vision or audition and (2) those in which the mode of revelation is an extra-terrestrial trip.

Not all these apocalypses is are alike. For example, *Jacob's Ladder*, *The Apocalypse of Peter*, and *The Shepherd of Hermas* involve public eschatology and destruction of the world but no cosmic transformation. The Apocalypse of St. John the Divine and The Apocalypse of Paul, on the other hand, talk also about cosmic renewal. Several Christian apocalypses discuss only personal eschatology; for example, *The Testa-*

ment of Isaac, The Testament of Jacob, Zosimus, The Apocalypse of James, and *The Apocalypse of the Holy Mother of God.* It seems that "the types involving only personal eschatology are somewhat later than those expressing cosmic and/or political eschatology" (Collins 66). In fact, all twenty-four texts contain expectation of a personal afterlife.

During the early three hundred years of the Christian religion, before the division of the Roman Empire into Eastern and Western, the Christian apocalyptic tradition was shared in common by the Christian communities of the entire Roman Empire which spread from Roman Britain to Syria and Africa. As a result, we find extant versions of many of these apocalypses in Greek, Latin, Syriac, and Ethiopic.

One important characteristic of the first three centuries of Christianity, before Christianity became the religion of the Roman Empire by the middle of the fourth century, was the adversarial, persecuted situation Christianity found herself vis-à-vis the Empire. It was during the confrontational phase of this period that the Apocalypse of John as well as most other Christian apocalypses were composed. It appears that most of these apocalypses with political and cosmic eschatology express an attitude of hostility toward the Roman Empire. The apocalypses that emphasize personal eschatology, like *The Apocalypse of Paul,* dwell rather on the themes of judgment, reward, and punishment. Two of the important apocalypses, which seem to have had significant influence on early Christianity and early English thought, are *The Apocalypse of Paul* and the *Sibylline Oracles.*[2]

The Apocalypse of Paul

The Apocalypse of Paul, written in the fourth century, was assigned to the authorship of Apostle Paul for the justification of its authority. Supposedly, the manuscript was stored in a sealed marbled box, along with Paul's shoes in Tarsus, under the foundation of his house. It was discovered during the consulate of Cynegius (388) and was translated immediately afterwards into Latin. It contains the notion of a heavenly journey on Lake Acherusia as in the Greek myth of the voyage of the golden ship *Parabola* to the holy island of Delos. What is remarkable here is that the author makes Lake Acherusia into the "Ocean of Milk" of Indian puranic mythology. The author also talks about ice-cold hell as in the Tibetan Buddhist tradition. He also uses the popular Indian motif of the suspended souls of the damned above a river of fire and a channel of water with their dry, parched tongues hanging out. The graphic details of heavenly joys and infernal tortures seem to have served as a wonderful tool for instruction in fire-and-brimstone sermons. The inspiration for the ascription of this work to Paul's authorship comes from 2 Corinthians 12, where Paul speaks of his flight into Paradise.[3]

The Sibylline Oracles

The second apocalyptic work which shows considerable dependence on various religious traditions and which was popular both in the East and in the West is the collection called the Sibylline Oracles (*Oracula Sibyllina*). These oracular utterances are found in Greek, Latin, Ethiopic, Coptic, and Arabic versions.[4] Their popularity even in later medieval times can be seen in the phrase *teste David cum Sibylla* of "Day of wrath...That will dissolve the world in flames, *as David and the Sibyl attest*" found in the hymn *Dies irae* ascribed to the authorship of the thirteenth-century Franciscan Thomas of Celano.[5]

The Sibyl speaks in the first person and in future tense. Both the figure and name of the virgin prophet are not originally Greek but Asian from the Persian region. Gradually, however, she became a popular prophetic figure first in Greek tradition and later in Latin literature. The best known Greek Sibyls were from Marpessas, Erithrea, and Cumae. The Erithrean Sibyl went to Delphi where she entered Greek mythology. Virgil describes the Cumaean Sibyl who lived in a cave by the citadel of Cumae. While the Jewish Sibyl and the Cumaean Sibyl of Virgil's *Aeneid* are well known, the Chaldean (Syrian) Sibyl of the Baalbek Oracles does not seem to have received sufficient attention.

The pagan Sibylline oracles survive today only in fragments.[6] The twelve Sibylline books that survive are of Jewish and Christian origin. The Greek-speaking Jewish Sibylline writers took over the Greek models and gave them a new content. According to Ursula Treu, "The Characteristic mark of the Jewish Sibyl, as of the Christian who is dependent on her, is the call to repentance, and then the prophecy and portrayal of future punishments down to the last judgment."[7]

Prophecies play an important role in these oracles. First, the Sibyl prophesies what has already happened during the life time of her audience and then what is yet to come, which is doom and punishments for sins and apostasy. The course of world history follows the Greek Herodotan sequence of empire states: Egypt, Assyria, Babylon, Media, Persia, Macedonia, and Rome.

The two Sibylline texts popular during the Middle Ages were the Tiburtine Sibyl and the Erythrean Sibyl, whom Augustine cites as the author of an acrostic.

The oracles of the Tiburtine Sibyl survive in 130 manuscripts, thirty of which come from before the thirteenth century.[8] The differences in the extant manuscripts indicate that the original text was revised and altered many times in subsequent centuries.

The second major Sibylline text is *The Prophecy of the Erythrean Sibyl* (*Vaticinium Sibyllae Erythraeae*), which became popular in Europe in the thirteenth century. Since thirteenth-century events are recorded in the surviving Latin manuscripts, the Erithrean Sibyl was considered to have originated in the thirteenth century. The text is a review of world history and a futuristic prophecy on the end of the world given by Sibyl to the Greek army after the fall of Troy. The Sibyl talks about the career of Alexander, Hannibal, Pompeii, Julius Caesar, and Augustus Caesar, who are "he-goats" (*hyrci*). Christ appears as the lamb of the Apocalypse. Then the Sibyl talks about the appearance of a mysterious, Antichrist-like beast appearing from the East. Like the dragon of the Apocalypse it has seven heads and 663 feet (years of reign). Two stars will attack the beast, and a lion from the West will check its advance; as a result, the dragon will die a little later.[9]

What is interesting about the popular texts of *The Prophecy of the Erithrean Sibyl*, as Paul Alexander has recently shown, is that they are revisionist texts produced in the Franciscan Joachimite circles in the thirteenth century.[10] In fact, both the Tiburtine and Erithrean Sibyls trace the origins of their apocalyptic thinking to the East, to the Syrian and Byzantine apocalyptic traditions. We will return to the Eastern apocalyptic tradition after briefly surveying the Western Apocalyptic literature.

East-West: A Shared Tradition

The earliest Christian writings of the West and of Rome were in Greek, the most famous of these being *The Epistle of Clement, The Shepherd of Hermas,* and the works of Hippolytus of Rome. Christian writings in Latin began to appear only in the second century. The official language of the Church in Rome continued to be Greek until the middle of the second century although Latin was used as liturgical language in Carthage, Africa. As the Latin Christian literary culture developed in the West under the tutelage of Tertullian, Cyprian, Commodian, and others, the Greek culture receded from Italy and Africa toward Byzantium in the East. We should note, however, that the rise of Byzantium as a cultural center even antedated May 11, 330, the formal inauguration date of the capital of the Roman Empire at Constantinople;

the very fact that Constantine chose Byzantium as his capital city was a clear recognition of Byzantium's importance as a pre-eminent city in the fourth century. With the subsequent division of the Empire into Eastern and Western spheres at the death of Theodosius in 395, the distinction between Western Christianity and Eastern Christianity became a *de facto* situation. However, until the time of the death of Constantine, at least it is hard to talk about a division between East and West in theology and religion because there really did not exist a separate Eastern brand and Western brand of Christianity and apocalypticism.

The first recorded reflections on the Apocalypse comes from Justin Martyr (d. 163). His writings indicate that the theory of the ages of the world played a role in early apocalyptic thinking especially in the context of millenarism (chiliasm), the literal doctrine of the reign of Christ on earth for a thousand years. Justin declares that this is the view of all orthodox Christians (*Dialogue with Trypho*, 80).[11]

There are two trends, according to Daniélou, in early millenaristic thinking: one developed in Asia Minor and reflected in the Johannine Apocalypse and Papias and the other developed in Syria. The first type emphasizes "the conception of an earthly reign of the Messiah which comes before the new creation" (403). Pleasant details of the nature of life in the new reign come from Genesis, chapters 2 and 3. In Syria and Egypt, on the other hand, messianic reign was based on Genesis 1 and on the cosmic week of seven millennia, and the sabbatical would constitute the thousand years of Christ's reign after his *parousia* and the repose of the saints. While the Asiatic view stressed the intensified creation of a new earth, the Syro-Egyptian view of Bardesan, Theophilus of Antioch, Hippolytus, and Sibylline Oracles implied *nirvana*-like sabbatical rest or the cessation of God's creative activity (Daniélou 403).

Ireneus (d. 202), who was born in Asia Minor and spent most his life in the West, is a spokesman for early apocalyptic tradition as well as for the changing political climate of the second century. He recognizes the importance of living at peace with the Empire, and so he refuses to identify the legendary number 666 with any Roman emperor. However, he is the first to identify the beast of Daniel 7 with the beast from the sea of Apocalypse 13 and recognize them as the present evil empire.[12] Yet Ireneus exhibits neither hostility nor affection towards Rome. Nonetheless, in fidelity to the prevailing interpretation of the Apocalypse, he reluctantly identifies the mysterious number 666 with the current regime as only "verisimilar" (*verisimile*), which he calls LATINUS.[13]

Hippolytus, who wrote his treatise *de Antichristo* (c. 200), has no reluctance whatsoever in identifying the fourth beast of Daniel 7 with Rome. Like Ireneus, he, too, allegorizes the number 666; he does not, however, identify the dead Nero with 666. He recognizes the seven heads of the beast with seven emperors; five have already fallen; the sixth is ruling, but the seventh is yet to come. He also makes use of the number seven to symbolize seven world periods of 1000 years each. Consequently, he argues against an imminent *parousia* because the gospel has not been preached yet to all the nations of the world.[14]

Tertullian of Carthage (160-220) insisted that Christians pray for the emperor, even though he is their mortal enemy and a persecutor of the faithful, because it is their duty to pray for enemies and persecutors, a practice that separates them from the pagans.[15] According to Tertullian, the Empire is a satanic invention because the persecution of the Christians is unjust and inspired by the devil. The Babylon of the Apocalypse is Rome.[16] Tertullian exhorts the Christian, who is a citizen of heaven, to flee the world rather than make oneself at home in the world;[17] however, he does not want to see Rome destroyed, for, citing 2 Thessalonians, he argues that it is the Roman Empire that delays the coming of Antichrist. So Tertullian recommends tolerating the Empire and praying for the emperor. He says that we should pray for Rome every day until the end of the world.[18]

The Latin poet Commodian, born in Syria and believed to have lived in the third century, was a strong millenarist and anti-Roman in his interpretation of the Apocalypse.[19] He taught that there would be two Antichrists, a revived Nero in the West who would be killed by the final Antichrist coming out of Persia and ruling over the Jews: "For us Nero is Antichrist..../Nero is the destruction of Rome; he of the world."[20]

Lactantius, who was born in North Africa before the middle third century, survived Diocletian's persecution and later became tutor to Emperor Constantine's sons. A convert to Christianity, Lactantius attacks Roman religion in his *Divine Institutes* (I and II) and summarizes the Christian doctrine of apocalypticism in Book VII. Like Hippolytus, he talks about the seven millennia of cosmic history, corresponding to the seven days of creation; Christ's birth comes in the middle of the fifth millennium, and the establishment of the millennial kingdom has to wait another two hundred years. The signs of the times forboded the collapse of the Roman Empire and the beginning of the end with the coming Antichrist. After the triumph of Christ over his enemies, the judgment, and the resurrection of the dead at the end of the sixth millennium, the joyous life of the blessed in Christ's chiliastic kingdom, which is a return to the Golden Age (VII.24), will begin. For his colorful description of chiliastic existence, he draws support from the Sibylline prophecies.[21] A glance at the sources of the *Divine Institutes* would indicate that Lactantius' apocalyptic vision is a fusion of Jewish, Christian, classical, Persian, and other texts.

Victorinus of Pettau (b. in Pannonia c. 300) wrote a commentary on the Apocalypse which was used and emended by Jerome.[22] Victorinus is also a millenarist who interprets literally the first beast of the Apocalypse as Nero redivivus and its seven heads as the emperors Domitian, Titus, Vespasian, and so on. He suggests also that the Apocalypse does not represent the succession of events in strict chronological order but that the same events are described under successive series. This way Victorinus introduces the theory of recapitulation in the interpretation of the Apocalypse.[23]   Later Jerome revised Victorinus' interpretation "into a form that better reflected a Church at peace with the Empire, if not always with the world. This he partially accomplished...by transforming a literal reading of the text into one with an allegorical framework."[24]

By the third century already, especially in the fourth century, apocalypticism began to show more variations in the thinking and writing of Eastern and Western writers.

Christian East

The great Origen of the Alexandrian Hellenistic school of thought (third century) tends to reject the strict literal interpretation of the Bible and attach to it spiritual meanings. There are no indications in Origen's work that support a literal identification of the beasts of the Apocalypse with the Roman Empire or with the Roman emperors; in other words, Origen was not interested in the literal interpretation of the Apocalypse.

Though most of Origen's works have not survived except for a small portion in translation done by Rufinus in the fourth century, Origen's views on Romans 13 have survived. There he makes an important distinction. Those who bear the sign of Caesar on their bodies render him what belongs to him; however, since the Apostles Peter and John do not possess Caesar's gold and silver (Acts 3: 6), they are not bound to submit to Caesar's orders. However, those who are engaged in the affairs of the world should obey the command of Rom. 13: 1: "Let every person be subject to the government authorities."[25] On the other hand, the non-law-abiding Christian gives the government cause to punish him/her even with death not on account of his/her Christian faith but because of his/her violation of laws. Such a death is not a meritorious Christian death.[26]

Against Celsus' accusation that Christians are bad citizens, Origen argues that the empire was unified by Augustus during the time of Christ through God's providential plan for the spread of the gospel and that, if the entire Empire were Christian and good, God would defend the Empire; nonetheless, Christians should reject the cult of the emperor and Satan. Thus Origen recognizes a place for the Christian in the Empire and by synchronizing Augustus and Christ he underscores the role of the empire in the expansion of Christianity. Origen was not hostile at all to Rome as Hippolytus was.

As for the Greek commentaries on the Apocalypse, only those of Oecumenius, Andreas, and Arethas of this period have survived, and they do not dwell on the literal interpretation of the Apocalypse but rather on its spiritual meaning. For example, Andreas, writing in the sixth century in his commentary on the Apocalypse chapter 13, like Oecumenius before him, does not identify either beasts or the dragon with Rome, as earlier commentators have done. He writes:

> There are those who call this beast [from the land] Antichrist; others prefer to call it one of the devils, and two horns are supposed to stand for Antichrist and the Pseudo-prophet. We prefer to think that the Dragon is Satan; the beast from the sea is Antichrist; the beast from the land is the Pseudo-prophet.[27]

As for the notorious number 666 of the Beast, Andreas refuses to identify him with any Roman emperors, as Hippolytus does. Andreas suggests that different names from different languages can be found to correspond to 666; for example, Greek LAMPETIS, TEITAN, Latin BENEDICTUS, Persian SARMUDEUS. Interestingly, Andreas' apocalyptic tradition is like the Syrian Ephrem's way of thinking, and he identifies Gog and Magog with the Huns.[28]

Arethas of Cappadocia (seventh century), likewise, shies away from a strictly historical interpretation of the Apocalypse. For example, he identifies the dragon with Satan and his ten horns as sins against the ten commandments. However, Arethas slips into historico-prophetical interpretation by saying that Antichrist appears in many forms at different times. For example, Julian and Valens, who came after Constantine the Great, were Antichrists; they were followed by the kingdoms of the Persians and Saracens.[29]

Arethas' commentary from the seventh century indicates that, in spite of the traditional spiritual interpretation of the Apocalypse prevalent in the East, tendency for historicizing the Apocalypse was creeping in on account of the changing political situation in the East, where the power of the Byzantine empire was gradually being eroded due to the ascendancy of Islam. The evidence for the historicizing tendency can be seen in the perception of the fact that the earlier empires and kingdoms are superseded by present ones like those of the Sasanid Persians and Muslim Arabs. Thus it is clear that the Alexandrian tendency of spiritualizing the Apocalypse did not totally snuff out the earlier tradition of historicizing found in Ireneus and Hippolytus.

What is most remarkable about the East of the period from the seventh century is that several apocalyptic works, which had considerable influence both in the East and the West, were published in the Byzantine empire, beginning with Pseudo-Methodius.

"The most consistent conception of world history with an eschatological perspective" is how historian Ernst Sackur evaluates Pseudo-Methodius' sermon *On the Kingdom of the Nations and the Last Times.*[30] The work was originally composed in Syriac in Mesopotamia between 674 and 678 after the conquest of the area by the Arabs. It was soon translated into Greek, and an unidentified monk Peter—perhaps a Greek or Syrian refugee—translated it into Latin in Merovingian Gaul before the end of the eighth century, for four of the Latin manuscripts date from that period.[31]

The Latin title is *Sermo de regnum Cantium* [read *de regno gentium*] *et in Novissimis Temporibus Certa Demonstratio.* As the title indicates, the work is divided into two parts. The first is a history of the world from Adam in the past tense to the Arab invasions, which is in the future tense. The second part records in the future tense eschatological events such as the victories of the Last Roman Emperor and of his sons over the Arabs, the attack of the peoples from the north, the activities of Antichrist, and the Last Judgment. There are two periods of rest: the first comes after the last emperor's victory over the Arabs, and the second prior to the appearance of Antichrist.

The second Eastern apocalyptic text that was translated into Latin before the Arabs invaded Sicily and southern Italy is a sermon attributed to "Pseudo-Ephrem."[32] The original language of the sermon could either be Syriac or Greek, and it was composed by the end of the sixth century; the Latin text in four manuscripts has been existence since 800.[33] The preacher stresses the imminence of the end of the world, the coming disintegration of the Roman Empire, the invasion by Gog-Magog, subsequent peace on earth, the surrender of the Christian empire to God, and the coming of Antichrist.

The third important Greek apocalyptic text, which was later translated into Latin and was made much use of in medieval Europe, is the Sibylline oracles of Baalbek (presently in Lebanon but formerly part of Syria), known in Latin versions as Tiburtine Oracles—from the Sibyl of Tibur, Rome. As mentioned earlier, the earliest Latin versions come from the eleventh century only. The discovery of the Greek manuscripts of the book and its textual analysis now point towards Baalbek in Lebanon as the originating point of the prophecies.[34] On the basis of material evidence, Paul Alexander assigns the Urtext to 502-6 (42-47). Though the Sibyl reportedly utters her prophecies on the Capitoline Hill of Rome among olive trees—there is no evidence for olive trees growing on the Capitoline Hill—, the Sibyl's references to the gigantic temples of Lebanese Heliopolis and to Mount Lebanon seem to suggest Baalbek as the more likely origination point of the prophecies (43-45). In many details the Sibyl's gospel differs from the canonical gospels. For instance, the Sibyl prophesies, as in Marcion, that Jesus will destroy, rather than fulfill, the Jewish Law (41).[35] Jesus' side is pierced by a stake rather than by a lance; three persons are crucified alongside Jesus; angels appear at Jesus' baptism; in an *agraphon*, Sibyl says: "The word you received from me preach to the people of the seventy-two languages"; in the canonical Gospels, on the contrary, Jesus sends out seventy-two disciples to preach (70).

As for the Sibyl's outlook on eschatology, the beginning of the end of the world is at hand in historical times during Emperor Leo I. The author invites puns on the bestial names of kings as in the case of Leo and Basiliscus. The reign of Emperor Anastasius will be followed by the end times. A good king from the East will be followed by a shape-shifting evil king (the ruler of perdition) who will kill the good king. Finally, after the death of Enoch and Elijah in war, Jesus will kill the evil king. Destruction by fire and Final Judgment will follow, paving the path for the reign of Christ.

Between the mid-eighth century and tenth century, several Greek and Latin truncated redactions of Pseudo-Methodius appeared, and they were attributed to the Prophet Daniel of the Hebrew Bible.[36] The redactors were less interested in Methodius' historical speculations than in his predictions of victories over the Arabs; they interpolated new historical materials in the prophecy section.[37] Interestingly, the Latin redactor of the abbreviated Pseudo-Methodius envisages a Western conqueror of the Arab forces rather than a Byzantine conqueror, but the last Emperor would be a king who would rule over both the Romans and the Greeks. In passing, it is interesting to note that the full text of Pseudo-Methodius' prophecy contains no references to or citations from the Book of Apocalypse.

Christian West

Emperor Constantine's conversion to Christianity and the gradual ascendancy and empowerment of the Church called for a revision of the literal, historical interpretation of the Apocalypse. The Alexandrian allegorical method of the scriptural interpretation hastened the new thinking.

Historian Eusebius of Caesarea (b. 263) of Emperor Constantine's court is stunningly favorable toward Rome in his *Ecclesiastical History*. He absolves the empire of many crimes committed against the Jews and Christians and shifts the blame on to imperial magistrates and the mobs.[38] Arguing for the salutary role of the Empire in the providential scheme of things, he thinks that the Empire and Christianity benefited from each other. He even condones the Diocletian persecution by suggesting that God was punishing the Christians for their sins through the emperor (8.1.7). Eusebius even develops a series of parallels between Christ's friend Constantine and Christ himself: As Christ rules forever, Constantine rules for a long time; as Christ redeems humans for the Father, Constantine leads people to Christ; as Christ vanquishes the demons, Constantine conquers his enemies; as Christ opens the portals of heaven to the faithful, Constantine opens the doors of the churches.[39] While Hippolytus viewed the Empire as a caricature of the heavenly kingdom and as a diabolical invention, Eusebius sees it as a figure of heaven and as God's means of human salvation.

As for the doctrine of millenarism, Eusebius disliked it, ignored it, and even ridiculed it as a crass materialistic error among the simple-minded.[40] For Eusebius, the impending *parousia* is not a catastrophe or a radical transformation and the end of Christian times but simply a feast, the glorious culmination of the triumph of Constantine, which is the end of history.[41]

The closing years of the fourth century, as Richard Landes observes, "marked a crucial moment in the history of millenarianism" (156). Alongside his contemporary St. Jerome, the theologian mostly responsible for the widespread decline and fall of millenarism in the West was largely St. Augustine of Hippo (354-430).

Jerome reedited Victorinus' Commentary on the Apocalypse to re-move millenarist statements from it and himself wrote a Commentary on Daniel. In the latter, though Jerome faithfully transmitted the tradi-tional apocalyptic teaching, on the interpretation of the Apocalypse ch. 20 he is a professed spiritualizer. However, Jerome's hesitation can be seen in his attempt, as in the case of Hippolytus, to account for a surplus of forty-five days between two reckonings in Daniel 12: 11-12 (1290-1310), for the time of Antichrist leads him to project a brief period of rest immediately before the end.

Augustine, as he himself admits in the *City of God*, was once a millenarist à la Apocalypse 20: 1-6, according to which the first bodily resurrection would be followed by the millennial sabbatical rest of the saints, which was often interpreted in highly sensual terms.[42] Later Augustine was compelled to combat against the unrealistic and ridicu-lous millenaristic tendencies of his episcopal days when a stream of apocalyptic due dates and events upset the morale of his people. Alaric's invasion of Rome in 410 was the most dramatic of these events. Some people preached: "Behold, from Adam all the years have passed...the 6000 years are completed...and now comes the Day of Judgment!"[43] The credulous folks watched for the signs of the End.

Augustine continuously preached against this apocalyptic hysteria by reminding his people that Jesus himself said that the Book of Apoca-lypse was to be understood as spiritual allegory, that the millennium had already begun with the birth of Christianity, that Jesus himself said no one was to know the hour of the End (Acts 1: 7), and that only the Father knew the exact hour of the Second Coming. And then, arming himself with the Donatist Tyconius' (330-390) exegetical strategies, he tirelessly propounded his spiritual interpretation of the Apocalypse of John.[44]

Tyconius had championed a typological, a-historical reading of the Apocalypse. According to him, apocalyptic symbolism is to be under-stood in terms of the constant struggle between the forces of good and those of evil within the Church in every age (McGinn 27). Tyconius postulated that every symbol is both positive and negative: just as there is light, there is also darkness. The Church necessarily entails the anti-church just as there is Antichrist to Christ. The Church itself is com-posed of believers and hypocrites from the beginning. Likewise, Anti-christ, false prophets, and sinful priests are at work in the world. Though, on one hand, Tyconius tended to view the End as at hand, he rejected the elusive literal-historical approach preferring the symbolical one which made more sense in understanding historical and metahistorical phenomena.[45]

Augustine argued that the earthly city and heavenly city would remain interlinked until the *eschaton*, which transcends time. Therefore, one cannot interpret any historical event apocalyptically and the prudent Christian should stay away from speculations about the end which no one—not even the Son of Man—is empowered to know. He interpreted Christ's 1000-year reign to be the present age, beginning with Christ's birth.[46] But the 1000 years is only a symbol of completeness just as the ten kings of Daniel symbolized full sovereignty rather than ten kings, numerologically speaking.[47] Likewise, Augustine refused to give any historical referents to Antichrist, Gog and Magog, and the beasts of the Apocalypse.

The Church of Rome found Augustine's symbolic interpretation of the Apocalypse more sensible than the historicist interpretations of the past and encouraged its dissemination throughout the Western world and at the Council of Ephesus (431) condemned belief in the literal millennium as a superstitious error. Church authorities even made determined efforts to suppress the chiliastic chapters from Ireneus' *Adversus Haereses*; remarkably, ecclesiastical censors seemed to have overlooked one manuscript of Ireneus' *Adversus Haereses* with chiliastic chapters discovered in 1575.[48] Primasius, Cassiodorus, Aspringius, Ambrose, Bede, Ansbertus, Beatus, Haymo, Walafried of Strabo, and Berengaudus followed Augustine in their exegeses of the Apocalypse. Consequently, the Tyconian-Augustinian reading of the Apocalypse, with its search for a-historical, moral, ecclesiological, and anti-millennial meanings and with its exclusion of attempts to find current events as signs of the end, dominated Western interpretation of the Apocalypse till about 1100.[49]

The immense popularity of Augustine and Jerome did not totally eclipse the earlier realistic eschatology of Ireneus and Hippolytus. Augustine's own disciple, Quodvultdeus, wrote the *Liber de Promissionibus* (c. 450), which systematically enumerated all the signs of the end times and declared them fulfilled; he even identified the Vandals and Goths as Gog and Magog.[50] Commentators, meanwhile, refused to forgo the obvious literal meaning of the 1000 years. At different times some disputed whether the 1000 years began with the birth or crucifixion of Christ. When Rupert of Deutz (c. 1100) interpreted the struggle between Pope Gregory VII and Henry IV as a prophecy or as a type of the conflict between the Woman and the dragon in chapter 12 of the Apocalypse, he was only working in the historical school of apocalyptic interpretation. A little later, Joachim of Fiore, the Calabrian abbot, set forth a fully developed historical reading of the Apocalypse in his extremely popular *Exposition on the Apocalypse*, which, according to him is "the key of things past, the knowledge of things to come; the opening of what is sealed, the uncovering of what is hidden."[51] As McGinn observes, Joachim's powerful exegesis introduced a new understanding of history in the West and influenced and challenged interpretations of the Apocalypse for centuries to come (533). What is to be noted here is that Rupert of Deutz and Joachim were only reemphasizing the earlier historical interpretation of the Apocalypse and not inventing something new.

The brief survey of early patristic apocalyptic thought given above shows that the belief in the imminence of the End did not necessarily die out either with the establishment of the Christian Roman empire or with the symbolic interpretation of the Apocalypse propagated by Augustine and his school. Faith in millenarism, indeed, is a fuzzy experience that does not follow one particular school of thought or is derived exclusively from it; it is compatible with different systems of theology. So we can say that, even though Augustinian historiographers and secular historians would like to assert that millenarism disappeared after Augustine's *City of God* appeared, "it survived in a variety of forms, elite and popular, at least in Latin Christendom" (Landes 203). As we shall see in the next chapter on Antichrist, the tenth-century *Letter of Adso on Antichrist* revives the historical interpretation of the Apocalypse by reaffirming the idea of the endurance of Rome to the end of time.

NOTES

1. See Adela Y. Collins, "The Early Christian Apocalypses," *Semeia* 14 (1979): 61-121 for a good bibliography of editions and studies. Most of these are accessible in English translation in Heinnecke and Schneemelcher, *New Testament Apocrypha* (Philadelphia, 1963), 1965) and M. R. James, *Apocryphal New Testament* (Oxford, 1924).

2. The Anglo-Saxon poem of *Beowulf* shows several instances of borrowing from *The Apocalypse of Paul* especially in the description of Grendel's lair. Dante also seems to have been familiar with this work.

3. See William Barnstone, *The Other Bible* (San Francisco, 1984), pp. 537-550, for an English translation.

4. See Bernard McGinn, "*Teste David cum Sibylla*: The Significance of the Sibylline Tradition in the Middle Ages," in B. McGinn, *Apocalypticism in the Western Tradition* (Norfolk, 1994), pp. 1-35.

5. See A. Kurfess, "*Dies Irae*," *Historisches Jahrbuch* 77 (1957): 328-38.

6. See McGinn, *Visions of the End* (New York, 1979), p. 20.

7. Heinnecke and Schneemelcher, *New Testament Apocrypha*, p. 654.

8. E. Sackur, ed. *Sibyllinische Texte und Forschungen* (Halle, 1898); according to Sackur, the present Latin text comes from no earlier than the eleventh century (134-5).

9. See O. Holder-Egger, "Italienische Prophetieen des 13 Jahrhunderts," *Neues Archiv* 15 (1890): 155-63.

10. Paul J. Alexander, The Diffusion of Byzantine Apocalypses in the Medieval West and the Beginnings of Joachimism," in *Prophecy and Millenarism*, ed., A. Williams (Harlow, 1980), pp. 53-106.

11. See Jean Daniélou, *The Origin of Latin Christianity* (London, 1977), *passim*; B. McGinn, *Visions of the End* (New York, 1979), pp. 17 ff.

12. *Adversus Haereses* 5.26.1: "Manifestius adhuc etiam de novissimo tempore et de his qui sunt in eo decem regibus, in quos dividetur quod nunc regnat imperium, significavit Johannes Domini discipulus in Apocalypsi, edisserens quae fuerint decem cornua quae a Daniele visa sunt."

13. *Adversus Haereses* 5.30.3: "Sed et LATEINOS nomen habet sescentorum sexaginta sex numerum; et valde verisimile est quoniam novissimum regnum hoc habet vocabulum. Latini enim sunt qui nunc regnant."

14. See François Paschoud, "La doctrine chrétienne et l'idéologie impériale romaine," in *L'Apocalypse de Jean* (Geneva, 1979), pp. 44-45.

15. *Ad Scapulam* I.3; Paschoud, p. 49.

16. *Adversus Judaeos* 9.15; *Adversus Marcionem* 3.13.10.

17. *Apologeticum* 41.4.

18. *Apologeticum* 32.1: "Romanae diurnitati favemus...Christianus...necesse est ut...ipsum [imperatorem]...salvum velit cum tot romano imperio quousque saeculum stabit; tamdiu enim stabit."

19. J. Martin, the most recent editor of Commodian (*Commodiani Carmina*, x-xii), places him in the third century; see also McGinn, *Visions of the End*, pp. 22-23.

20. See McGinn, p. 23.

21. See McGinn, *Apocalyptic Spirituality* (New York, 1979), pp. 25-80, for a readable translation of Lactantius' *Divine Institutes*, VII.

22. *CSEL* 49.

23. See R. H. Charles, *Studies in the Apocalypse* (Edinburgh, 1915), p. 11.

24. F. Ann Matter, "The Apocalypse in Early Medieval Exegesis," in *The Apocalypse in the Middle Ages*, ed. R. K. Emmerson and B. McGinn (Ithaca, 1992), p. 39.

25. *Commentaria in Epistolam ad Romanos 9:25*.

26. *Commentaria in Epist. ad Rom.* 9:30.

27. *Commentaria in Apoc. Sermo* 13; *PG* 106: 335.

28. See W. Boussset, *The Antichrist Legend* (London, 1890), p. 92.

29. Arethas, *Comment. in Apoc. PG* 106:671.

30. Ernst Sackur, *Sibyllinische Texte und Forschungen* (Halle, 1895), p. 7. See Paul J. Alexander, "The Diffusion of Byzantine Apocalypses in the Medieval West and the Beginnings of Joachimism," in Ann Williams, ed., *Prophecy and Millenarism* (Burnt Hill, Harlow, Essex, 1980), p. 55.

31. Sackur, pp. 60-96; Monk Peter's preface is on pp; 59 ff.

32. C. P. Caspari, ed. *Briefe, Abhandlungen, und Predigten* ... (Christiana, 1890), pp. 208-20; Paul J. Alexander, *The Byzantine Apocalyptic Tradition* (Berkeley, 1985), pp. 136 ff.

33. Alexander, "Diffusion...," p. 60.

34. Paul J. Alexander, *The Oracle of Baalbek: The Tiburtine Sibyl in Greek Dress* (Washington, DC, 1967), *passim.*

35. In the Marcionite Lucan Gospel, a charge brought by the Jews to Pilate is that Jesus was trying to destroy the Jewish law and the prophets, a charge which would make Jesus a Nasorean (heretic or rebel) deserving of death, as the cause of Jesus' death is indicated in John 19: 19; see Tertullian, *Contra Marcionem* iv.7.4 (*CCSL* 1.554.22): "Venisse se, non ut legem et prophetas dissolveret, sed ut potius adimpleret. Hoc enim Marcion ut additum erasit"; see also A. Harnack, *Marcion: Das Evangelium vom fremden Gott* (Leipzig, 1924), pp. 80, 261; cited by Alexander, p. 72.

36. V. M. Istrin, *Otkrovenie Mefodiia Patarskago...* (Moscow, 1897); see Alexander, "Migration," p. 95.

37. See Alexander, *The Byzantine Apocalyptic Tradition*, pp. 62-95.

38. *Historia ecclesiastica* 2.21-3; 2.22.8; 3.33; 4.8.6; 7.30.21; 2.23.2; 8.1.7; see Paschoud, p. 62.

39. *The Eulogy of Constantine*, 6 ff; see Paschoud, p. 64.

40. *Historia ecclesiastica* 3.28; 4.14; 7.25; Richard Landes, "Lest the Millennium Be Fulfilled: Apocalyptic Expectations and the Pattern of Western Chronography, 100-800 CE," in Werner Verbeke et al., *The Use and Abuse of Eschatology in the Middle Ages* (Leuven, 1988), p. 150.

41. See J. Cirinelli, *Les vues historiques d'Eusèbe de Césarée durant la période pré-nicenne* (Dakar, 1961), pp. 455-86; Paschoud, p. 66.

42. *De Civitate Dei* 20.7.1; Paula Frederiksen, "Tyconius and Augustine on the Apocalypse," in R. K. Emmerson and B. McGinn, *The Apocalypse in the Middle Ages*, p. 29.

43. *Sermo* 113:8; PL 38:576.

44. Paula Frederiksen, "Tyconius and the End of the World," *Revue des Études augustiniennes* 18 (1982): 59-71.

45. See Walter Klaasen, *Living at the End of the Ages* (New York, 1992), p. 4.

46. *City of God*, 20.7.9.

47. *City of God*, 20.23.

48. Norman Cohn, *Pursuit of the Millennium* (Fairlawn, 1957), p. 14.

49. Bernard McGinn, "Revelation," in Robert Alter and Frank Kermode, eds., *The Literary Guide to the Bible* (Cambridge, 1987), p. 531.

50. *Liber de Promissionibus*, iv.13.22; *CCSL* 60: 207; see Landes, p. 158.

51. Joachim, *Exposition*, fol 3r; cited by McGinn, p. 532; on Joachim's exegesis see McGinn, *The Calabrian Abbot: Joachim of Fiore in the History of Western Thought* (New York, 1985), chaps. 4 and 5.

CHAPTER FOUR

Antichrist: East and West

Among the several important eschatological themes and images of the Apocalypse discussed in the earlier chapters—like the Second Coming, millenarism, attitude toward the Roman Empire, and Last Judgment— probably the most popular one is that of Antichrist. In religious discussions and popular imagination all these themes are closely interrelated; that is, Christ would come again to save the faithful from the persecution of the satanically controlled Roman Empire, whose emperors were more or less closely identified as Antichrist in the early centuries of the Christian era by the persecuted and disenfranchised Christians. With the defeat of his enemies, followed by the Last judgment, Christ would come again to establish his kingdom on earth, more or less a synonym for earthly paradise, for a millennium.

As St. Augustine provided a view of world history as a gradual unfolding and final resolution of the dramatic conflict between the Earthly City and the Heavenly City, one could look at the same conflict as a struggle between Christ and Antichrist, as early and medieval Christian writers had viewed it. Christian writers and preachers saw Antichrist at different periods as Nero, Justinian, Mohammed, Frederick II, Pope John XXII, Luther, Napoleon Bonaparte, Hitler, Stalin, Saddam Hussein, and so on—all as enemies of God and Christ. Antichrist was now conceived as one, then as many; now as fully human, then as part devil; now as gentile, then as Jew; now as the principle of evil in each human being, then as an external agent; now as heretics and schismatics outside the Church, then as hypocrites and wicked priests inside the Church.[1]

Though *Antichrist* may appear very Christian in his appellation, his origins lie in pre-Christian cultures and times. Having been christened by the Christian tradition—canonical and apocryphal—, Antichrist's legend started flourishing in early patristic Christianity. After the Germanic invasions of Western Europe, the colorful legend of Antichrist went through a period of retarded growth under the blistering attack of the Augustinian school of thought which frowned on the literal-historical interpretation of the Apocalypse and Antichrist. During the same period, however, the legend enjoyed a luxuriant growth in the East. Gradually the Eastern views of Antichrist migrated to the West and infiltrated the preaching of Englishmen like Aelfric and Wulfstan and literary works like Anglo-Saxon (Old English) *Beowulf* and culminated in Adso's treatise on the life of Antichrist.

Our previous survey of pre-biblical and parabiblical apocalyptic literature indicates that in general both Jewish and Christian apocalypses have generously borrowed from earlier eschatological traditions like Persian and Indian. As Gunkel, Bousset, and Dibelius have shown years ago, Antichrist is a mythical monster, the adversary of God in creation, who at the end of time will appear again and take up his struggle against God but will be finally dislodged, whereas in primordial times he was only temporarily defeated and imprisoned.[2] A. H. Keane, English translator of Wilhelm Bousset, the premier scholar on the Antichrist tradition, echoes the master's view that:

> Antichrist legend is nothing less than a later anthropomorphic transformation of the Babylonian Dragon myth....[The] primeval dragon presents so many features in common with the dragon of Revelation, as well as of the independent Antichrist legend, that the descent of one from the other can scarcely any longer be denied.[3]

Bousset finds the connecting links between Antichrist and the Babylonian Tiamat in the biblical books of Daniel, Enoch, and the Prophets. The Hebrew-Assyrian connection can be seen in the cognate Hebrew/Assyrian names such as Mardochai (Murdoch)/Marduk, Samuel/Shamailu, Ishmael/Ishmaelu, Methuselah/Metushaili, and Gamaliel/Gamalili. Bousset agrees with Gunkel:

> The apocalyptic writers do not themselves create or invent their materials, or even merely weave them together of all sorts of scattered threads.... These seers simply reveal the sacred lore of primeval times. They, of course, modify here and there; but their function consists essentially in adaptation, not in invention, in application (to the times), not in fresh creations. (Bousset 6)

The pre-Christian Antichrist figure is the classical adversary of the gods, and he appears in different forms. He appears as Tiamat, Leviathan, the Serpent of the Garden of Eden, Satan, Ahirman, and Asuras. In a monotheistic religion, the adversary of God is typically one person, while both God and Satan have their followers: Michael and the angels fight for God against Satan and his comrades, who are the fallen angels. In a polytheistic religion like Hinduism, Antichrist-like enemy is plural, the Asuras in general, with each side having different leaders at different periods and with power shifting from one side to the other side and the cycles repeating endlessly. Historian McGinn shows the interplay of myths, legends, and history in the polymorphous development of the Antichrist-myth within the apocalyptic traditions of the intertestamentary or Second Temple Judaism (200 BCE - 50 CE).[4] The Christian writers of the New Testament tradition built upon the foundations of past literature and created the fascinating figure known as Antichrist.[5]

Antichrist in the New Testament

In the New Testament the title "Antichrist" appears only in 2 John 7 and in 1 John 2: 18, 22; 4: 3. It is more than likely that Presbyter John derives the term from existing Christian apocalyptic preaching rather than invents it. The persona, though not the term, of Antichrist appears as an apocalyptic figure or as false prophet elsewhere in the New Testament, as mentioned earlier; he is expected to perform signs and wonders to deceive the faithful. Here Antichrist is linked to the Jewish tradition of the false prophet of the end time as the opponent of the true prophet.[6] He is also a false teacher or heretic; 1 John 2: 22 indicates that a heresy, like Doceticism which claimed that Jesus' body was not real but only apparent, is an Antichrist. The conception of Antichrist as a world ruler is largely borrowed from Daniel, chapter 7 (Mark 13: 9-19; Apoc. 13; 1-11). Daniel's reference to the Seleucid Empire and Antiochus Epiphanes becomes Roman Empire and its emperor in New Testament apocalyptic thought.

2 Thessalonians 2: 1-12 and St. Paul

The canonical New Testament Epistle 2 Thessalonians, attributed to the authorship of St. Paul, addresses the issue of the Antichrist-like figure in the context of the *parousia*. Though the epistle does not use the term "Antichrist," "the lawless man" or "the Son of Perdition" has always been regarded in hermeneutic thought as Antichrist. Here he appears as a single figure, the human agent of Satan. In a hand-to-hand combat the "breath of the mouth of the Lord Jesus" (Ps. 2: 9; Is. 11: 4) will slay him. Antichrist's arrival is described as a *parousia* (coming) at the end time.

> And now, brothers, about the coming of the Lord Jesus Christ and his gather-
> ing of us to himself: I beg you, do not lose your heads or alarm yourselves
> whether at some oracular utterance, or pronouncement, or some letter pur-
> porting to come from us, alleging that the Day of the Lord is already here. Let
> no one deceive you in any way whatever. That day cannot come before the
> rebellion [apostasia] against God, when the Man of Lawlessness will be re-
> vealed, the Son of Perdition. He is the Enemy. He rises in his pride against
> every god, so called, and every object of men's worship, and even takes his seat
> in the temple of God claiming to be God himself. You cannot but remember
> that I told you this while I was still with you; you must now be aware of the
> restraining hand [katechon] which ensures that he shall be revealed only at the
> proper time. For already the secret power [mysterion] is at work, secret only
> for the present until the Restrainer [katechon] disappears from the scene.
> And then he will be revealed, that lawless man [ho anomos] whom the Lord
> Jesus will destroy with the breath of his mouth, and annihilate by the manifes-
> tation of his coming [parousia]. But the coming [parousia] of that wicked man
> is the work of Satan. It will be attended by all the powerful signs and miracles
> of the lie [pseudos], and all the deception that sinfulness can impose on those
> doomed to destruction. Destroyed they shall be, because they did not open
> their minds to the love of the truth, so as to find salvation. Therefore, God puts
> them under a delusion, which works upon them to believe the lie, so that they
> may all be brought to judgment, all who do not believe the truth but make
> sinfulness their deliberate choice.

The crux of this passage is the "restrainer" or "restraining hand or force"
(katechon of verses 6 and 7). In the West, as early as Tertullian (c. 200),
Christians living under Roman persecution tended to identify katechon
with the Roman Empire. In the East, Theodore of Mopsuestia (fifth
century) of the Syrian Church identified katechon as the necessity of
preaching the gospel throughout the world (Matt. 24: 14).[7]

John's Apocalypse

John describes the coming of Antichrist in chapter 12 of the Apocalypse, in the famous vision of the Divine Mother or the Woman clothed
with the sun, the antithesis of the harlot of the book. A huge red dragon,
identified as Satan (ch. 13) with seven heads and ten horns, attacks the
woman in order to devour her son. While heaven saves the son and she
flees into the desert, a fierce war breaks out in heaven between Archangel Michael's forces and the dragon's minions; the defeated dragon is
flung down to earth. It goes down to the beach looking for help. It is
not disappointed. A leopard-like beast with ten horns and seven heads
rises from the sea and is empowered by the dragon to reign for 42
months over all mankind in utter defiance of God. Then a land beast

with two horns but roaring like the dragon appears. It is a wonder-worker, life-giver, and ally of the first beast. He enforces the worship of the beast whose name is 666. God decides that he has had enough of the beast's misrule. He sends out plagues, and the angels pour out vials of divine wrath on the sinful world. As the seventh angel executes God's orders, divine vengeance falls on the great harlot of Babylon, who is riding a scarlet beast with seven heads and ten horns. God punishes the sinful scarlet harlot, the city on seven hills, by burning it to the ground. As the city burns, the smoke from its ruins becomes visible for miles around, and God's vindication is complete:

> "Alas, alas! thou great city,
> thou mighty city, Babylon!
> In one hour has thy judgment come."

> And the merchants of the earth weep and mourn for her, since no one buys cargo any more, cargo of gold, silver, jewels and pearls, fine linen, purple, silk and scarlet, all kinds of scented wood, all articles of ivory, all articles of costly wood, bronze, iron and marble, cinnamon, spice, incense, myrrh, frankincense, wine, oil, fine flour and wheat, cattle and sheep, horses and chariots, and slaves, that is, human soul. "The fruit for which thy soul longed has gone from thee, and all thy dainties and thy splendor are lost to thee, never to be found again!" The merchants of these wares, who gained wealth from her, will stand far off, in fear of her torment, weeping and mourning aloud.

> "Alas, alas, for the great city that was clothed in fine linen, in purple and scarlet, bedecked with gold, with jewels, and with pearls! In one hour all this wealth has been laid waste." And all shipmasters and seafaring men, sailors and all whose trade is on the sea, stood far off and cried out as they saw the smoke of her burning, "What city was like the great city?" (18: 10-18).[8]

There is near-unanimous agreement among the Apocalypse scholars that the author means the Roman Empire by the image of the first beast, whose wounded head represents Emperor Nero, the Antichrist figure. From another perspective, the unholy trinity of the dragon, the first beast, and the second beast (described also as the false prophet in 16: 13 and 19; 20) reveals the multidimensional personality of Antichrist.

Antichrist of the Apocalypse appears in Jerusalem (chapter 11), which is the theater of many events such as the killing of the two witnesses by the beast from the sea (11: 7). The Jerusalem association indicates that there is also an Antichrist who seems to have little to do with Rome, as Bousset points out (22). The abomination of desolation or profanation that Matthew (24:15) speaks about should be Antichrist who takes his seat in the Temple in Jerusalem. The connection between the Roman factor and Jerusalem factor finds some clarification not in the writings of apologists and Apostolic Fathers but in the later writings of Ireneus, Hippolytus, and others.

An Early Tradition

Ireneus views Antichrist as the embodiment (*recapitulatio*) of all evil while Christ is the embodiment of all good. If Christ became man to save humankind, the apostate Antichrist will become man to destroy mankind (*Adv. Haer.* 5.28.2); he is almost like the Hindu avatar of Kalki during the *kaliyuga*. When he is charting the career of Antichrist, he departs from the Nero legend and claims that Antichrist will be born a Jew from the tribe of Dan, citing Jeremiah 8: 16 (*Adv. Haer.* 5.302); he even points out the fact that the tribe of Dan is conspicuously absent from the list of the tribes saved in Apocalypse ch. 7. Ireneus associates him with the heresies of Gnosticism and Marcionism along with apostasy, which is the hallmark of Antichrist.[9]

Presbyter Hippolytus, writing in Rome about 235, portrays Antichrist as Christ's alter ego in many details. He subscribes to the tradition on the birth of Antichrist from the people of Israel, a tradition taught by Ireneus. Hippolytus writes:

> A lion is Christ, and a lion is Antichrist; king is Christ, and king is Antichrist.... In the circumcision came the Redeemer into the world, and in like manner will the other come; the Lord sent Apostles unto all nations, and in the same way will the other send false apostles; the Savior gathered the lost sheep, and in like manner will the other gather the scattered people. The Lord gave a seal to those that believed in him, and a seal will the other likewise give; in the form of a man appeared the Savior, and in the form of a man will the other also come; the Lord stood up and exhibited his holy body as a temple, and the other will also set up the temple of stone in Jerusalem.[10]

While discussing the Last Enemy's career, Hippolytus identifies the first beast of the Apocalypse with Rome and one of the horns of the second beast as Antichrist, who will establish his sway after the fall of the Roman Empire (*Antichrist* 49; McGinn 61).

After the period of Ireneus and Hippolytus, most Christian writers could no longer realistically portray Antichrist as a pagan Roman emperor, so they started painting him as one belonging to the Jewish race. Victorinus may be an exception, for he tenaciously holds on to the view that Nero is Antichrist but disguised as a Jew:

> He will lust after no women, and acknowledge no God of his fathers, for he will be unable to beguile the people of the circumcision unless he appears as

the champion of the law. Nor will he summon the saints to the worship of idols, but only accept circumcision should he succeed in leading any astray. Lastly, he will so act that he will be called Christ by them. (*Antichrist* 13; Bousset 29)

Thus the historicist interpretation of Antichrist in the early Church goes beyond the identification of the Roman Empire or of one of the emperors with Antichrist and alludes to the possibility even of a second Antichrist of Jewish origin.

One way to account for the appearance two Antichrists in Christian apocalyptic thinking is that since the Apocalypse talks about two beasts there must be two Antichrists. The two persecutors the early Christians encountered were, as is evident from the Gospels and the Acts of the Apostles, were the Roman Empire and Pharisaic Judaism. While Rome is the first Antichrist, the second one must be of Jewish origin especially since in traditional Jewish view the false messiah was a Jew (McGinn 65). The problem with this position is simply that Judaism ceased to be a threat to Christianity after the destruction of Jerusalem and the dispersion of the Jews.

It is more than likely that it is the presence and rule of the beast in Jerusalem in end times that necessitated the invention of the second Antichrist with Jewish connections. Commodian is probably the first one to spell out the doctrine of the double Antichrist. In his *Instructions* (1:41) he identifies Antichrist as Nero raised from Hell. Then in his *Carmen apologeticum* he predicts that after the three-and-a-half year rule of Nero redivivus and the fall of the Roman Empire, a king from the East (Persia) will march on Rome, kill Nero and his two adopted caesars (Daniel 7-8) and set the end times in motion (Bousset 79-81). Then the second Antichrist will march to Jerusalem where he will be welcomed by the Jews in whose favor he will reestablish the Old Law. Commodian writes:

A man from Persia claims to be immortal.
For us Nero is the Antichrist, for the Jews the other is.
These two are prophets at the very end.
Nero is the destruction of Rome; he of the whole world;
I tell only a few of the secrets I have read about him. (932-6)[11]

The last line of the poem suggests that the idea of the double Antichrist is an ancient tradition, which means Commodian did not invent it. Support for the same idea comes also from the fourth-century North African writer Lactantius. His first persecutor of the Christians is Rome to be followed by "a mighty enemy from the North"—Lactantius is writing in North Africa—who would destroy Daniel's legendary three kings in the East and tyrannize the world.[12] Though Lactantius does not call the last emperor from Syria Antichrist, in effect he is one, as McGinn also convincingly argues (67–68). The Lactantian view receives support from Sulpicius Severus, who has left the oral tradition of St. Martin of Tours (313–397), who also preached about two Antichrists; according to Martin, the second one will appear in Jerusalem and will kill Nero.[13]

Spiritual Antichrist in the West

The Johannine epistles, as mentioned earlier, identify heretics with Antichrist. Origen's allegorical interpretation could easily accommodate this view. Origen calls Antichrist "the son of the evil demon, who is Satan and the devil" (*Contra Celsum* 6.45); since the devil is a liar and heretics are also liars, heretics can be allegorically called the archliar devil's offspring, one of whom is the lying Antichrist.

In the fourth century the spiritual view of Antichrist, adumbrated and obscurely indicated by Origen, began to take firm shape in Western Christendom as the political landscape changed. With the edict of Milan in 313, under Constantine's benevolent eye, the once-persecuted Christian religion became the state's favored religion, Rome the persecutor became the protector, and the ghost of Nero faded away never to return again. Rome was no longer the accursed Babylon of the Apocalypse and the sworn enemy of the Christian God but the eternal city. If Rome could no longer confidently be identified as Antichrist, where were the faithful to look for him?

Augustine provided the answer. Without in any way denying or compromising the Catholic belief in a future Antichrist, Augustine called on the faithful to look for Antichrist also here and now in the Church, outside the Church, and in each one of us. In his homilies on 1 John, Augustine echoes John's view that heretics are all Antichrists or enemies of Christ since *Antichrist* literally means "enemy of Christ." Though heretics are outside the Church, many enemies of Christ— those who deny Christ by their sinful deeds—are in the Church: "There you have Antichrist—everyone that denies Christ by his works" (Hom. 3.8). For Augustine, Antichrist is already at work in the world. Antichrist is us![14]

Antichrist in the East

Antichrist is a well-established figure in the East and is known also

by a series of circumlocutions such as "shape-shifter," "prince of iniq-
uity," "son of perdition," "head of pride," "master of error," and "pleni-
tude of wickedness."[15] It is important to note at the very beginning that
Antichrist develops into a very colorful figure in the Eastern tradition
much more so than in the West, which itself gradually adopted many
features of Antichrist from the East, including his physical features.

The fifth-century Syriac *Testament of the Lord*—based on a third-
century Greek original—describes the physical features of Antichrist as
follows:

> And these are the signs of him: his head is as a fiery flame; his right eye is shot
> with blood, his left eye is blue-black, and his eye has two pupils. His eyelashes
> are white; his lower lip is large; his right thigh is slender; his feet are broad; his
> great toe bruised and flat. This is the sickle of desolation.[16]

The Coptic (originally Greek) *Apocalypse of Elijah* from the third
century describes Antichrist as a human but protean creature:

> He is a small person (*pelec*) who has lean legs…with a tuft of grey hair on his
> forehead, which is bald, while his eyebrows reach to his ears, and there is a
> leprous spot on the front of his hands. He will transform himself in the
> presence of those who see him: at one time he will be a young boy but at
> another time he will be an old man. He will transform himself in every sign,
> but the sign of his head he will not be able to change. (3: 15-17)[17]

Pseudo-Ephrem also characterizes Antichrist as a human monster,
clever and crafty like a serpent, rapacious and murderous like a serpent
and a destroyer of souls:

> But the accursed destroyer of souls rather than of bodies, a crafty serpent
> while he grows up, appears in the cloak of justice before he assumes power.
> For to all men he will be cunningly gentle, unwilling to accept gifts or to place
> [his own] person first, lovable to everybody, peaceful to all, not striving after
> gifts of friendship, seemingly courteous among his entourage, so that men will
> bless him and say he is a just man—they do not realize that a wolf is hidden
> beneath the appearance of a lamb and that he is inwardly rapacious under the
> hide of a sheep.[18]

Pseudo-Ephrem's description of Antichrist is in agreement with the
views of Ireneus, who also views him as an apostate, wicked one, mur-
derer, and thief (Adv. Haer. 5. 25).

As for Antichrist's personal identity, Eastern testimonies coalesce with
the earlier views that he is a man of Jewish origin, an incarnation of
Satan, a monstrous dragon or serpent in form, and the enemy of God.

Jerome had already said before in his *Commentary on Daniel* 7: 8:
"Nor let us think that [Antichrist]…is the devil or a demon, but one of
men in whom Satan is wholly to dwell bodily."[19] St. Chrysostom of the

Eastern Church concurs in his Homily 2 on 2 Thessalonians 2: "But who is this one? Think you, Satan? By no means, but some man possessed of all his energy." Bousset points out that Eastern writers like John Damascene, Oecumenius, and Theophylactus accept the authority of Chrysostom on this question (139).

Antichrist is, therefore, not Satan, pure and simple, but satanic, demoniac, and superhuman; he is Satan incarnate as Christ is God incarnate. Pseudo-Ephrem puts it thus:

> Let us learn, my friends, in what form shall come on earth the shameless serpent since the Redeemer...was born of a virgin and in human form crushed the enemy....This then the enemy having learnt...shall be...born of a defiled woman, his instrument.[20]

All the Byzantine apocalypses agree that Antichrist will be of Jewish origin and will be born of the tribe of Dan—a view dissonant with the gentile descent of Antichrist in the legend of Nero redivivus. The Jewish origin of Antichrist is a very ancient one found in Ireneus and Jerome, as noted earlier. The latter on Daniel 11:21 comments that "Antichrist...is to rise up from a small nation; that is, the nation of Jews."[21] Pseudo-Methodius writes: "And immediately the Son of Perdition will be revealed, who is from the tribe of Dan.... [He] is a man of sin clothed in a body from the seed of man and he will be born from a married woman from the tribe of Dan."[22] Antichrist's arrival from Babylon underlies the assumption that the tribe of Dan was deported to Babylonia where they continued to reside (Alexander 195).

Antichrist is also frequently represented as a dragon. Pseudo-Ephrem begins his homily by announcing his intention to speak "on the most shameless and terrible dragon who is to bring disorder into the world" (Bousset 145); he is again referred to as "the most wicked and detested dragon."[23] "The serpent that sleepeth shall awaken," is how the Greek Apocalypse of Daniel (116.35) characterizes Antichrist (Bousset 145). He is Cyril's "fearful beast, the great dragon" (iv.15; Bousset 146). Pseudo-Ephrem describes the exploits of the Dragon-Antichrist:

> A great conflict, brethren,—in those times
> Amongst all men—but especially amongst the faithful
> When there shall be—signs and wonders
> [Wrought] by the Dragon—in great abundance
> When he shall again—manifest himself as God
> In fearful phantasms—flying in the air
> And [show] all the demons—in the form of angels
> Flying in terror—before the tyrant,
> For he crieth out loudly—changing his forms also—

> To strike infinite dread—into all men [24]

The association of Antichrist with the serpent is found, according to Pseudo-Methodius and other apocalypticists, in the exegesis of Jacob's blessing of Dan in Genesis 49: 17: "Dan shall be a serpent in the way, a viper by the path, that bites the horse's heel so that his rider falls backward." Given the tradition of identifying Dan's offspring with Antichrist, commentators find in this passage not only the image of the serpent for Antichrist but also a rationale for his Jewish origin. Additionally, Pseudo-Ephrem finds in the serpent's biting of the horse's heel the miracles performed by Antichrist.[25]

All the Byzantine apocalypses, except *The Oracle of Baalbek*, talk about a double Antichrist or rather about the twofold appearance of Antichrist. The latter view is probably an attempt to accommodate the earlier view that there are two Antichrists—Roman and the Eastern emperors. Pseudo-Ephrem has the following explanation: Antichrist first appears before his assumption of imperial power; he appears the second time after becoming emperor.

Pseudo-Methodius has a different explanation. According to him Antichrist first appears after the Last Emperor of the Greeks has taken up his residence in Jerusalem. His second appearance takes place after the King of the Greeks ascends Golgotha, surrenders his imperial power to Christ, and dies:

> And immediately when the Son of Perdition is revealed, then the King of the Greeks will go up and stand on Golgotha. [here follows a lengthy account of surrender and death]. And immediately the Son of Perdition will be revealed.[26]

The length of the time of the residence of the Last Emperor in Jerusalem is twelve years in the Slavonic Daniel, whereas Pseudo-Chrysostom omits the activities of the Last Emperor in Jerusalem altogether.[27] Pseudo-Ephrem makes two surprising and apparently contradictory statements about Antichrist. First, he says that "the Lord will slay him with the breath of his mouth," and then he says, "He will be bound and plunged alive into the abyss of eternal fire together with his father Satan."[28] Perhaps Antichrist's death is supposed to take place after his being thrown into the fire, as in the Old English poem *Beowulf*, wherein Beowulf mortally wounds Grendel and sends him to his fiery abode in the netherworld, where he dies.

When Antichrist appears in Jerusalem, he will sit in the Jewish Temple and demand to be worshipped as God. This feature, based on 2 Thessalonians 2:4, is found in most Byzantine apocalypses. For example, Pseudo-Ephrem writes: "And entering that [Temple], he shall seat himself as God, and command all nations to worship him."[29] What is of some interest regarding this motif of Antichrist's being seated in the Temple of Jerusalem is the assumption that the Temple must exist, that it must have been rebuilt after the destruction of Jerusalem in the year 70 CE. In this connection there arose the tradition that Antichrist will rebuild the Temple of Jerusalem (Bousset 162). Antichrist will also issue the edict of imposing universal circumcision, "according to the rite of the ancient law," as Pseudo-Ephrem puts it.[30] The period of the depredation of the Temple during Antichrist's tenure is forty-two months, according to the Apocalypse itself (11: 2).

While Antichrist is holding court in the Temple, according to the Erithrean Sibyl, he will stretch out his hand to get hold of the Most High. When the earthlings see him challenge the Almighty, they will say: Is he not the Son of the Highest? They will then begin to worship him as the Messiah.[31] Antichrist, of course, fails in his effort to arrest God.[32]

During his reign in Jerusalem, Antichrist will unleash a terrible persecution against the believers. This time God will send his messengers Enoch and Elijah to announce the imminent coming of Christ. According to the Latin version of the Tiburtine Sibyl, Antichrist will slay them both, but Christ will resurrect them three days later.[33] The messengers become stars in the prophecy of the Erithrean Sibyl. These stars will rise up in the East against the beast, whose roars could be heard as far as the African shores. He will blaspheme against the Lamb and his Testament. The whole world will be terrorized by the beast which has seven heads and 663 feet, and the two stars will not prevail against it until the plan of the Almighty is fulfilled.[34] Obviously, the seven heads of the beast remind us of the beast of the Apocalypse, while the 663 feet should remind us of the association of the beast with Islam because Christians of the time believed that Mohammed, who symbolizes Antichrist in this passage, was born in 663!

According to many Byzantine apocalypses, Elijah and Enoch will eventually succeed in saving the followers of Antichrist (Alexander 216); even though Antichrist will slay them, Christ will revive them later. Finally, the crucified Christ will kill Antichrist and all his hosts, according to *The Oracle of Baalbek* (220). At this point it is useful to know that there is considerable variation in the Byzantine apocalypses as to the final fate of Antichrist. The Tiburtine Sibyl says that Michael will kill him on the Mount of Olives, while Pseudo-Ephrem thinks that

Christ's breath (spiritus) will slay him (Alexander 216).

The basic scheme of the sequence of events of the last days, according to Pseudo-Ephrem, is the following:

1.	Attacks by the wicked, warlike nations	21.13-21.17
2.	Surrender of the empire	214.1
3.	Appearance of the evil and abominable dragon	214.4
4.	Blessings of Moses and Jacob on Dan	214.6
5.	Antichrist as a young man and legitimate king	216.2,11
6.	Sitting in the Jewish Temple	217.1
7.	The great tribulation of three and a half years	217.14
8.	Mission of Enoch and Elijah	219.10
9.	Second Coming of Christ and Antichrist's fall	220.2[35]

What is notably present in Pseudo-Methodius but lacking in Pseudo-Ephrem is a long passage on the Arab invasions, a section on the three woes pronounced by Jesus on Chorazin, Bethsaida, and Capernaum (Matt. 11:21; Luke 10:13)—places associated with the conception/birth, growth, and reign of Antichrist—and a section on the rise of Antichrist. While all the apocalypses follow the basic pattern outlined above, the Greek and Latin Pseudo-Methodius, with the exception of the earlier original Syriac version, have the nine-part sequence and the three additions mentioned above.[36]

The Legend of the Last Emperor

The legend of the Last Emperor who will vanquish all the enemies of God, establish a kingdom of peace, and will surrender his crown and power to Christ is a staple of the Byzantine apocalypses.[37]

After the accession of Constantine to the throne of Rome, the empire was seen in a positive light and was interpreted as the "Restraining Force" of 2 Thessalonians, preventing the rule of Antichrist. In the legend of the Last Emperor, the emperor becomes a positive personification; by means of his victories over Christ's enemies, he prepares the way of the Lord as the Precursor John the Baptist did for Christ. He does this by surrendering his imperial power and office to God and thus puts an end to the Roman Empire. The old era ends and the new era begins.

The common designation for the champion of God against Antichrist is emperor or king (basileus, rex) followed by the name of his subjects: Greeks, Romans, and/or both. In the Latin version of the

Tiburtine Sibyl, the king is referred to as *rex Graecorum* (185.1), as *rex Romanorum et Graecorum* (185.2), and *rex Romanorum* (186.5). In Pseudo-Methodius, he is the king of the Greeks throughout. Only the Latin Sibyl gives him a name: Constans. *The Visions of Daniel* uses the image of the lion for the Last Emperor. When he defeats his enemies, he defeats the first Antichrist or overcomes the first manifestation of Antichrist; after the Last Emperor's death, the second manifestation of Antichrist will appear on earth, but Christ will slay him during his Second Coming.[38]

In Pseudo-Ephrem's *Sermon on the End of the World* (sixth century), the preacher emphasizes the wars between the Greeks and the Persians and announces the imminent end of the world after the fall of the Roman Empire:

> And when the days of the times of those races have been completed, after they shall have corrupted the earth, the kingdom of the Romans will also rest and the empire of the Christians "will be taken from their midst and handed to God and the Father." Then will come the consummation, when the kingdom of the Romans will begin to be consumed and "every principality and power" will have ended.[39]

Islam as Antichrist

Pseudo-Methodius (c. 691) uses Psalm 78:65-66 ("The Lord will awake from his sleep like a man who shakes off his wine and he will put his adversaries to flight") as his starting point. The enemies against whom the Greek king directs his campaigns are not Persians but Arabs. Further, he changes the Psalmist's past tense into future tense and transforms past facts into future prophecy:

> Then suddenly there will be awakened perdition and calamity as those of a woman in travail, and a king of the Greeks will go forth against them in great wrath, and he will be aroused against them like a man who shakes off his wine, and who plots against them as if they were dead men. He will go forth against them [Arabs] from the sea of the Cushites and will lay desolation and ruin in the desert of Jethrib and in the habitation of their fathers. And the sons...of the king of Greece will seize the places of the desert and will destroy with the sword the remnant that is left of them in the land of promise. And fear of all those around them will fall upon them They and their wives and their sons and their leaders and all their camps and the entire land of the desert of their fathers will be given into the hands of the king of the Greeks, and will be surrendered to desolation and destruction and to captivity and murder. And their servitude will be one hundred times more severe than their yoke had been.[40]

In Pseudo-Methodius the prophecy section is largely fulfilled prophecy (*vaticinia ex eventu*), the story of the Muslim invasions of the Near East, which began in 634. He also mentions an earlier Ishmaelite (Midianite) conquest of the world: "And in vessels of wood they flew over the waves of the sea and they went to the lands of the West and came as far the great Rome" (Alexander 38). He also talks about the Roman conquest of the Ishmaelites (39). Now he couches the story and details of the Arab conquest in prophetic terms. His familiarity with the post-conquest details seems to indicate that he lived not long after the beginning of the invasion, probably after the accession of Caliph Uthman (644-56), who built the first navy for the land-locked Arabs. Since he does not mention the Arab failure of the siege of Constantinople in 678 or the story of the Arab Civil War (656-661) between Ali and Muawiya, Paul Alexander argues for c. 676 as the date of the composition of Pseudo-Methodius (24-25). The details of the repressive measures of the conquerors, such as the enslaving of men, beasts, birds, and even waste places with the statement that the tyrant will record them as his as in the *Doomsday Book,* confiscation of natural resources (fish, trees, fruits, land, and crops), collection of poll taxes, destruction of cities, and defilement of Christian sanctuaries also point to a period when the conquest was in progress (24-5). Pseudo-Methodius records the progress of the Muslim conquest over the Persians, Greeks, and Christians as follows:

> It is in the last millennium, which is the seventh, that is brought to nought the kingdom of the Persians and that the sons of Ishmael will depart from the desert of Jethrib and come and assemble, all of them, there at Gabaot the Great. And there will be fulfilled the word of Our Lord who said We are like the animals of the field and the birds of heaven and call them saying: Assemble and come because today I shall make a great sacrifice for you [Ezekiel 39: 17]. Eat the flesh of the fattened animals and drink the blood of the mighty men. For at Gabaot the fattened animals of the kingdom of the Greeks, who destroyed the kingdom of the Hebrews and of Persia, will be exterminated. And thus they too will be exterminated in Gabaot by Ishmael, the wild ass of the desert, who was sent in the wrath of ire against men and against animals and against cattle and against trees and against plants. And it is a punishment in which there is no love.... Also it was not because God loves these sons of Ishmael that he granted to them that they enter the kingdom of the Christians, but because of the iniquity and sin perpetrated by the Christians. (Alexander 44)

The Greek versions of Pseudo-Methodius mention also the Muslim invasion of Africa but not of Spain 711, but they do talk about Muslim raids against Sicily and Greece.[41] Pseudo-Methodius also prophesied that the Arab domination would end after some "year-weeks" or intervals of seven years as in Daniel 9:24: "And after those ten weeks of years they [the Arabs] also will be overpowered and subjected to the kingdom of Rome."[42] Of course, Muslim rule in Mesopotamia did not end either after the seven-year weeks around 689 or after the ten-year weeks around 710. What is important to note here is that Pseudo-Methodius prophesied that a Byzantine emperor would put an end to Arab domination in the Near East and drive them back to the desert and impose on them a yoke a hundred times heavier than the one the Muslims had imposed on the Christians.[43]

Three points, though apparently insignificant in the present context, are relevant in the larger context of the apocalyptic dimensions of *Beowulf* and should be noted below.[44] They are (1) observations on some persons' view of the "worthlessness" of the Last Emperor, (2) the Emperor's sojourn in Jerusalem, and (3) the utter worthlessness of treasures.

The Greek Pseudo-Methodius observes that many thought that the Last Emperor was utterly useless:

> There then will suddenly arise against them [Ishmaelites] with great fury an emperor of the Greeks or Romans. He will awaken from his sleep like a man who had drunk wine, whom men considered like one dead and utterly useless.[45]

What is remarkable about this passage is the important change the translator introduced: he speaks of the Emperor resembling a dead man, while Syriac originally characterizes his enemies as being "like dead men." The translation introduces the element that the Emperor acts with extraordinary vigor in spite of his reputation for uselessness. The net effect of the translation is to enhance the miraculous aura surrounding the Last Emperor: he inflicts a decisive defeat on the Arabs, Rome's mortal foe.[46]

After the victory over the Arabs, the king of the Greeks will reside in Jerusalem for ten and a half years and will hand over his kingship to God on the hill of Golgotha and then give up his spirit.

As the cross is raised to heaven, Antichrist will appear one more time. During the ensuing reign of Antichrist, the earth will be tormented by all sorts of natural disasters like famine, floods, drought, and so on. Then money and treasures are worthless and useless. Pseudo-Ephrem says:

> In those days gold and silver, valuable garments, precious stones and all

kinds of pearls will be scattered on the streets and lanes of cities. No one will even try to collect them nor wish to carry them away for they will be totally regarded as useless.[47]

Byzantine Date of the End of the World

In the West, the fall of Rome in 410 to Alaric and in 455 to Gaiseric prompted much lamentation and forboded the end of the world in the minds of some. Though Jerome could not bring himself to forecast the end of the world, he was devastated as were his contemporary Augustine and the hermit Arsenius in one of the remote monasteries of the Thebaid in Africa, after the sack of Rome in 410 by Alaric the Visigoth.[48] Jerome wrote in one of his letters: "I have long wished to attack the prophecies of Ezekiel and to make good the promises which I have so often given to curious readers. When, however, I began to dictate I was so confounded by the havoc wrought in the West and above all the sack of Rome that, as the common saying has it, I forgot even my own name. Long did I remain silent knowing it was a time to weep (Ecclesiastes, 3:4)."[49] Part of the reason for such distress was the *idee fixe* of the eternity of Rome (*Roma aeterna*), propagandized by Poet Tibullus in the first century before the birth of Christ. After Emperor Constantine decided in 324 to found the city of New Rome (*he Néa Romé* or simply *he Néa*) on the shores of the Bosphorus, Constantinople took over the place of Rome and was destined to last till the second coming of Christ.

Evidence for the conception of the eternity of the new city comes from a description of the ceremonies celebrating the consecration of the new city which has the following passage: "Then the city that was called Constantinople was saluted with acclamations, when the priest cried aloud, 'Oh Lord! Guide it well for infinite ages.'"[50] That the Byzantines seemed to have believed that their city, which is also called New Jerusalem, would endure to the end of the world can be seen in *Life of St. Andrew the Simple* (*Vita Sancti Andreae Sali*).[51] This hagiography contains a conversation between St. Andrew and his disciple Epiphanius:

> Epiphanius began to interrogate the Blessed One and said: "Tell me, please, how and when the end of this world shall occur? What are the beginnings of the throes? And how will men know that the end is close, at the doors?... And whither will pass this city, the New Jerusalem?..." The blessed one said: "Concerning our city, know that it will in no way be terrified by any nation till the consummation of time, for no one will ever ensnare it or take it; because it has been given to the Mother of God, and no one will tear it from Her holy

arms."[52]

The notion that Constantine was the architect of the final Roman empire and that it would end only with the end of the world entered Byzantine theological tradition and into the apocalyptic tradition popularized by Pseudo-Methodius.[53]

According to the Byzantine era, the history of the world begins in September 1, 5509 BC; that is, 5508 years and four months before the beginning of traditional Christian era computed by Dionysius Exiguus in the sixth century and is expected to last for six thousand years before the start of the reign of Christ and his saints.[54] Therefore, they tended to believe that Antichrist would come in 492 if the 6000-year computation is used.[55] The Byzantine chroniclers do not regard this year as connected with any universal catastrophe; for instance, for the year 6000, Theophanes and John Malalas mention only the construction by Anastasius of the wall against the Persians around the city Dara in Mesopotamia (Vasiliev 469). If the 7000-year computation is used for the end of the reign of the saints, then the predicted end would be 1492; further, if the 8000-year model is used, then the end would come only in 2492.

Migration of Apocalypses from East to West

The migration of the apocalyptic preaching of the Syrian priest called Pseudo-Methodius of the Sassanid kingdom in Syria toward Western Europe was rather fast. The seventh-century Syriac work was translated into Byzantine Greek some time before 800 by a cleric who substituted Greek texts for the Syriac Pshitta quotations from the Bible.[56] The translator removed details of Syrian topography and unflattering references to the clergy. A Slavonic version (Slavonic Daniel) was produced in Sicily between 821 and 829. Another Greek text, known as Pseudo-Chrysostom, appeared c. 842. Other Greek versions also appeared in the ninth century (Alexander 77).

Even before most Greek versions appeared, Peter the monk translated Pseudo-Methodius into Latin in Merovingian Gaul during the late seventh or in the eight century.[57] In his little preface (*Praefaciuncula*), Peter says that he translated the work for the benefit of his fellow monks "because [Pseudo-Methodius' predictions] have been rather aptly made for our time...so that by means of the happenings which we observe with our own eyes we may give credence to what has been predicted by our fathers."[58] Probably the Greek Peter was alarmed by the Muslim incursions into Spain and Gaul and was holding out hope for delivery from Islam by means of a "king of the Greeks or the Romans" who would defeat the Muslims and surrender the empire to God.[59] What we notice here is the change from "the king of the Greeks" of the Greek version to "the king of the Greeks or the Romans" and then to "the king of the Romans" in the Latin version. Obviously, the translator is trying to accommodate prophecies to his own time and place. We find a similar transformation of time and place in the prophecy's later adaptations as given below.

In 968, Liudprand, bishop of Cremona who visited Constantinople as the ambassador of Emperor Hugo, saw the book of the prophecy of the Sicilian bishop Hippolytus who predicted that "not the Greeks but the Franks would crush the Saracens."[60] It seems that Liudprand, who had little affection for the Greeks, probably decided to revise the prophecy himself. Before Liudprand became aware of the Byzantine prophecies, the monk Adso of Montier-en-Der, wrote his *Epistola de Ortu et Tempore Antichristi* for Gerberga, wife of the Carolingian king of the Western Franks, Louis IV d'Outremer (936-54) and sister of Otto I of Germany. The work was composed between 945 and 954.[61] In this work Adso discusses the success of the Frankish kings and predicts that one of them would restore the Roman empire and be the Last Emperor of the prophecies:

> Some of our teachers say that one of the kings of the Franks who will come at the end of time, will rule the Roman empire in its entirety. And he will be the greatest and last of all kings. After he has prosperously governed his kingdom, he will finally come to Jerusalem and take off scepter and crown on the Mount of Olives.[62]

Adso's expression "some of our teachers say" indicates that the Byzantine prophecies were modified on the Continent and fairly well known at least in the Frankish kingdom, where Pseudo-Methodius was translated into Latin in the eighth century.[63] What is most remarkable about Adso's work, as in the case of Liudprand, is the "translatio imperii" from Byzantium to the Franks—the common neo-historicizing tendency of apocalyptic writing. Adso's Epistle should be seen as a case of the Germanization of Eastern apocalypticism. As I shall argue later, we see a similar Germanizing tendency of apocalypticism in *Beowulf.*

In fact, the myth of the restorer of the Roman Empire, the victory over Muslims, and the surrender of crown at Jerusalem played a powerful role in Germanic history from the crowning of Charlemagne on Christmas Day in the year 800 as king of the Holy Roman Empire by

Pope Leo. Peter Munz has shown that "in the period immediately preceding the First Crusade, more and more people began to identify the
Last Emperor's journey to Jerusalem with a crusading army for the
reconquest of the Holy Sepulcher" and that in the early twelfth century
"by the time Frederick [Barbarossa] was a young man the Antichrist
speculation was the universal topic of conversation."[64] In the thirteenth
century, Barbarossa's grandson Frederick II became the subject of the
myth of the *imperator redivivus* from death. It was believed that he was
alive on Mount Kyffhäuser and would return to rule as the last emperor
(Alexander 62). In the fourteenth century, Frederick Barbarossa replaced his grandson as the subject of the myth.[65]

Above all, it is important to note that "the influence of Pseudo-
Methodius was immense," to quote the preeminent apocalypse scholar
of today, Bernard McGinn.[66] The text is found in numerous vernacular
translations in the West, including a Middle English version. The text
was used, as mentioned above, for imperial propaganda and during
confrontations with Islam and the Mongols (McGinn 73). Indeed, the
colorful Byzantine legend of Antichrist had an equally colorful career
in Western Europe. No wonder, then, that the legend found its way
into Early English sermons and literary works like *Beowulf,* as we shall
see later.

NOTES

1. Bernard McGinn, *Antichrist: Two Thousand Years of the Human Fascination
with Evil* (San Francisco, 1994), *passim.*

2. See Hennecke and Schneemelcher, p. 577.

3. Bousset, *The Antichrist Legend,* xii–xiv.

4. McGinn, *Antichrist,* pp. 9–32.

5. Surprisingly, the Jewish tradition also mentions the figure—not the name—
of Antichrist a few times in the Jewish apocalypses; for example, the Sibylline books
(I:167) state: "Beliar shall come and work wonders."

6. Hennecke and Schneemelcher, II: 578.

7. McGinn, pp. 43, 291.

8. This section from the Apocalypse is evocative of the memorable lines where
Beowulf is cremated with his treasures in the barrow.

9. McGinn, p. 60.

10. Hippolytus, *Antichrist* 6; cited by Bousset, p. 25.

11. Translation of the poem is by McGinn, p. 66; see Josef Martin, *Commodiana
Carmina* (Turnhout, 1961), Corpus christianorum 128: 33–34; Josef Martin,
"Commodianus," *Traditio* 13 (1957): 1–71; M. Sordi, "Commodianus, *Carmen
apologeticum* 892 ss: *rex ab oriente,*" *Augustinianum* 22 (1982): 203–10; McGinn, p.

66.

12. *Divine Institutes* 7.16.

13. "Ipsum denique Neronem ab Antichristo esse perimendum"; see Bousset, pp. 83, 267; McGinn, p, 68.

14. McGinn, pp. 76-77.

15. Paul J. Alexander, *Byzantine Apocalyptic Tradition*, p. 194. Some of these Eastern titles of Antichrist seem to refer to the Beowulfian monsters, who are also Antichrist-figures.

16. See James Cooper and Arthur J. McLean, *The Testament of the Lord* (Edinburgh, 1902), pp. 57-58.

17. See O. S. Wintermute in *Old Testament Pseudepigrapha*, I: 721-53; David Frankfurter, *Elijah in Upper Egypt: The Apocalypse of Elijah and Early Egyptian Christianity* (Minneapolis, 1993); McGinn, p. 69.

18. See Caspari, pp. 216.1-9; translation in Alexander, *Byzantine Apocalyptic Tradition*, pp. 194-5; on physical descriptions, see Bousset, *Antichrist*, pp. 101 ff.

19. Cited by Bousset, p. 139.

20. Pseudo-Ephrem, III. 134C; cited by Bousset, p. 141.

21. Bousset, p. 135.

22. See Alexander, p. 195.

23. Pseudo-Ephrem, ch. 8; "Ille nequissimus et abominabilis draco," as cited in Bousset, p. 145.

24. Bousset, p. 146. The flight of Simon Magus of Samaria is reminiscent of this passage. At the command of Peter, Simon fell down and died. The legend seems to go back to an older Buddhist story wherein a monk flew in the sky to show off his *sidhi* or yogic powers, and Buddha rebuked him for such a display of vanity and pride.

25. See Alexander, p. 202, for more details.

26. See Alexander, p. 198.

27. Alexander, p. 199; it is noteworthy that in *Beowulf*, Grendel rules in Heorot for twelve years!

28. "Interficiet eum Dominus spiritu oris sui; alligabitur et demergetur in abyssum ignis aeterni vivus cum patre suo satana"; cited by Alexander, p. 199.

29. See Bousset, pp. 160-63, for more patristic testimony. English scholars will note that Grendel seems to do exactly this when he invades Heorot, a play on the word *Hierusalem*.

30. Alexander, p. 206: "Proponet enim edictum ut circumcidantur homines secundum ritum legis antiquae. Tunc gratulabuntur ei Judaei eo quod eis reddiderit usum prioris testamenti."

31. O. Holder-Egger, "Vaticinium Sibyllae Erithreae," *Neues Archiv* 15 (1890): 172: "Os et palatum eius usque ad celos, et manus suas extendet, ut apprehendat altissimum. Et cum viderint terrigene sanctorum excidium, scandalum perfectorum, vestes humiliatas dare testimonium, clamabunt et dicent: 'Ve, ve! diutina derisio, et nonne hic est, quem prescii nunciaverant in leonem? Nonne hic est filius altissimi? Et aperiet abhominatio os suum in contumeliam agni, ut nomen eius deleat, et sibi

primevam superbiam applicabit. Et dicens verba intollerancie conscribetur undique sceleribus et nominibus blasphemie, donec tres pedes semique abbreviati discurrant." Antichrist's attempt to capture God is probably an allusion to the Dragon's attempt to capture the son of the Glorious Woman of Apocalypse 12.

32. In Christian theology, Antichrist is a creature subject to God's authority; in Hindu theology, however, demons are equally powerful as the gods, and demons can win over the gods at least temporarily, with the cycle repeating itself in reverse.

33. Sackur, p. 186; Alexander, p. 211.

34. Holder-Egger, p. 162: "Erit autem bestia horribilis ab oriente veniens, cuius rugitus usque ad gentes Punicas audietur, cuius capita VIIem, sceptra innumera, pedes sexcenti sexaginta tres. Hic erit contradicens agno, ut blasphemet testamentum eius, augens draconis aquas. Reges autem et primates seculi erunt in sudore terribili, et non diminuent pedes eius. Stelleque due consimiles prime insurgent contra ipsam et non obtinebunt, usque dum veniat abhominatio, et voluntas altissimi consumetur, sicut inferius distinguemus."

35. Schedule according to Alexander, pp. 218-9.

36. Alexander, pp. 220-1.

37. See Paul J. Alexander, "Byzantium and the Migration of Literary Works and Motifs: The Legend of the Last Roman Emperor," *Mediaevalia et Humanistica*, n.s. 2 (London, 1971): 47-68; Alexander, *The Byzantine Apocalyptic Tradition*, pp. 151-84.

38. Alexander, p. 152. In the Greek model of the Slavonic *Daniel* the lion (*leon*) becomes a dog (*kuon*): "And there will be fulfilled the saying that the dog and its whelp together will pursue the field (Alexander, p. 152). *Beowulf*-scholars will notice here the parallel between this passage and the pursuit of the dragon by Beowulf and Wiglaf.

39. Translation by McGinn, p. 307.

40. Alexander, p. 48.

41. See Istrin, 42.8; cited by Paul Alexander, "Medieval Apocalypses as historical Sources," *American Historical Review* 73 (1968): 1000.

42. Codex Vaticanus Syrus 58, fol 222v; cited by Alexander "Medieval Apocalypses," p. 1001.

43. Istrin, 41.1; Alexander, "Medieval Apocalypses," p. 1001.

44. The poet of *Beowulf* seems to have made clever use of these ideas in the poem; that means, the English poet was quite familiar with the Eastern apocalypses.

45. Cited in translation by Alexander, *Byzantine Apocalyptic Tradition*, p. 153. The Latin translation is faithful to the Greek: "et exiliet super eos rex Gregorum sive Romanorum in furore magna et expergescitur tamquam homo a somno vini, quem estimabant homines tamquam mortuum esse et in nihilo utilem profecisse (Sackur, p. 93).

46. See Alexander, p. 153; this passage makes much sense for *Beowulf*, where the old and weak king, Beowulf, inflicts a mortal blow on the dragon; the king's helplessness is indicated in the fact that the dragon has already dealt the king a fatal bite and that the king needs the help of Wiglaf in finishing off the dragon.

47. See C. P. Caspari, p. 451; this passage strikes a close resemblance to the passage

at the end of *Beowulf,* where the poet notes about the worthlessness and uselessness of the treasures hoarded by the dragon and carried over to Beowulf as the king lay dying.

48. Augustine's *City of God* reverberates with his pain for the fall of Rome. As for Arsenius, see *Life of Arsenius the Great,* ed. G.Tsereteli (Saint Petersburg, 1899); cited by A.Vasiliev, "Medieval Ideas of the End of the World:West and East," *Byzantion* 16 (1942-43): 462-3.

49. Jerome's Letter 126:2; PL 22:1086; CSEL 56:144.; *A Select Library of Nicene and Post-Nicene Fathers* (New York, 1893), 6: 252-3; see also Jerome's Letter 127:12; *CSEL* 56: 154.

50. *Scriptores originum constantinopolitanarum,* ed.Th.Preger, I (Leipzig, 1908), p. 57; cited by A Vasiliev, p. 464.

51. *PG* 111: 621-888.

52. *PG* 111: 853; the long reply of St. Andrew has been abbreviated here; see translation in Vasiliev, p. 465.

53. See V. Istrin, *Revelation of Methodius of Patara and Apocryphal Visions of Daniel in Byzantine and Slavo-Russian Literature* (Moscow, 1897) (Russian)II: 17; Vasiliev, p. 466.

54. According to Annianus' Alexandrian era, the world was created in 5492 B.C.

55. Vasiliev, p. 500.

56. Alexander, p. 77.

57. Alexander, "Byzantium and the Migration of Literary Works and Motifs," *Medievalia et Humanistica* 2 (1971): 61.

58. Sackur, p. 59; cited by Alexander, p. 61.

59. Sackur, p. 93: "et exiliet super eos rex gregorum sive Romanorum in furore magna.... Hic exiet super eos a mare Aethiopeae et mittit gladium et desolationem in Ethribum...ascendit rex Romanorum sursum in Golgotha, in quo confixum est lignum sanctae crucis...et tollet rex coronam de capite suo et ponet eum super crucem, et expandit manus suas in coelum et tradet regnum Christianorum Deo et patri."

60. Josef Becker, *Liudprandi episcopi cremonensis opera,* scriptores, MGH (Hanover, 1915), p. 196: "Scribit etiam praefatus Hippolytus Graecos non debere Saracenos, et Francos conterere."

61. See Robert Konrad, *De Ortu et Tempore Antichristi:Antichristvorstellung und Geschichtsbild des Abtes Adso von Montier-en-Der* (Kallmünz, 1964); Sackur, pp. 104-13.

62. Sackur, 110.10; translation in Alexander, "The Diffusion," p. 68.

63. Alexander thinks that the source Adso is relying on here is a Latin translation of Pseudo-Hippolytus' version of Pseudo-Methodius known as *The Vision of Daniel* mentioned by Liudprand (68). If that is the case, then the *Beowulf*-poet could easily have encountered *The Vision of Daniel* and could have use the expression of the twelve-year reign of Grendel in Heorot as in the case of the Last Emperor in Jerusalem.

64. Peter Munz, *Frederick Barbarossa: A Study in Medieval Politics* (London,

1969),p.376.

   65. See Norman Cohn, *Pursuit of the Millennium*, pp. 107-112.

   66. McGinn, *Visions of the End* (New York, 1979), p. 72.

PART II

APOCALYPTIC TRADITION
OF EARLY ENGLAND

CHAPTER FIVE

The English of the Millennium: A Heresy

In general, the Christian population of both Western Christendom and Eastern Christendom were more or less aware of the aforementioned views on the Apocalypse and Antichrist. The monasteries and cathedrals preserved the tradition of learning—classical, biblical, and patristic—and continued to pass it on to generation after generation of monks, preachers, priests, and children in monastic and cathedral schools. All monasteries and cathedrals had access to books and libraries since no teaching or preaching was feasible without access to libraries. Monks, priests, seminarians, and lay brothers discussed apocalyptic ideas in the contexts of their times; priests continued to preach apocalyptic sermons based on the readings of the liturgy of the Sunday. During the reign of tyrannic kings and times of war and famine—which were not infrequent in medieval Europe—the ghost of Antichrist was naturally the topic of conversation, as it was during the Gulf War of 1991, when Saddam Hussein of Iraq was almost invariably portrayed as Antichrist, like his earlier cousins Napoleon, Hitler, and Stalin. Tyrannical times also served as the wellspring of hope for better times; for example, the impending millennium (the year 1000) and its environs gave rise to endless speculations. Frequent travels of monks, priests, bishops, merchants, and workers between the British Isles and mainland Europe, both of which were under papal jurisdiction, kept Britain as an integral cultural part of Europe. Therefore, it is impossible to view the British Isles as insular and isolated from European mainstream. Evidence for constant cultural contacts can be found in records of travels, correspondence, and historical works, like in Bede's *Ecclesiastical History of the English People*, not to mention archeological evidence. Besides, the early English folks, whom historians fondly call Anglo-Saxons, are a motley group of people coming from different parts of Europe, including the Iberian Penin-sula—a heresy of sorts.

Anglo-Saxon Invasion: Facts and Fiction

The story of the English people begins with the decline and fall of Roman rule in Britain in the fifth century, the increasing presence of Germanic settlers in Britain during the same century, and the gradual control of Britain by the Germanic powers by the end of the seventh century; English ascendancy comes to an end with the Norman con-quest of the island nation in 1066. It seems then that the Germanic immigrants gradually transformed the political and cultural landscape of Roman Britain while the Norman invasion dramatically changed the face of England in doomsday fashion. Yet the country, which is officially called United Kingdom today, is not just English but multicultural like the USA—if the English language with its different strata is any indication.

The term *Anglo-Saxon*, which is a modern one, conveniently refers to a period in British history from 500 to 1000 and attributes a non-existent degree of ethnic unity and identity to the people of England for political reasons. In fact, the term is very much like "American," which refers to the myriad racial and ethnic groups and religious com-munities that live on the North American continent. The population of Anglo-Saxon England was made up of many British tribes and Ger-manic tribes and Romano-British people, not excluding the descen-dants of Picts who were in Britain before the coming of the Germanic tribes and Huns who came to Europe about the fourth century. Such considerations raise the question about the ethnic origins of the En-glish nation, for which we have no reliable historical sources. A case in point is the identity of the mysterious Mercians, a study of whose ori-gins may help clarify the earlier identity of the English people.

As for the period from the seventh century, we have literary sources, which give detailed and contemporary accounts of the political and ecclesiastical history of the Anglo-Saxons. There are chronicles, biogra-phies, laws of the kings, and land charters. But the two intervening centuries (430-630) are truly dark ages in Anglo-Saxon history. On the Anglo-Saxon side there is no contemporary evidence at all. It is true that in *The Anglo-Saxon Chronicle*, compiled during the reign of King Alfred, there are annals attached to the dates in the fifth and sixth centu-ries. These dates and entries simply give the legendary story of the

settlement of Kent, Sussex, and Wessex, but not of Mercia! Bede compiled his own *Ecclesiastical History* only in 731, almost three centuries
after the settlement without the benefit of any historical records con-
temporaneous with the settlement times since Bede himself does not
identify his own historical sources for the early settlement history. Further, his own interest was not in the pagan age of the settlement but in
the age of the conversion of the English to Christianity, as the very title
of his historical work indicates. Bede, as Patrick Wormwald reminds us,
was not concerned with charting reality but with idealism.[1] Therefore,
"gone are the days when a historian felt able to write...as if he had
been present at the landing of the Saxons, and had watched every step
of their subsequent progress' [Charles Plummer]."[2]

Where did the invaders or settlers come from? In what parts of
England did they settle? These two important questions raise more
difficulties than solutions. But Bede tries to give clear-cut replies to
both questions in a passage as celebrated as confusing. The *foederati*
(Anglo-Saxon invaders) whom the British king invited and settled in
Kent came, Bede says,

> from three powerful German peoples, the Saxons, Angles, and Jutes. From the
> Jutes are descended the Cantuarii and Victuarii, that is, the people which
> holds the isle of Wight and that which to this day is called the *Jutarum natio* in
> the province of the West Saxons set opposite of isle of Wight. From the Saxons;
> that is, from that region which is now called that of the Old Saxons, came the
> East Saxons, South Saxons, and West Saxons. Moreover from the Angles, that is
> from the country which is called Angulus, and from that time to this is be-
> lieved to remain inhabited between the Provinces of the Jutes and the Saxons,
> the whole stock of the Northumbrians...and the other Anglian peoples.
> Their first leaders are believed to have been two brothers Hengest and Horsa.
> (*HE* 1.15)

The final statement in the excerpt given above," Their first leaders
are believed to have been...Hengest and Horsa," sets the conjectury
nature and skeptical tone of Bede's historiography of the early settlement of the Anglo-Saxons. Probably the direct location of the Jutes
right across the sea from Kent and Wight in Jutland made sense to a
direct route from Jutland to Wight (*HE*, I:xv); this kind of direct topography is also appealed to in the case of the Angles and Saxons.[3] The
problem, however, as Collingwood and Myers say, is that this clear-cut
migration hypothesis is "difficult to reconcile with the archeological
remains or with other literary evidence not inferior in authority to his
[Bede's] own."[4]

Unlike Bede, the sixth-century writer Procopius divides the invaders between the Angles and the Frisians (*Gothic War* 4. 20). Tacitus does not mention the Saxons at all, but other writers do. Ptolemy refers to the Saxons in his *Geography* (ii.11.7). Constantius in his *Life of St. Germanus* (c. end of fifth century) calls the Germanic peoples in Britain Saxons (ch. 47); so does Gildas fifty years later (*De Excidio* ch. 23) like Jonas of Bobbio in the middle of the seventh century. The *Life of Fursey* written in the seventh century as well as the anonymous *Life of Cuthbert* (seventh century) and Adamnan's *Life of Columba* retain the same usage. What is important about these authors is that they were neither Saxons nor Angles! As Michael Richter's study of the Irish annals and the Welsh chronicles shows, the term *Saxons* is almost invariably used for the Germanic settlers of the northern part, where, according to Bede, the Angles settled. Remarkably, the Gregorian nomenclature *Angli*, which Bede follows, does not appear in the sources written in England before the eighth century.[5] Though Bede did not coin the term *Angli*, he adopted what Pope Gregory had created on the basis of a misunderstanding, as narrated in chapter nine of the *Anonymous Life of Gregory the Great*. When Gregory queried about the ethnic origin of the fair-haired boys he found in the slave market of Rome, he was told that they were Angles; Gregory added, "They are angels of God" (*Angeli Dei*). The same Gregory would also allegorize Aelle's name as *Alleluia* and the country of Deira as *De Ira*.

Saxon was a name of terror, as they raided British shores continually before and after the fifth century. Eventually, the term *Saxon* was applied to all Germanic settlers of Britain. The Celtic people, even to this day, following their Latin-speaking ancestors, label the Germanic inhabitants of the island as Saxons. Interestingly, Penda of Mercia appears in Welsh annalists not as Angle but as "Penta the Saxon" (Collingwood and Myers 343). Even Bede, who places the Jutes with precision in Kent, speaks of the invaders of the region as "Anglorum sive Saxonum gens." The Kentish Hengest appears as Saxon and Angle, from Jutland/Gothland, but Kent itself seems to be more closely connected socially and dialectally to Frisia—Frisian is closely related to Gothic—than to any other part of the Continent. There is no echo of Jutish (from Jutland) placenames in Kent, nor is there any evidence that they ever referred to themselves as Jutes; they are always *Cantware* or people of Kent. As Britain came to be called "Engla land" or England in legal and other documents, more and more people came to identify themselves as Angles/English; this phenomenon is similar to the American, Indian, and Native-American phenomena: all immigrants call themselves Americans because they live in America; all immigrants from India, even though they belong to numerous ethnic groups and come from different states, call themselves Indians; all Native Americans call themselves—whether Iroquois, Hopi, Ojibway, or Potowatomie—ironically "Indians." Similarly, the Mercian royal house of Penda and his successors as well as the kings of Wessex traced their ancestry to the Anglian group. Thus the West Saxons also came to call themselves English and their language English. For example, Alfred, though a Saxon, called the whole population living between the Humber and the Thames "Angelkynn" and their language "Englisc." This kind of detribalization is often a political phenomenon, which is a way to unify different tribes into one mega tribe in order to repel aggression from abroad; Alfred must have used this political strategy against Viking aggression. This phenomenon can be effectively brought about in one single generation. Such is the case of typical American immigrants, whether they be from Costa Rica, Germany, India, or Australia, who consider themselves American; nonetheless, just their name American does not mean they or their ancestors have been American citizens for generations. We find a similar situation in Germany: all the descendants of the various Teutonic tribes are called "German."

Archeological evidence, as Collingwood and Myers argue, also does not suggest a division of the country along quite the lines suggested by Bede (348); that is, if we look for bronze and pottery artifacts paralleling proposed areas of emigration and immigration. For example, the saucer brooches of the Saxon homeland are found in a striking manner in parts of Middle Anglia.[6] Similarly, Saxon window urns are found prominently in Middle Anglia and Kent (Collingwood and Myers 349). Barbara Yorke writes:

> Considerable ingenuity has been shown in attempts to reconcile the written and archaeological evidence, but the difficulties of such reconciliation increase as the number of archaeological studies grows. Even if the annals are seen as only describing the activities of the dynastic founders, and not of the bulk of Saxon settlers in Wessex, difficulties abound, for as recent studies have stressed the early annals contain serious internal inconsistencies and chronological distortions. (84)[7]

The place names Swaffenham in Norfolk and Cambridgeshire indicate that Swabians settled there. The Hwicce of Severn Valley are another example; that great tribe has no place in the settlement tradition, and its origin is obscure. Bede includes the Freppingas among the Middle Anglians. Ancient charters relating to the territory of the Hwicce mention the Pencersaetan of the country southwest of Birmingham, the

Stoppingas around the country of Woolton Wawen, and Usmere who lived in the woods east of Kidderminster (Stenton 44). To the south of Phepson, the stream Whitsun Brook derives its name from the Wihsan, associated with the Gyrwe of the Fens.[8] Metalwork belonging to the Franks of the Continent found in graves "testifies to the presence of some Franks in the initial phase of the Anglo-Saxon settlement which began in 443.[9]

It is also known from literary sources such as Gildas' *De Excidio Britanniae* that there were Alamannic leaders with their army in Britain long before the invasion. It was a Roman practice to employ German mercenaries to protect the country against its various enemies in the frontier regions like the diocese of Britain.[10] These mercenaries were known as "federates" (*foederati*), i.e., military contingents furnished under treaty by tribes in alliance with the Empire and serving under their own leaders. Historian Jones describes the nature of this relationship:

> Such allied tribes could form buffer states against enemies farther afield and act as a curb on recalcitrant neighbours on the frontier itself: at least their treaties bound them to refrain from raiding the provinces. Such paper guarantees were by no means always effective, but the Roman government reinforced them not only by punitive actions against treaty-breakers, but by periodic gifts...to loyal chiefs.[11]

These *foederati* existed all along the frontiers of the Roman Empire: among the Germanic and Sarmatian tribes along the Rhine and the Danube, among the moors in the fringes of the African desert, among the Nobadae of Egyptian desert, and among the tribes of Caucasus. As for Britain, an Alamannic chieftain, commanding his own countrymen in Britain, "played a decisive role...in Constantine's proclamation in 306" (Jones II: 612). Later Valentinian I appointed Fraomarius to the command of an Alamannic unit in Britain (Jones II: 621).

As for southern Britain, there is archeological evidence for the presence of Saxons before 410, for example, in Winchester, long before the Anglo-Saxons forced a landing in Wessex 495, according to the testimony of the *Anglo-Saxon Chronicle*. Thomas Shippey writes:

> Archaeologists do not think that the Anglo-Saxons forced a beachhead in Wessex in 495, fighting the same day, as the *Chronicle* asserts. They think that the Saxons had arrived in Southern England well before, as paid auxiliary soldiers—a sort of early Brigade of Gurkhas, as it were—under the late Roman Empire. They also point out that there is strong evidence of an early Saxon presence in what became the *northern* Wessex border, along the Thames valley; and that Saxon immigration was just as likely to come from Berkshire as from the Solent. The view now put is that up to about the year 410—close to

the traditional date for the abandonment of Britain by the Roman Empire—Winchester was an important place, well-fortified, with a partly Saxon garrison, and a large *gynecaeum* or textile factory producing goods for the Roman army.[12]

Add to this early presence of Germanic tribes in Britain the curious phenomenon that not all the names of the Wessex kings sound English; for example, Cerdic is a Saxonized form of the famous British name Caractatus/Caradwg, and Caedwalla bears the name of the Welsh Cadwallon (Shippey 9). Barbara Yorke's observation that the persistent tradition, partly confirmed by place names that the Isle of Wight and parts of Hampshire were settled not by Saxons but by Jutes.[13] The implication is that tribal distinctiveness of both Germanic people as well as of the British people was very fuzzy at least by the seventh century. The fifth-century King Arthur's Roman name could indicate that he was a Briticized Roman or a Roman of British origin! Of course, the British, who lived in the Roman Empire and were citizens of the Empire, could always be called Romans. Incidentally, the Old English word *Wealas* meant not only the "Welsh" but also "Romans" and ironically "foreigners." The ninth-century West Saxon king Alfred's mother was allegedly a member of the Jutish (Gothic?) tribe since king Aethelwulf of Wessex married Osburh, a woman of royal Jutish descent.[14] Intermarriages and relocation were probably the real reasons for this phenomenon. As a result, Alfred could trace his Saxon ancestry conveniently from his Saxon father, but his mother's dynastic connection with the Jutes/Goths provided him access to Jutish loyalty and friendship. Alfred, of course, could call himself English because he lived in England. Such association of the interlinking of tribes in the person of Alfred certainly helped him unify the various tribes of England.

The practices of Germanic people serving as mercenaries under the Romans and moving about the empire serving the Romans as well as changing their names and taking non-Germanic spouses, as in the case of the famous Vandal Consul Stilicho who married Emperor Theodosius's adopted daughter Serena, indicate that the Germanic tribes were neither ethnically "pure" nor politically "tribal" in their lifestyle. There were frequent fights among the Germanic tribes and within tribes not only in Europe, as *Beowulf* attests, but also in Anglo-Saxon England, as Bede's *Ecclesiastical History* records. Many of the migrant mercenaries lost touch with their own people and became completely assimilated as the case of Stilicho indicates.

The process of assimilation involved also the learning of the vernacular languages as well as Latin. All the German soldiers had to learn some Latin, the language of the army. In his life of St. Hilarion of Gaza (22), St. Jerome tells the story of a Frankish soldier who visited the saint to be exorcized of a devil. Jerome says that the soldier spoke Frankish and Latin only, but when the saint spoke Syriac, the soldier miraculously replied in Syriac (Jones 622). The story suggests that some Germans knew even Syriac!

There exist no records to suggest that the German mercenaries returned home after completing their military service. As Jones points out, "All seem to have preferred to pass their declining years among the comforts of the Roman civilization rather than return to the...insecurity and squalor of Germany" (II: 622). The case of Frank Silvanus, reported by Historian Ammianus Marcellinus, is singular. This German officer, accused of seeking imperial honors, thought of seeking refuge among fellow Franks; upon reconsidering the possibility that he might be betrayed by his own tribesmen, he decided to take the risk of appealing to his Roman troops (xv.v.6). The reason for such actions seems to be that a mercenary became *persona ingrata* among his own people against whom he often had to fight while carrying on his commander's orders and that the mercenary would be accused of being a collaborator with the enemy, which was the Roman Empire for the Germanic nations.

In view of the presence of Germanic people on British soil in the fourth and fifth centuries, one can suggest that the settlement of Britain by the Anglo-Saxons was also a gradual process of the members of the Roman Empire moving from one diocese to another, from the Continent to Britain—similar to the case of the British Empire in the nineteenth and twentieth centuries when the English or Indians, for example, holding British passports could travel from one part of the British Empire to another part. The settlement of Britain by the Germanic peoples, thus, was not necessarily a simple case of military incursion, invasion, or posting. It was also a case of finding living space and agricultural base and employment opportunities. This theory, made popular by Colin Renfrew in the case of the settlement prehistory of the Indo-Europeans, finds indirect support between the lines of the *Anglo-Saxon Chronicles*, which report on the arrival of the Germanic peoples in Britain.[15] The E version of *Chronicle* states:

> And in their days Vortigern invited the English hither, and they then came in three ships to Britain at the place Ebbsfleet. King Vortigern gave them land in the south-east of this land on condition they should fight against the Picts.

They then fought against the Picts and had the victory wherever they came. They then sent to Angeln, bidding them send more help, and had them informed of the cowardice of the Britons and the excellence of the land. They then immediately sent hither a greater force to the help of the others. Those men came from three tribes of Germany: from the Old Saxons, from the Angles, and from the Jutes.[16]

The invitation of King Vortigern after 410 gave the Germanic people the legal right to be in Britain especially since the validity of the previous Roman landgrants became questionable with the departure of the Romans. The expression "the excellence of the land" shows the real purpose of the Germanic settlement, implying the condition of poverty and destitution in Gaul. The phrase "the cowardice of the Britons" suggests that the British were intimidated into surrendering more land and privileges to the Germanic people whom the British were afraid of. Naturally, reports and rumors on the fierceness of the Saxons were fairly well known to the panicking British who moved out of their way to make more room for the Saxons. The new immigrants also took advantage of this situation and moved into the land vacated by the British.[17]

It is quite possible that the availability of much land in Britain as well as the unavailability of sufficient fighting men among the British were the result of the loss of a large British population due to the ravages of the plague, which is reported by Gildas: "A pestilential disease mortally afflicted the foolish people, which, without the sword, cut off so large a number of persons, that the living were not able to bury them" (22).[18] Without totally denying the military factor of the settlement process, we can say that it was primarily for economic reasons— for greater opportunities and better living conditions—that the Germanic tribes had been moving to Britain over a long period of time, probably from the time of the Roman occupation of Britain in the first century. This theory of the gradual movement of Germanic peoples to Britain does not discount the fact of increased military activity and even military campaigns against organized British resistance under leaders like Arthur against the Anglo-Saxon occupants, as there were military uprisings against Romans in Britain under Boudicea. In other words, the Anglo-Saxons were living in Britain for hundreds of years more than mentioned in Bede's eighth-century *Ecclesiastical History*, Gildas' sixth-century *De Excidio*, and the later *Anglo-Saxon Chronicle*. It looks as if the Germanic folks had been in the process of becoming British long before the "invasion" of the fifth century. John Myers addressed a similar issue in his book *Who Were the Greeks?* and answered: "They were always in the process of becoming."[19]

The purpose of *The Anglo-Saxon Chronicle* and of Bede with regard to their description of the Anglo-Saxon settlement is perhaps to give an apologia of legitimacy to the English presence in Britain. The English always had to answer this question: "What right do you foreigners have to be in Britain?" If they answered that the Romans had invited them to come to Britain, the spontaneous riposte of the natives would be: "The Romans don't live and rule here any more; we threw them out; they left; you mercenaries too should have left with your masters the Romans." Now, after 450 or so, the English could answer: "You invited us in to help fight your wars, and you told us to stay here. That is why we are here." Bede finds support to this view in Gildas' *De Excidio Britanniae*, 23, which he uses in his own narration of the coming of the Anglo-Saxons to Britain:

> They [the Britons] consulted what was to be done and where they should seek assistance to prevent or repel the cruel and frequent incursions of the northern nations, and they all agreed with their king Vortigern to call over to their aid, from the parts beyond the sea, the Saxon nation; which…appears to have been done by the appointment of Our Lord Himself. (*HE*,I,14)

Thus Bede finds not only legal justification but even a divine imperative in the coming of the Anglo-Saxons to Britain: The Anglo-Saxons came to Britain to preach the Gospel! Bede even goes further. Following Gildas, he even finds an excuse for the warlike behavior of the Saxons who accused the British of breaking the terms of their contract. The Saxons pretended that the British were breaking the treaty which stipulated that the British would supply them with provisions, though the British thought otherwise. Gildas writes:

> Yet they [the Saxons] complain that their monthly supplies are not furnished in sufficient abundance, and they industriously aggravate each occasion of travel, saying that unless more liberality is shown them they will break the treaty and plunder the whole island. In a short time they follow up their threats with deeds. (*De Excidio* 23; Bede, *HE*, I, xv)

While Bede finds a divine plan in the Anglo-Saxon attacks, the Anglo-Saxon chronicler tells its readers "a hero-tale about the glorious founding and rise to power of Wessex, through its dauntless and legitimate royal dynasty, the Cerdingas or descendants of Cerdi…who invaded the land from the south 495 and 'fought with the Welsh the same day' and whose ancestry is carefully traced back to the god Woden" (Shippey 7-8). So much for the epic, extra-historical dimension of historiography.

Preacher Gildas saw the pathetic plight of the British at the hands of the Anglo-Saxons as situated between Scylla and Charybdis: "The Barbarians drive us into the sea, and the sea drives us back to the Barbarians; and between one and the other we are either slain or drowned" (*De Excidio* 20). Thus, from Gildas and from Bede who faithfully follows Gildas, one may get the impression that the British who did not flee to Wales, Cornwall, Scotland, or Brittany were mostly slaughtered and the rest of them enslaved. One could also infer that those British who tried to establish ethnic British kingdoms did not succeed while the vast majority of the British population opted to live by the rules laid down by the new ascendant Anglo-Saxon culture and accept their language, customs, and religion not only for survival but also for social advancement and for the future well-being of their children and grandchildren. Isn't that also the case of Spain and other romance-language-speaking countries of Europe? It looks like history was repeated in the case of Ireland at a much later time.

It is salutary to be a little skeptical about the invasion-theory regarding the occupation of Britain by the Germanic peoples especially since there exists no reliable dates and records for the dark settlement period of fifth and sixth centuries. That seems to be the real reason that Historian Bede himself refrains from assigning any datable events to the period between 449 and 538.[20]

The upshot of this advocacy of healthy skepticism is simply the acceptable theory that the unity of the Anglo-Saxons and the native British or the emergence of the Anglo-Saxons as a nation, as *gens Anglorum*, was a phenomenon of gradual development—politically, linguistically, and religiously. The political notion of "Bretwalda" (ruler of Britain), the adoption of "English" as a unifying language under Alfred of Wessex and his successors, and the adoption of Roman Catholicism as the official religion of the British Isles were all gradual developments. Suffice to say that the people of Britain gradually considered Britannia as their patria, English language as their mother/father tongue and national language, and Catholicism as their official religion and patrimony. Indeed, for the rulers of England it was quite expedient politically, for forging national unity, to have a single *ecclesia*, a single *gens Anglorum*, and a single *English* language.

The *gens Anglorum* was not a single tribe but a complex of tribes speaking the English language, much like the English-speaking peoples of today. There is one group mentioned among the Angles (*gens Anglorum*), the Mercians, who seem to have a tantalizing history, which

goes back not just to present-day Germany but to the Gothic kingdoms of the Iberian Peninsula.

The Mercian Heresy

In 1935, historian Hodgkin wrote that "the early history of Mercia is
so dark that it is better to pass it by and admit the impossibility of
putting together any trustworthy history."[21] In spite of the absence of
contemporary written evidence as to the origin of the Mercians, fuzzy
logic leads me to postulate the theory that the Mercians are of Iberian
origin.

As for quasi-historical records, there are three post-Norman-Con-
quest chronicles that throw light on early Mercia, according to Wendy
Davies. They are Henry of Huntington's *Historia Anglorum* (1129) and
two *Flores Historiarum* of Roger of Wendover and Matthew of Paris
(1234). These records are 600 or more years removed from the time of
the original settlement. These chronicles are probably useful for the
later history of the Mercians. As Stenton points out, "No traditions have
come down from the peoples of the Trent Valley who formed the original kingdom of the Mercians. They first appear [in recorded history]
under a king named Cearl, of unknown ancestry, whose existence was
only remembered because he gave his daughter (Quenberga) in marriage to Edwin, the exiled heir of the royal house of Deira (*HE* 2: 14)."[22]
This mysterious Cearl does not appear in the pedigree of the later
Mercian dynasty, and there is no record of a king of Mercia before
Penda's accession in 626 or 633. This means that there exists no historical or literary record for the Mercians for the first 200 years of Mercian
existence on the British Isles. My hypothesis will, hopefully, change
this assessment.

The tribal name *Myrce/Mierce,* Latin *Mercii*—the only name known
to Bede—to which the Latin name *Mercia* (in Mercian dialect *Mercia*
should be *Murcia*) is related, is supposed to mean "borderers" or "boundary folk," as people on the borders of British holdings. Of course, *the
Marches* in English stands for the borderlands between England and
Scotland and between England and Wales; *march/Mark* means in Germanic "border" or "frontier"; a person who lives in the borderland is
called a "marcher." It is true that the late historian Blair Hunter argued
that the term *Suthanhymbre* ("Southumbrians"), which is found in annals which derive from a Northumbrian compilation of the early eighth
century, was indeed a name for the Mercians.[23] However, later Mercians
describe their king on their coins only as *Rex Merciorum* but never as

the king of Southhumbrians (Brooks 160). *A pari*, there is no reason to believe that the Mercians considered themselves as "borderers" since the extensive tract of land of Mercia or Midland England can hardly be seen realistically as a frontier. For example, when "Bede described Raedwald of East Anglia's defeat of Aethelfrith in 616 by the River Idle, he stated that the battle on the east bank of the river was *in finibus gentis Merciorum*. As Brooks argues, "the location of the north-eastern boundary of the Mercian kingdom there in Bede's day is no indication of the whereabouts of the original *mearc*," (160). It looks like we apply the meaning of "borderland" to Mercia rather very loosely from some erroneous notion of "borders" and "borderers" which finds no support whatsoever in documented history except in the writings of modern historians. Instead of trying to identify the tribe which has given the kingdom of Mercia its name, we lump together a bunch of nations like Wigesta, Magonsaete, Nox, Oht gaga, Henrica, Unecunga, Hwicce, Gifel, Spale, Gyrwe, and so on and call them "*borderers*," because we know next to nothing about them. That is why Brooks notes: "It is certainly difficult to envisage when or how the whole of this area was a frontier" (161). It looks rather like historians have somehow tried to gentrify the Mercians who carry the unsavory title of the so-called "Borderers" by assimilating them and the other tribes to the Angles/English, a catchall for all the English-speaking Germanic tribes, though their Welsh neighbors still continue to call the present-day Mercians "Seaxe," and then we turn around and say that the Angles are a separate tribe including the Mercians. It does not seem to make much sense, so I suggest that the *Myrce* are so called after Mercia, the kingdom, which is a transplanted name from the Swabian/Visigothic kingdom called Murcia in the Iberian Peninsula and that the Mercians are probably the same tribe as Myrgingas celebrated in *Widsith*. There is also some linguistic evidence to suggest that the Mercian dialect may carry features of East Gothic, which has left its many traces on the Spanish language spoken in the ancient land of the Visigoths and Swabians. Who are really the Mercians?

The historic Offa, known as Offa II who reigned over Mercia during the latter half of the eighth century and who is celebrated as the founder of the great abbey of St. Albans, had a remote ancestor, Offa I. He is supposed to have lived in the latter half of the fourth century (twelve generations earlier). Offa I ruled over the Mercians in their Continental home. His name appears in *Beowulf*, and he is the father of Waermund and the grandfather of Eomer (Geomer). *Widsith* mentions this Offa I:

Offa ruled Angel (*Ongle*), Alewih the Danes; he was the boldest of all these men, yet did he not in his deeds of valor surpass Offa [II], but Offa gained, first of men, by arms the greatest of kingdoms whilst yet a boy; no one of equal age ever did greater deeds of valor in battle; with a single sword he settled Mercia with the Myrgingas as far as Fifledor. The Angles and the Suevi afterwards continued to abide by it [Offa's judgment] even as Offa had brought it about by fighting. (lines 35-44)

The *Widsith*-poet says that Mear also ruled the Myrgingas (23). He also says, "When I came home, as reward to the dear one…, the prince of Myrgingas gave me land, my father's dwellings." The implication seems to be that Myrgingas live in England, where the poet's home is. The poet, in fact, says that his race springs from the Myrgingas "Him from Myrgingum / aethelo onwocon" (4-5); he also says that he even once opposed the Myrgingas (85).[24] Does he mean that he opposed some policy of the Myrgingas? Was he exiled for his opposition and then became a wanderer on the face of the earth? The poet says that he came home and gave his lord Eadgils rich gifts (to make amends?). Most importantly, he engages in the word-play "merce" and "Myrgingas" and brings the Mercian Offa into the context: "Merce gemaerde with Myrgingum" (He settled Mercia with the Myrgingas) and separated them from the Angles and the Suevi, who moved east.[25] This event seems to have taken place on the Continent.

What we find here is a federation of Swabians, Angles, and Myrgingas; they are like the Gewissae, the federation, to which the West Saxons belonged. One of the famous kings of a group of Swabians is called Mir after whom are named a province and a city in Spain called Murcia. This Mir appears as Geomer in *Beowulf* and Eomer in the Mercian genealogy and as Meara in *Widsith* (23). The Myrgingas seem to be followers of King Mir. As for other place names in Spain, sometimes the name of the chief who established the community is preserved as in *Villabalde* (Lugo), named after Baldus; *Vilabertran* (Gerona), named after Bertrand; *Villeza* (Leon), named after Leon; *Castro Adalsindo* (Lérida), named after Adalsind, *Casaldoufe* (Viana do Castelo), named after Nandus. Murcia seems to be a similar case: a town and province are named after the chief/king. It is probable that the ancestors of the Mercians are Myrgingas from Murcia, which was founded by or named after Mir.[26]

Historically speaking, the people of Murcia, Myrgingas, entered Spain in 406 and established themselves there by giving the placename of Murcia, as the Swabians, Alans, and Vandals poured over the frontier along with the Myrgingas. Their immigration into Gaul/Spain along with the Vandals and Alans was forced on them by the Visigoths who were on the war path, aided and abetted by the Romans, who naturally followed the traditional imperial policy of divide-and-conquer. In 418 the Roman Emperor Honorius allowed the Myrgingas to stay in Gaul. The Swabians, Silings, and Myrgingas sought refuge in Galicia, northwestern Spain, on account of the Visigoths. Some of the Swabians and Alans joined the Vandals led by Gaiseric and crossed over into Africa in 429. The Vandals took Rome itself under Gaiseric; later their power was weakened by Justinian's generals and finally obliterated by the Arabs and Berbers in North Africa. In northwestern Spain the Swabians, who accepted Arianism, were hounded by the Visigoths and were subdued after the long and bitter war of 456-470.[27] It was probably during this time that many of them crossed over to Western Britain along established trade routes connecting North Africa, Spain, and Western England. The Myrgingas and Swabians probably entered Britain via Bristol Bay along the Severn.

Besides introducing some three hundred or more Germanic words into Romance languages, the Germanic tribes have left their names on places in Spain. *Andalucía*, the *al-Andalus* of the Muslim historians, seems to have been named after the Vandals. *Andalíes* near Huesca may also commemorate the Vandals, and *Catalonia* (Spanish *Cataluña*) means "the land of the Goths."[28] The name of Alans remains in *Puerto del Alano* (Huesca), *Villalín* (Vallodolid), and perhaps *Catalonia* (Goth-Alania). Swabian names appear in the northwest; for example, *Suevos* occurs four times in Coruña, *Suegos* in Lugo, *Puerto de Sueve* in Oviedo; and the element *Sab-*, *Sav-* or *Jab-* found in *Agro de Savili, Sabín, Sabegode, Villasbariego, Jabariz, Jabalde, Saboy*, etc. (Entwistle 78). Gothic place names are found in Galicia, north Portugal, and northwest generally, with Gothi, Gotha, Gothones, etc., in village names like *Goda, La Goda* (near Barcelona), *Gudin, Gude, Godos, Gotones* (Entwistle 78). Germanic names ending in *-ing*, which are fairly common in Kent along River Medway, are rare in Spain and even in those instances they are Romanized as in *Soenga*(s) in north Portugal from Suninga and *Villa Albarenga*. In passing, it may be useful to note that Spanish personal names of men are either Gothic names (for examples, *Alfonso, Bermudo, Elvira, Frederico, Fernando, Francisco, Gonzalo, Matilde, Ramiro, Richardo, Rodrigo*) or names of saints (Entwistle 79), and very likely the Spanish surnames such as *Fernandez, Suarez, Juarez, Lopez*, etc. seem to have rather the Germanic genitive ending rather than the Latin genitive ending which is *-is* for the third declension as in Maro-Maronis. In short, as the Swabians and the Goths have stamped their names on places, so did the Myrgingas on Mercia. The *c* of *Mercia* is simply a variant of *g* as in the case of Gothic *g* becoming *k*/*c*; for example, *Grecos* becomes *Crecos* in Gothic and appears as *Crecas* in Old English. Gradually the Mercians were re-integrated among the Angles and came to be known as English.

Linguistics and Mercians

Linguistics offers support to the Spanish connection of Mercia to Murcia via the Gothic language spoken in Spain during the Visigothic period. The substance of the argument is that the Mercian dialect— often assimilated into Anglian and Northumbrian—is related to Gothic in the sense that it is a spin-off from Gothic but was amalgamated into Old English while retaining some features of Gothic just as the Northern dialect of English retains features of the Scandinavians (Danes and Norwegians) because of the English contact with the Scandinavian dialects during and after the Danelaw period (ninth and tenth centuries) of English history. The real difficulty in being too dogmatic about this hypothesis is the absence of written English documents from the fifth, sixth, and seventh centuries, the crucial period of dialectal interaction. The best we can do here is to rely on linguistic archeology, piecing together surviving linguistic fragments, and on fuzzy logic which postulates that as the whole contains its parts so does the part contain the whole albeit partially. There is a fuzzy or gray area in the interstices or interfaces where Mercian English and Gothic interact. Now, in order to understand the Spanish/Gothic connection of Mercian, it is necessary to address briefly the problem of the grouping of Germanic dialects.

The widely used handbooks on Germanic dialects divide the Germanic languages/dialects into three groups: North, East, and West Germanic, a division based on the distribution of Germanic nations in the fourth-fifth centuries of the Common Era.[29] Since the only surviving literature for the Gothic language comes from the fourth-century Bishop Wulfila (311-383), Gothic is considered as the most archaic of the Germanic group (as a written language) as it became separated from the other Germanic dialects at a very early period and not represented at all in later Germanic speech and "shows no traces of some developments that appear in all the other known Germanic languages."[30] Such a view ignores the fact that Gothic speakers in fact thrived in the fifth century in Italy, and in the sixth century in Gaul and Spain, where they remained dominant until the coming of the Moors in 711 and spoke

Gothic, even though for political administration they used the Latin language. They traveled all over Europe and migrated to England as Mercians and Swabians and Juti (Goti) from Spain and gave some features and words of their speech to Old English, especially to the dialect known as Mercian, which has developed to a large degree as Modern English.[31] It is highly likely that since the days of Wulfila, over a period of some two hundred years, East Gothic changed due to constant contact, during migratory movements across Europe, with West Germanic languages both on the Continent and Britain and became what we call today Mercian. On account of the dialectal similarities found between Kentish (Jutish/Gothic) and Anglian/Mercian (Gothic), Karl Brunner says that Kentish and Anglian are more closely connected lexically and phonologically with North Germanic—comprising Gothic and Norse—than West Saxon.[32]

The traditional division of Germanic languages into East, West, and North bespeaks separation and ignores similarities and frequent contact. Jakob Grimm writes: "The Gothic language is closely related to High German, though it maintains at the same time a certain connection with the northern languages."[33] Grimm's remark finds support in Wrede's statement of 1924, which led to the regrouping of Germanic languages:

> I view the entire Germanic language area as a large continuous complex extending from the southeast to the northwest, whose individual members were of every conceivable irregularity and were shifted and displaced again and again in the course of centuries. The vanished Gothic forms the beginning. The Gothicized West Germanic of the later German adjoins it; thereupon follows the purer West Germanic of Northern Germany, which since the days of the Heliand poet has been increasingly Germanicized; this German impact is lacking Anglo-Saxon...; this, however, reaches over to the East Germanic Nordic. And in its way the Germanic languages have always been in movement, always in unrest and mutual influence. (Lehmann 25)

The new grouping is based not on the late geographical location of the group but on the basis of linguistic evidence and migration history, which fostered the spread of cultural features such as linguistic items. Two factors account for linguistic agreement among dialects: inheritance and contact.[34] For example, similarities between Spanish Gothic and Crimean Gothic as well as between Gothic and Mercian are due to inheritance in spite of distance caused by migration. On the other hand, similarities between Mercian and West Saxon are due to contact. As explained above, evidence from *Widsith* seems to indicate that the Mercians came from Spain. Historically speaking, from around 650 to

825, Mercia was the most powerful kingdom in England, reaching its zenith of power in the eighth century under King Offa. The Mercian ascendancy in politics and language came to an end during the reign of King Alfred who promoted West Saxon as the unifying language for the English nation as a whole; as a result most surviving manuscripts are of the late tenth and eleventh century. One wonders, whether there took place even a large-scale destruction of Mercian manuscripts for the purpose of promoting West Saxon as a national language, as outlined in Alfred's educational reform encoded in his Preface to Gregory's *Pastoral Care*. We shall never know except that most surviving Old English manuscripts are in West Saxon and hardly any in Mercian, Kentish, and Northumbrian.

A new regrouping of the Germanic languages links Gothic and Old Norse which share many more common features than recognized before.[35] This theory suggests a Gothic-Norse speech community, scholarly disagreements notwithstanding (Robertson 254). Perhaps contact theory may account for these similarities between Norse and Gothic, leading to a basic division between North Germanic and South Germanic, with Gothic being part of the North Germanic group. Meanwhile the similarities found among Low German languages and Gothic postulate the theory of the Gothicization of West Germanic, including Anglo-Saxon but excluding High German dialects, a conclusion arrived at by Theo Vannemann.[36] In this regrouping Scandinavians, Goths, and Vandals form one subgroup closely related to the Anglo-Saxons and Frisians.

This regrouping will account for the many similarities found between Gothic and Old English represented by its Mercian dialect. There is no evidence or probability that the Gothic language became extinct between Wulfila's time (fourth century) and the fifth century when the Goths and Mercians migrated to Britain. It is this Gothic/Mercian migration from Spain that gives the Mercian dialect of Old English some Gothic features; that is, the Gothicization of Anglo-Saxon took place to some extent on the Continent before the fifth century but to a larger extent after the arrival of the Anglo-Saxons in Britain in the fifth century. In this highly non-technical work, I can only hint at some Gothic features of Old English.[37]

One interesting feature of Gothic and Old English is that among all Germanic languages only they both have reduplicative preterits as in *lacan*—OE *leolc* vs. Gothic *lailaik*, *letan*—OE *leort* vs. Gothic *lailot*; *hatan*—OE *heht* vs. Gothic *haihait*. In addition, there is the rounded *hw* as *hwaet* etc. found both in Gothic and in English. One may wonder whether both these linguistic phenomena are due to the fact that Mercian and Gothic were sister languages or that Mercian was influenced by Gothic.

One tantalizing example found in Modern English, which is slightly different from Old English is worth speculating about. It is the English word *much*, which is, of course, related to the Old English word micel/ mickle. The intriguing aspect of this word is that *much* without the *l* of *micel* is Mercian/West Midland; the corresponding Spanish form is muchos/ *muchas*/ *muchacho*. *Muchos* certainly can be derived from the Latin *multos*, which is perfectly in accord with romance phonology, as Menendez Pidal shows.[38] I wonder whether the Mercian form comes from the Iberian branch of the Mercians. If my hypothesis of the Iberian ancestry of the Mercians is tenable, it would easily explain the *u*-forms (versus Northumbrian *i*, West Saxon *y*, and Kentish *e*) found in the Mercian/West Midland dialect of Old and Middle English. My only hope is that perhaps a more careful comparative study of Gothic and English (Old and Modern) of the Mercian variant will doubtless reveal many more fascinating insights, which is beyond the scope of this study.[39] Unfortunately, we do not have any Mercian texts dating from the fifth, sixth, or seventh century or even the eight century. The most representative of the Mercian texts, the interlinear gloss of the Vespasian Psalter, in current opinion, dates only from the first third of the ninth century (Dresher 5).[40]

Revisionist Conclusion

To sum up revisionist history: Historiographers seem to have misinterpreted Bede regarding the identity of the Germanic peoples who came to Britain. Bede gave a simplified version of the tangled web of the numerous Germanic tribes that came to Britain over a long period of time by reducing their number to three. The three nations (*gentes*) of Bede were three powerful federations rather than three individual tribes. They were the Saxon Federation (East, South, and West), the English Federation (including Swabians and Mercians), and the Jutish/ Gothic Federation; the last group, including the Frisians, eventually formed an alliance with the Saxons in the South and formed a single federation and disappeared from history, leaving behind just two federations Angles and Saxons—our current "Anglo-Saxon" nomenclature—probably even before the time of Bede.[41] Eventually, by the time of Alfred, the Saxon Federation and Angle Federation merged into one:

the English Federation or England. As for Bede's report of the Continental home of these federations, he seems to have deliberately mentioned only their legendary original home rather than their whereabouts during the fifth century, when they were practically on the move all over Europe and North Africa. Since the Germanic federations were constantly moving, Bede could not and would not identify the ports from where they embarked at various times and stages for Britain. Bede had to ignore by necessity and for brevity's sake the complex history of the pagan Germanic tribes (except for an introduction, probably included at the request of his powerful, patriotic patrons) simply because his historical intention was solely writing a Church history of the English nation in Britain. Finally, the purpose of raising objections to Bede's legendary version of the early settlement narrative of the Anglo-Saxons, or rather to the traditional historical interpretation of Bede, and propounding the heresy of the Iberian origin of the Mercians is only to suggest that the Early English people were much more cosmopolitan than we had ever been led to think from our biased reading of Bede's works and later works of the interpreters of the history of the first millennium with regard to the roots of the so-called Anglo-Saxons. Not only were the early English from several parts of Europe but they also maintained cultural contacts with the rest of Europe consistently. The cultural world of the Early English even went farther afield to embrace the vast domains of the East, which is the subject of the next chapter.

NOTES

1. Patrick Wormwald, "Bede, the Bretwaldas, and the Origins of *Gens Anglorum*," in Patrick Wormwald, ed. *Ideal and Reality in Frankish and Anglo-Saxon Society* (Oxford, 1983), pp. 99-129.

2. Barbara Yorke, "The Jutes of Hampshire and Wight and the Origins of Wessex," in Steven Bassett, ed. *The Origins of Anglo-Saxon Kingdoms* (Leicester, 1989), p. 84.

3. The place name *Ytingstoc*, modern Bishopstoke, on the east bank of the Itchen, certainly refers to the *Jutes*, which word is simply the Mercian form of the West Saxon *Ytes*, which is another word for Goths/Guths.

4. R. G. Collingwood and J. N. L. Myers, *Roman Britain and English Settlements* (Oxford, 1936), p. 337.

5. It is quite possible that the story of Pope Gregory is a good political propaganda tool to call the nation "English," because the nomenclature is sanctioned by the supreme authority of the Pope himself!

6. E. T. Leeds in *Archaeologia* 63 (1912): 159-202.

7. See in particular G. J. Copley, *The Conquest of Wessex in the Sixth Century* (1954), J. N. L. Myers, *Anglo-Saxon Pottery and the Settlement of England* (1969),

and J. Morris, *The Age of Arthur* (1973), K. Harrison, *The Framework of Anglo-Saxon History to A. D. 900* (1976)—Resources cited by Barbara Yorke.

8. See A. H. Smith, "Place-Names and the Anglo-Saxon Settlement," in *British Academy papers on Anglo-Saxon England*, ed. E. G. Stanley (Oxford, 1990).

9. S. C. Hawkes and G. C. Dinning, "Soldiers and Settlers in Britain," *Mediaeval Archaeology* 5 (1981): 410.

10. "The Archaeology of Anglo-Saxon England in the Pagan Period: A Review," *Anglo-Saxon England* 8 (1989): 297-8.

11. A. H. M. Jones, *The Later Roman Empire* (Oxford, 1964), II: 611.

12. T. A. Shippey, "Winchester in the Anglo-Saxon Period and After," in *Winchester: History and Literature*, ed. Simon Barker and Colin Haydon (Winchester, 1992), p. 8.

13. Barbara Yorke, "The Jutes of Hampshire and Wight and the Origins of Wessex," in Steven Basset, ed. *The Origins of Anglo-Saxon Kingdoms* (Leicester, 1989), pp. 84-96.

14. Asser's *Life of King Alfred*, c. 2; B. Yorke adds: "Osferth, a royal kinsman who received estates in King Alfred's will and was a leading ealdorman in Wessex in the early years of the ninth century, may also have been related to Osburh (263 n 100); see *Alfred the Great*, ed. Keynes and Lapidge, 177, 322 n.79.

15. Colin Renfrew, *Archeology and Language: The Puzzle of Indo-Europeans* (New York: 1987).

16. Dorothy Whitelock, trans. *Anglo-Saxon Chronicles* (London, 1961).

17. The history of the Israeli occupation of parts of Palestine and Syria is an excellent current example of this historical phenomenon.

18. See J. A. Giles, *Six Old English Chronicles* (London, 1878), p. 310; Bede repeats this episode almost verbatim in *HE*, I. 14.

19. J. L. Myers, *Who Were the Greeks?* (Berkeley, 1930), p. 538; see also G. Copley, *Early Place-Names of the Anglian Regions* (Oxford, 1988), p. 19; S. C. Hawkes, "The South-east after the Romans: The Saxon Settlement," in *The Saxon Shore: A Handbook*, ed. V. Maxfield (Exeter, 1989), p. 85. The Anglo-Saxon invasion theory is similar to the "Aryan"-invasion theory of North India. On the basis of references to horses and chariots and Indra as "sacker of cities," critics have concluded rather uncritically that the superior fighting race of the Aryans defeated their enemy the Dasyus. The Vedic hymns do not warrant such a conclusion; similarly, the accounts of the coming of the Anglo-Saxons to Britain do not present a true picture of the story of the migration of Germanic people to Britain.

20. See Collingwood and Myers, *Roman Britain*, pp. 118-45; N. J. Higham, *The English Conquest: Gildas and Britain in the Fifth Century* (Manchester, 1994), pp. 118-45; Patrick Wormwald, "Bede, the Bretwaldas…," pp. 99-129.

21. R. Hodgkin, *A History of the Anglo-Saxons*, II: 194.

22. Venerable Bede's *Historia ecclesiastica gentis anglorum* (HE) is the pseudo-historical source for the early settlement of the Anglo-Saxons.

23. See Nicholas Brooks, "The Formation of the Mercian Kingdom," in Bassett, p. 160.

24. R.W. Chambers, *Widsith: A Study in Old English Heroic Legend* (New York, 1965), p. 159:"More than once in our poem mention is made of the Myrgings, a tribe to which, it would seem, Widsith himself belongs. Unfortunately the text is not clear.... Who these Myrgings were it is not easy to say. We should gather that, on the north, their boundaries touched those of the Angles, for a frontier dispute was settled by Offa with the sword at Fifeldor.... Again the word *Swoefe* seems to be used as synonymous with *Myrgingas*. We should conclude then...that they were members of the wide-spread Suevic stock." The identification of Myrgings with Mauringas is doubtful (160); the derivation of *Mauringa, Mauringani* must remain unsettled (236).

25. Some people would translate the passage as "He drew the boundary against the Myrgingas."

26. This Mir (god or hero) seems to have bequeathed his name to two Swabian kings Theodmir and Ariamir. Some scholars, as in Juan Bernal Segura, *Topónimos árabes de la provincia de Murcia* (Murcia, 1952), pp. 27-32, think that it is the Moors who are responsible for the name of Murcia, perhaps meaning "the firm place, the strong place." I thank Andrew Breeze of the University of Pamplona for calling my attention to this point.

27. William J. Entwistle, *The Spanish Language* (New York, 192), p. 77.

28. Robert K. Spaulding, *How Spanish Grew* (Berkeley, 1943), p. 44.

29. The handbooks are Streitberg, *Urgermanische Grammatik* (1896), Hirt, *Handbuch des Urgermanischen* I (1931), and Prokosch, *A Comparative Germanic Grammar*, see Winfred P. Lehmann, "The Groupings of the Germanic Languages," in *Ancient Indo-European Dialects*, eds. Henrik Birnbaum and Jaan Puhvel (Berkeley, 1966), pp. 13-27.

30. W.H. Bennett, *An Introduction to the Gothic Language* (New York, 1972), p. 18.

31. It is very likely that the mysterious *Iuti* (Juti, Giuti) of Bede and the Geatas of *Beowulf* could very well be the Visigoths from Spain. My reason for suggesting this unorthodox theory is that *Goti* could appear as *Guti/Juti* in Gothic for the simple reason that in Gothic the Goths are known as *gutthioda*, and in classical writers as *Gutones/Gotones*; they are known as Goths only in later writers. If Bede had consulted a chronicle written in Mercian or Gothic or Latin, he probably found the name of the Goths spelled as *Iuti*. We know that the Goths were one of the most powerful Germanic tribes of Germania, which included Spain in those days. Bede may be quite right in stating that the Jutes/Goths settled down in the Kent area. It is the same Goths who would appear as Geats in *Beowulf*. I wonder whether Bede deliberately changed *Gothi* into *Iuti* probably for the reason that the word by the eighth century had acquired a pejorative meaning as is the case in Spain, where *Gothic*, like *Vandal* in English, has come to imply all that is reactionary, out of date, and behind the times; in modern Spanish, the phrase *niño gótico* means "childish or puerile youth" (Spaulding, p. 48). In support of my Goths/Geats theory, may I point out that Benjamin Thorpe translates Geats as Goths in his translation of *Beowulf*. See Jane Acomb Leake, *The Geats of Beowulf: A Study in the Geographical My-*

thology of the Middle Ages (Madison, 1967) and Zacharias P. Thundy, "*Beowulf*: Geats, Goths, and Asiatic Huns," *Littcrit* 17 (1983): 1-8.

32. Karl Brunner, *Altenglische Grammatik*, 3 2; see Hans F. Nielsen, *Old English and the Continental Germanic Languages* (Innsbruck, 1985), p. 65. If Kentish and Mercian/Anglian are closely related, the so-called Jutish could very well be the same as Gothic. Let me cite R. W. Chambers, *Widsith*, p. 237: "*Ytum* = Early West Saxon *Ietum*, corresponding to which the Anglian or Kentish form would be *Eotum*, *Iotum*. These *Yte*, *Iotas*, *Eote*, *Ytan...* are identical with the *Iutae*, *Iuti* whom Bede mentions as conquering and colonizing Kent, the Isle of Wight, and the adjacent parts of Hampshire.... The words *Ytena...*, *Eota...* are used to render *Iutarum* in the Old English version of Bede's History, iv, 18, "*ea (gens) quae usque hodie in prouincia Occidentalium Saxonum Iutarum natio nominatur, posita contra ipsam insulam Vectam*." As Chambers reminds us, "Moeller's attempt to prove that the original tribal name underlying all these later forms cannot be identical with that from which the name of Jutland is derived has not succeeded" (240). I would go further and argue for the identification of *Geatas* of *Beowulf* and Bede's *Iuti* with the Goths; as for the variations of *g*, *j*, *i*, and *y*, look at the following words derived from the same root *mag-* "great": *magnus*, *major*, *mayor*, *maius*, and *maximus*.

33. Cited by Streitberg, p. 10 in Lehmann, p. 2.

34. August Schleicher, *Die deutsche Sprache* (Stuttgart, 1866), is the well-known proponent of the inheritance theory; he assumes that features found in all Germanic languages also existed in the "*Deutsche Grundsprache*." He assigns agreements counter to the genealogical to coincidence or lexical borrowing. Johannes Schmidt prefers contact or his "wave theory" to account for a larger number of agreements among neighboring members of the family than among more distant ones; that is, linguistic changes spread concentrically like waves, becoming weaker like ripples as they travel farther.

35. See Orrin W. Robertson, *Old English and Its Closest Relatives* (Stanford, 1992), pp. 252-55.

36. Theo Vannemann, "Hochgermanisch and Niedergermanisch: Die Verzweigungstheorie der germanisch-deutschen Lautverschiebungen," *Beiträge zur Geschichte der deutschen Sprache und Literatur*, 106 (1964): 1-45; Roberts, p. 262; Lehmann, p. 16.

37. The theory has to be worked out more in detail. Meanwhile, may I point out the following controversial similarities between English and Gothic:

English	Gothic
crecas	*krekos*
twa	*twa*
thaet	*thata*
beorn	*barn*
willed	*wilda*
each	*all* (singular)
according to	*bi*
was	*was*
then	*than*

she	*si*
at	*at*
from	*fram*
am	*im*

38. Menendez Pidal, *Manual de Grammatica Historica Española* (Madrid, 1944), *passim.*

39. On Mercian dialect, see Bezalel E. Dresher, *Old English and Theory of Phonology* (New York, 1985); see the bibliography on Mercian studies found in this dissertation.

40. Specimens of language antedating those found in the Vespasian Psalter are recorded in three manuscripts of a glossary containing materials of diverse origin: the *Corpus Glossary*, the *Epinal Glossary*, and the *Erfurt Glossary*. Though Sherman Kuhn assigns the *Corpus Glossary* to the eighth century, there is no general consensus on that issue (Dresher 5). In spite of the pessimism of Dresher and others, we may have to consider the charter (composed between 672 and 674) of the Mercian sub-king Frithuwold who grants land to Abbot Eorcenwold, later bishop of London, for the minister at Chersey as a genuine Mercian document. The document retains many Mercian words with the vowel *u* in place of the West Saxon *ie* *Fullinga dic* and *Sunninges.*

41. Linguistically and ethnically speaking, the term "Anglo-Saxon" should be used inclusively to incorporate the Goths and the Gothic language, which is related to the Frisians and the Frisian language.

CHAPTER SIX

The World of Anglo-Saxons: West-East

Anglo-Saxon England was not an isolated island any more than Ireland was; it had commercial ties with Europe; like the Irish, the Anglo-Saxons traveled back and forth to Europe and beyond; their sphere of knowledge embraced certainly the Western world and bordered on the Eastern.

Evidence from Archeology

Anglo-Saxon England, by and large, thrived on an agrarian economy, leading essentially a self-sufficient existence. The English produced most things such as fuel, food, clothing, and building materials at home, and there is no evidence they imported raw materials from abroad.

There is indisputable evidence, nonetheless, that many commodities came from the Continent and even from farther afield. Some of the imported items like amethyst, beads, gold coins, garnet, rock crystal spheres, and pottery have Continental or Mediterranean sources.[1] For example, amber found in graves must have come from the shores of the Baltic Sea, Rumania, or Sicily. Some seventy examples of ivory rings are found in graves. These pieces of ivory—fragments of elephant tusk, walrus tusk, or the tusk of wild boar may have originated from Africa, India, and or the Scandinavian coasts.[2] Most of these luxury items found in graves date from 600 C.E. (Arnold 61). From the early sixth century onwards, large quantities of garnet are found especially in Kent; garnet may have come from several sources: Egypt, Turkey, Scandinavia, Sri Lanka, and/or parts of Europe. Some scholars suggest Bohemia as a source for garnet (Arnold 63). Archaeologists suggest Italy, Yugoslavia, and Spain as the source of mercury found in Anglo-Saxon England.[3] Leeds thinks that the amount of Anglo-Saxon metalwork found in the Bordeaux region points toward exchange of that commodity for Spain's mercury.[4] The presence of Britons in Syria in the fifth century, the sixth-century reference to Britain found in Procopius' *Gothic Wars*, and the two seventh-century Egyptian references to Cornwall indicate probably trade contacts between Britain in the Mediterranean region.[5]

One import, the cowrie shell, found in some grave sites in Cambridgeshire and Kent, has its origins in the Indian Ocean or the Middle East (Arnold 64). Another item, pepper, mentioned by St. Cuthbert, which Bede distributed to his confreres on his death bed came all the way from India.[6] The Coptic bronze bowls found in Anglo-Saxon England may have come through Frankish contacts through Frankish lands (Dark 211). Dark writes:

> There are Frankish objects among the finds from western Britain, possibly suggesting Frankish traders in the sixth century, and textual evidence combines with the wide distribution of E-ware pottery to make this probable in the seventh. (212)

Mercantile interests do not seem to have been the only incentive for Byzantine contacts with Anglo-Saxon England. The Byzantine policy of the reconquest of the Western Roman Empire initiated by Justinian could have involved diplomatic contacts for the purpose of enlisting support from the former provinces and allies of Rome.[7] Ann Bowman has shown that voyages exclusively for trading purposes were not cost-effective simply because of sailing time involved; however, sherds of Byzantine ships' water-jars and amphora-stoppers found in Britain suggest also direct contact with Byzantine merchants (Dark 211). Too, Charles Thomas's study of archeological remains shows the presence of Eastern Mediterranean pottery (fifth to seventh centuries) in Cornwall, Wales, and southern Ireland and arguably provides evidence for "direct, if casual and irregular, trade" between the Mediterranean and the British Isles.[8] This trade, which came through the Straits of Gibraltar, was in Thomas's words "a raft for transmarine contact" which could involve "ideas as well as trade goods."[9]

Archeological evidence reflects primarily the activities of corporate groups involved in trade with the Continent and the Mediterranean world, not excluding Arab traders dealing with South Asia. Though there is not sufficient evidence to argue for large-scale commercialism between Anglo-Saxon England and the rest of Europe, the presence of foreign goods on English soil from the seventh century indicates Anglo-

Saxon contacts with the mercantile world of Europe and Asia.

Travelers and Scholars: West and Beyond

The travelers from the Age of Discovery in the fifteenth and six-teenth centuries were more than businessmen; they were missionaries, explorers, soldiers, linguists, and royal ambassadors. The Middle Ages were really no exception to this rule. Take, for instance, the case of the arrival of the "first" missionaries in the historical narrative of Bede.

The Anglo-Saxons' place in Roman Church history began conveniently on a spring day in the year 597 in the market place of Rome with Pope Gregory the Great. The Pope saw products and people from Britain for sale. When he found out that the fair-haired boys on the slave block were English boys (Angles), he exclaimed that they would henceforth be called "Angels"—*engle* means "Angles" as well as "Angels" in Anglo-Saxon. Maybe Gregory put a temporary end to the slave trade of English boys then and there, but England continued trade with the rest of Europe and Asia in commodities other than humans to deserve later the uncoveted title of "nation of shopkeepers" from Napoleon. Through this story Bede put an indelible stamp of English identity in lieu of all other unsavory Germanic tribal names—like Saxons and Goths—on the Germanic tribes of Britain as though they were all called "Angles" or English.

Gregory sent Augustine (later the first archbishop of Canterbury) and forty monks to preach the Roman Christian religion in Britain. The story certainly is an exercise in simplicity because there were already many Christians in Britain, among whom the preeminent ones were St. Helena, her son Constantine the Great, Pelagius, St. Alban, the legendary king Arthur, and his mentor Sage Merlin. The early plantation of the Roman legions and the later establishment of Roman Catholic religion on the British soil started a great deal of intercultural communication between the Continent and Britain. Shortly Britain became a diocese of the Roman Empire, another member of the Catholic communion of saints, and an integral part of the European commonwealth.

Travelers went back and forth between Britain and Europe as the Roman legions did earlier during the first four centuries of the Common Era. Even after the Romans left in 410, as the British left India in 1947, Roman roads continued to be used in Britain and Roman trade routes were utilized by non-Roman traders and Churchmen and Christian pilgrims. It was a case of mutual interdependence both for the

European mainland and England, both needing each other as in any cultural commerce. *The Anglo-Saxon Chronicle* and Bede's *Ecclesiastical History* give dates and details for some of these cultural transactions from classical antiquity through the early Middle Ages between England and Ireland and between England and Europe.

Bede relates in a famous passage of his *Ecclesiastical History* (III: 27) how "large numbers...of the English race" (*multi...de gente Anglorum*) left England and fled to Ireland in the first half of the seventh century in order to study or to pursue a life of sanctity at the feet of Irish masters. Bede, in fact, gives the names of a dozen or so, including the names of Ecgberct and Willibrord.[10]   Aldhelm says that Heafrith studied in Ireland; Aethelwulf states that a certain Eadfrith was his teacher in Ireland.[11]   Bede notes that English students who studied in Ireland in the later half of the seventh century were supported by the Irish themselves and that they travelled from master to master (*HE* III; 27).[12]   Bede even mentions the principal site or monastery where these English aspirants stayed, Rath Melsigi.[13]   It may very well be the place from where the Frisian mission of Willibrord was masterminded and dispatched by Ecgberct (O. Cróinin 23).   Naturally, Because of the close proximity and longlasting ties among the British Isles, travels between Ireland and England were fairly frequent; probably several ships plied between England and Ireland on a daily basis.   Sometimes travelers fared back and forth simply due to their *Wanderlust*, according to *The Anglo-Saxon Chronicle*, in 891 three Irishmen came to King Alfred in a boat secretly without any oars from Ireland simply because they wished to go to foreign lands.

In addition to Bede, *The Anglo-Saxon Chronicles* also records visits of the English to the Continent and of foreigners to England, starting with the mission of the Italian monk Augustine in 601. Augustine himself would not have come to England but for the European wife of Aethelberht of Kent.   In 675 Bishop Wilfrid went to Pope Agatho in Rome.   In 688 King Caedwalla journeyed to Rome and received baptism from Pope Sergius; in 688 Caedwalla's successor, Ine of Wessex also went to Rome and spent his last days there.   Benedict Biscop, Bede's mentor, made regular journeys to Rome and brought back large quantities of books from Italy and Gaul for the Monk Wearmouth monastery, which he himself founded. The extent of the library's holdings can be guessed at from various writings of Bede who spent most of his life at Jarrow; Bede's writings show his familiarity with a wide range of authors like Ambrose, Augustine, Cyprian, Jerome, Gregory, Cassiodorus,

Isidore, and others.[14]

It seems that Anglo-Saxons traveled as pilgrims not only to Rome and the Holy Land but also to India. According to *The Anglo-Saxon Chronicle*, in 883 Sigehelm and Aethelstan took alms to Rome and also to the shrines of St. Thomas and St. Bartholomew in India that King Alfred had promised when they [the Vikings] besieged London.

The purpose of many of the early medieval travelers, especially of the monks, was the pursuit of wisdom. Some of the early Irish monk-travelers are known in history as exiles (*peregrini*); some of the brightest among them were Columbanus, Dicuil, Dingal, Sedulius Scotus, and John Scotus Eriugena. These travelers left their imprint on every aspect of European learning in the works they had composed, in the manuscripts they had acquired in Europe, and in the schools they had taught. The frequency of the travels of scholars from country to country on the Continent and their constant acquisition, transcription, and transmission of manuscripts gives the impression of the existence of a commonwealth of letters all over Europe, including the British Isles, from the middle of the seventh century onwards. Much of this was facilitated by the network of Benedictine monasteries found all over England and the Continent.

In England a new generation of lettered men sprang up with the arrival in Canterbury in 669 of the African Hadrian and of the Greek Theodore, who reorganized schools in England after the disastrous plague of 664, which decimated the clerical and monastic population.[15] The presence in England of these Easterners indicates the truth that political boundaries no longer hindered the travels of scholars and of ideas across borders. Anglo-Saxons and Irish men passed through Gaul to Italy at will. Besides Benedict Biscop, Wilfrid went to Rome again in 704; Willibrord was there in 692 and in 695; Ceolfrid of Jarrow was buried at Langres; two Anglo-Saxon kings spent their last days in a Roman monastery.[16] It is possible that the "Franks Casket" found at Brioude was made for a Northumbrian pilgrim who was on his way to Rome.[17] Some Anglo-Saxon and Irish travelers chose to remain in Europe; for example, Peronne (Perona Scotorum) in northern Gaul and Willibrord at Echternach.[18] It is useful to note here that after the Arab conquest of Spain in 711, a flood of Spanish refugees bearing manuscripts fanned beyond the Pyrenees to the British Isles, Gaul, and Italy (Riche 368-9).

The Anglo-Saxons' appetite for knowledge is clearly evident in their attempts in acquiring books overseas and in their pursuit of education in Ireland, for example. They also transmitted this acquired knowledge through the establishment of schools in all parts of England as early as the seventh century, the most important ones being in Kent, Wessex, and Northumbria. Between Theodore's arrival in England in 669 and Alcuin's departure for Europe in 778, four generations of students received excellent education at these schools: the generations of (1) of Aldhelm, (2) of Bede and Boniface, (3) of Lull, Cuthbert, and Egbert, and (4) of Alcuin's born around 730. At Theodore's episcopal school at Canterbury, the program of education included metrics, astronomy, computus, medicine, exegesis, and even Greek (Riche 371). The presence of Coptic and Syrian vases and Byzantine jewels in Kent suggests cultural exchanges between England and the East during the seventh and eighth centuries.[19] The monastic school of Saints Peter and Paul founded by Benedict Biscop and directed by the African Hadrian was equally famous. Aldhelm, Hadrian's student, says in a letter to Bishop Eleutherius that he learned meter, chant, arithmetic, astronomy, and Roman Law at Canterbury.[20]

Perhaps the most famous of Anglo-Saxon schools was the episcopal school at York, directed by Bede's disciple Alcuin. The York school had a rich library, which Alcuin celebrates in a famous poem dedicated to the bishops of York; in this poem Alcuin recalls the subjects and authors taught at the school.[21] It would be misleading to think that Alcuin himself received all his academic education at York; in fact, Alcuin's formal education took him to Murbach, Pavia, and Rome (Riche 383). Though Alcuin's case is probably atypical, his situation indicates that the opportunity for seeking and obtaining higher education in different parts of the Continent was there at least for select members of the Benedictine Order.

Of course, the Anglo-Saxon intellectual renaissances of the seventh, eight, and ninth centuries touched only the elite monks. Probably there were no more than twenty episcopal and monastic schools throughout England during this period for which there is historical evidence. Even among the six hundred monks who lived at the Jarrow monastery, there were the "simplices fratres" and the "illiterati."[22] The clergy were not even "required" to know Latin provided they knew how to preach in the vernacular, baptize, and hear confessions.[23] Though some monks recited the psalms without knowing Latin, some laymen who were educated in monastic schools knew Latin and could exchange letters with abbots and bishops.[24] It seems that Bede wrote his Latin *Historia* also for the benefit of lay people, some of whom could read Latin.[25] In fact,

Bede sent an early draft of his *Historia* to King Ceolwulf for a critical reading and approval (*ad legendum ac probandum*), and the king was reportedly interested in the study of the Bible and noble deeds of the ancients. Aelfred of Mercia was a student of the Bible and geography; his teacher Adamnan of Iona gave him a copy of his *de locis sanctis*, which the king in turn gave to his courtiers (*HEV*: 15). All these cases of lay learning suggest that there were literate lay people among the Anglo-Saxons who were educated well enough to compose poems like *Beowulf* for the education of young nobles and princes.

Skeptics and moderns who believe by seeing clearly written testimony and place little credence on the principles of fuzzy logic will ask: How much did the Anglo-Saxons know? What kind and degree of erudition did they have of Western and Eastern apocalyptic thought? It is hardly possible to answer these two questions satisfactorily just on the basis of manuscripts surviving in England from the ninth century, for example.[26] Broadly and negatively speaking, if all the surviving Latin manuscripts from the entire England of the seventh and eighth and even ninth centuries were collected, they would not even fill one large book case, whereas England in the eighth century alone had hundreds of monasteries possessing hundreds of manuscripts not to speak of episcopal and royal libraries! If we include the tenth-century books to the list, we may have a little over thousand manuscripts with only a few duplicates of texts![27] Since that is the case, and if Bede and Alcuin and their times can be used as a benchmark, it will not be hard to answer the questions.

The Anglo-Saxons and Continental brethren surprisingly knew a great deal not only of the Western intellectual tradition but also of Eastern thought comprising Byzantium, Syria, and Islam even though it is impossible to identify each and every literary work they consulted. Undoubtedly, as the extant booklists indicate, many books—Greek, Latin, Classical, Byzantine, etc.—were not available in England on account of the high cost of reproducing them; however, Anglo-Saxon scholars could have easily consulted them in European libraries or could have borrowed them from the Continent through inter-library loan. The presumption, then as now, is in favor of the availability of more books for use than are accounted for in Anglo-Saxon library catalogues. The situation was no different then than now. A person living in Marquette, Michigan, can travel to the Newberry Library, Chicago, Illinois, or overseas to England and Europe and use manuscripts available there—as I have done myself many times. The ongoing work in the "Study of the

Sources of Anglo-Saxon Literary Culture," sponsored annually by the International Medieval Conference in Kalamazoo is increasing our knowledge of the books the Anglo-Saxons knew. Helmut Gneuss and Michael Lapidge's useful lists of books and authors known in Anglo-Saxon England from surviving booklists is a good endeavor. All these lists, nonetheless, do not and will not be able to include even a quarter of all the books and authors the Anglo-Saxon writers cited by name or used intertextually as sources, references, and allusions, which will continue to elude readers and scholars except for occasional discoveries that will be published in scholarly journals and presented at conferences.

As for Bede, he had access to a number of books besides the Scriptures and works on Scriptures. He quotes from classical authors like Cicero, Plautus, Terence, Virgil, Pliny, and several others. Bede was also familiar with the writings of the Church Fathers since his own works consist largely of borrowings from them. More importantly, Bede, the historian, collector, and narrator, used oral traditions such as he brought together in the differing accounts of Edwin's conversion.[28] At the end of his History Bede himself describes how he "put together the account of the Church of Britain and of the English people in particular, gleaned either from ancient documents or from tradition or from my own knowledge" (V:xxiv). This confession of Bede's indicates not only how elusive are many of his literary sources but also how challenging and promising are the searches for subtexts.

Alcuin himself provides an interesting list of books, which he acquired from the generous distribution of Archbishop Aelberht, in his long poem on the saints and bishops of York. The list includes the works of Jerome, Hilary, Ambrose, Augustine, Athanasius, Orosius, Gregory the Great, Pope Leo, Basil, Cassiodorus, Chrysostom, Bede, Aldhelm, Victorinus, Virgil, Statius, Lucan, Priscian, Donatus, and so on.[29]

Naturally, both the libraries of Bede and Alcuin should be seen only as limited fontes of knowledge rather than as the exhaustive sources of all the knowledge the Anglo-Saxons possessed. To a very large extent, from childhood through old age, most of human knowledge, especially in the pre-print culture comes from sources other than books—from observation, hearsay, church sermons, oral instructions, school teachers, folksongs, village festival performances, story telling, and daily conversations, all of which form part of the normal transmission of culture and learning from generation to generation then as now. This kind of learning process often lacks necessarily profound understanding of a subject or knowledge of a language acquired through library research and pro-grammed learning.[30]

Thus, though many Anglo-Saxons knew Latin, the Bible, and the lives of saints well, their knowledge of classics, the Greek language, Is-lam, and the East, in general, was rather limited. Mario Espositio writes:

> The whole question of the extent of the knowledge of Greek existing in Western Europe during the early mediaeval period has been singularly con-fused by the lack of a precise definition of what is meant by "knowledge of Greek." If this means the possession of and the ability to read such authors as Homer, Euripides, Xenophon, etc., it certainly is safe to assert that Greek was unknown. If on the other hand it merely signifies the ability to understand and make use of a number of Greek terms, mostly of a theological nature, introduced into the Latin language during the early Christian centuries, or to quote isolated Greek words or phrases from the pages of certain grammarians, then it may certainly be conceded that knowledge of Greek existed not only in Ireland, but all over Europe.[31]

Esposito's judicious assessment does not imply that all Anglo-Sax-ons were rather ignorant of Greek, the East, and the classics. There were always exceptions; for example, Scotus Eriugena knew Greek well. The situation is similar to that of most American Universities, where one professor or two may know his Greek and Latin well, a handful of other professors may have a smattering of Greek and Latin (little Latin and less Greek, like Ben Jonson's Shakespeare), and most none at all, not to mention the ninety-nine percent of American students not knowing any Greek or Latin at all. It is the one or two Greek scholars that hold up the torch of Greek learning high above the heads of most of us, giving the impression that Greek is alive and well in America. That was precisely the case in Anglo-Saxon England. In a large Benedictine monastery, one or two monks knew their Greek, whereas the vast ma-jority did not need to know Greek nor cared to learn it nor were en-couraged to learn it for obvious practical reasons. Their services were required elsewhere, on the farm, for instance, and not in the classroom or the scriptorium. The carefully written book *The Name of the Rose* by Umberto Eco is perhaps the best fictional representation of the po-sition I outlined above.

There is enough evidence to indicate that Greek was alive and well in Anglo-Saxon England, if not among the clergy at large, at least among a few scholars if manuscript evidence is any indication. As Mary Catherine Bodden points out, "more than five hundred of these [thou-sand] manuscripts contain Greek matter" (56). Though only few con-tain continuous Greek prose, Boethius' *De Consolatione Philosophiae*, which is preserved in fourteen copies, contains several examples of continuous prose (Bodden 57). There are also hundreds of Early English manuscript volumes containing Greek glosses, a valuable index to the Greek vocabulary amassed by the Anglo-Saxons (Bodden 59). Suffice it to say that some Anglo-Saxons knew Greek well enough to read Greek classics as in Modern-day America, where a handful of professors in the classics and religion departments can read and understand Greek and Latin classics, while the vast majority of the educated class know little or no Greek at all and could care less about Latin and Greek as in Anglo-Saxon England.

Anglo-Saxons and the East

That the Anglo-Saxons were aware of the Eastern world and Islam is patently an understatement. First of all, Eastern Christianity had always been part of the larger Catholic tradition of which the British Isles were an integral part just as part is in its whole and the whole in each of its parts. Each part contains the whole partially or to some degree. That means the Eastern world was always a part of the intellectual tradition of the Anglo-Saxons. Weren't most of the earliest Ecumenical Councils, beginning with the Jerusalem Council held on Eastern soil? That is why Alcuin acknowledges the Anglo-Saxons' knowledge of the writings of Eastern Fathers like Chrysostom and Cyril. The same holds true of the Syrian writers like Ephrem of Edessa and Theodore of Mopsuestia. Just as the West Saxon Psalms show the influence of Theodore, *Christ III* (lines 1379-1532) shows dependence on Ephrem's Sermon called *The Day of Judgment*.[32]

Likewise, there is evidence for Anglo-Saxon interest in and curiosity about the marvels of the East. By far the most fascinating of the Old English works with Oriental themes is the version of Greek-Latin romance *Apollonius of Tyre*.[33] The story's popularity can be gauged by the presence of many earlier Latin manuscripts of the text and two Middle English versions. There are three other prose texts of Eastern interest—the *Wonders of the East,* Prose *Solomon and Saturn,* and the *Letter of Alexander to Aristotle*—which appear in Ms Cotton Vitellius A xv. These texts are in the same hand that also penned the first 1399 lines of the *Beowulf* poem. The same manuscript also contains a fragmentary *Life of St. Christopher*.[34] One may naturally wonder why *Beowulf* and *Christopher* are found alongside the other Oriental works. I would go beyond Kenneth Sisam's suggestion that the *Beowulf* codex was compiled as a book about monsters and argue that *Beowulf* is also about the Orient.[35] In its use of the Eastern apocalypses like the *Vision of Pseudo-Methodius* and in its inspiration to include Islam as an Antichrist figure in the poem, *Beowulf*, as I argue in the last chapter, is also an Eastern poem. Further, St. Christopher is an Eastern saint—an avatar of the Bodhisatva as Prince Sutasoma of the Jataka Tales—with Buddhist origins. It seems, then, that the entire *Beowulf* codex is in a sense a work about the East. More explicitly, *The Letter of Alexander* is supposedly from India and describes magnificent palaces, elephants, water monsters, two-headed serpents, talking trees, and so on. What is remarkable about the *Prose Solomon and Saturn* is that it consists of exchanges between two disputants representing Eastern and Western wisdom.[36]

There are probably three channels that provided lines of communication between the British Isles and Eastern thought.

The first would be the books and pictures Benedict Biscop brought to England during his trips to the Continent. We do not know the titles of these books; it is more than likely that some of these books were written by the Eastern Fathers who are mentioned in Anglo-Saxon booklists referred to earlier.

The second channel would be Theodore of Tarsus, who came to England with the African Hadrian. These two Oriental Churchmen certainly served as a conduit between the East and England. Theodore, who at the age of sixty-seven commenced a glorious twenty-two year career as Archbishop of Canterbury, introduced the teaching of Greek at Canterbury; being from Tarsus of the Antiochene Patriarchate, he was probably also aware of his Syriac-speaking neighbors and their developed literature containing the works of Ephrem, Jacob of Serugh, and Theodore of Mopsuestia, for instance.[37] As Michael Lapidge points out, "The Canterbury biblical commentaries are wholly Antiochene in orientation" (5) since these commentaries dwell on the literal sense of the Bible as opposed to Alexandrian preoccupation with allegorical sense. The Vulgate text is elucidated by reference to the Greek Septuagint version. Frequent appeals are made to Greek and Syriac etymology. John Chrysostom is cited seven times by name; indirect references are made to the writings of other Eastern Fathers like Theodoret of Cyrrhus, Severian of Cabala, and Theodore of Mopsuestia (Lapidge 5). The Canterbury Commentaries carry striking parallels to Ephrem's *Commentary on Genesis* as well as the Syriac book of the *Caves of Treasures*, a sixth-century exegetical work (Lapidge 8). Indeed, Theodore imported Eastern "perspectives and experiences which were unique to the Western world in the seventh century" (8). With Theodore's infusion of Greek learning and Eastern thought into England, "it becomes legitimate to regard the seventh-century school of Canterbury as one of the high points, perhaps the acme, of intellectual culture in the early Middle Ages (29). It seems that the intellectual tradition of fusing Eastern thought with English sensibility introduced by Theodore continued to flourish in England if evidence of the influence of apocalyptic work by Pseudo-Methodius and Ephrem in subsequent Anglo-Saxon preaching and literature is any indication.[38]

East influenced not only the literary works of the seventh-century Anglo-Saxons but also their artistic expressions. A case in point is the Anglo-Saxon interlaced work. Nils Aberg emphasizes:

> The Germanic interlaced work does not go back to the beginning of the migration period and does not derive from imperial classical art, but will originate chiefly from Byzantine prototypes…. Only through the close connections with Byzantine culture, which flourished with the Lombard penetration to the Mediterranean, was interlaced work seriously incorporated into Germanic art. Its time of greatest development fell therefore after the year 600.[39]

Interlacing flourished in Anglo-Saxon territories in metal objects, grave finds, stone crosses, and illuminated manuscripts, especially in Kent. Interlacing was so prolific that the seventh and eighth centuries might justly be known as the interlace period, as Leyerle suggests.[40] He continues:

> In the visual arts of the seventh and eight centuries interlace designs reached an artistic perfection in England that was never equalled again. Interlace appears so regularly on sculpture, jewelry, weapons, and in manuscript illuminations that it is the dominant characteristic of this art. There is clear evidence that a parallel technique of word-weaving was used as a stylistic device in both Latin and Old English poems of the period. (7)

The style, not necessarily of Irish origin, seems to have been developed and perfected by the Irish. The Anglo-Saxons even incorporated this Oriental interlacing technique into their literature especially into *Beowulf* as the study of John Leyerle has demonstrated.[41] We see the same technique employed also in the Saxon gospel *Heliand.*[42]

There is every reason to believe also that the Roman Apocalyptic icons that Benedict Biscop brought to England were inspired by the East. Bede writes about this in his *Lives of the Holy Abbots:*

> He [Benedict Biscop] brought home sacred pictures to adorn the church of the blessed Apostle Peter built by him, namely, the icon (*imaginem*) of the Blessed Mother of God and EverVirgin Mary, and also of the twelve apostles…,

icons (*imagines*) of the visions in the Apocalypse of the blessed John for the ornament of the north wall in like manner in order that all men having, as it were before their eyes, the peril of the Last Judgment might remember more closely to examine themselves.[43]

These Roman images could very well be Oriental in inspiration since much Roman art after the sack of Rome by Alaric and Gaiseric in the fifth century was Oriental. As Dalton puts it, "All the culture and art of the fallen city was now Eastern, and remained so for two hundred years."[44] Dalton continues:

> The rich ornament of animals and foliage in which the Syrian took delight, the oriental treatment of reliefs in which gradation of planes abandoned in favour of contrasting light and shadow, all these things came out of Asia, and were eagerly adopted in the West. The bearded Oriental type of Christ is but the most conspicuous of iconographic forms which the world inherited from the Christian East during these centuries; the solemn monumental attitudes, the formal groupings of the figures in larger compositions, were borrowed from the same source: the Persian costumes rich with pearls and stiff embroideries came into the Byzantine world through her provinces of the East. (12)

The Oriental features of Anglo-Saxon and Irish art—the use of interlace and anti-realist attitude in the portrayal of human figures—stem from the use of the same Eastern—Coptic and Byzantine—models.[45] What is remarkable about the Eastern influence on the art forms of the British Isles is the likelihood that Spain, as well as Italy and Gaul, acted as principal intermediary between these two regions.[46]

Archeological evidence points toward the possibility of direct intellectual, literary, and artistic relations between the East and British Isles by way of Spain. The popularity of the Visigothic author Isidore's *Etymologiae* in England is a good example for literary contact between England and Spain. The Byzantines had a significant military presence in southern Spain till the year 624. Ships coming from Alexandria or Constantinople could go to southern Spain or sail up to Braga, Galicia, and the north. These ships carried traders, travelers, and artists. Some of these ships continued on their way to the British Isles, in all probability together with Spanish ships. We know this from the record of the experiences of Arculf who was shipwrecked near Britain on his way from Italy to France in the 680s.[47] The presence of Eastern Mediterranean pottery in the British Isles, notably on monastic sites in north Cornwall and South Wales adds support to the Spanish connection (McNally 202).

It is also important to note the influence of Mozarabic liturgy on the Irish and English liturgical books. The practice of singing the Creed at Mass came from the East to Spain to England and Ireland.[48] C. W. Jones has shown how the African tracts dealing with the date of Easter passed through Spain before reaching Britain before 633.[49] Galicia in north of Spain probably seemed as one of the major connecting links in the Atlantic sea-route; Galicia was an independent kingdom under the Swabians from the fifth century until 585, and the Swabians even settled down in Cambridgeshire, England, leaving the place name Swaffenham on the map.[50]

The influence seems to have been mutual if the evidence of the works of the English author Aldhelm is an indication. Andrew Breeze has shown that the writings of Aldhelm (c. 635-c. 709), one of whose poems contains the oldest statement linking Spain with the tradition of Santiago de Compostella, were widely known in early Spain.[51] Paul Alvarus (d. 861) notes in his account of the life and martyrdom of Eulogius, the discoverer of the anonymous life of Muhammed at the monastery of Leire, that the holy bishop brought back several books from Pamplona, including a collection of the epigrams of Aldhelm, a standard schooltext of the times, along with the works of Augustine, Horace, Virgil, and Juvenal.[52] Breeze also shows close links between Aldhelm's *Carmen de Virginitate* and Paul Alvarus's poem on the nightingale and suggests that Aldhelm was taught at Cordoba in the ninth century and that he formed part of the curriculum of northern and southern Spain alike (13).

The influence of the East on the British Isles is obvious in the seventh and eighth centuries; evidence indicates that even in Roman times the British had some Oriental connections. A small church of the Roman period discovered at Silchester is definitely of the Oriental type in contrast to the church styles found in the western provinces.[53] The mosaic pavements in Britain have affinities with Eastern types and the "Sacred Monogram" found on British stones of the fourth and fifth centuries is a type similar to those found at Delphi, Ravenna, and Antioch.[54] In Scotland the first monastery was called the "White House" probably after the White monastery near Akmin, Egypt, founded in the fourth century.[55]

The cause of this phenomenon is not far to seek, for from the Roman period, people from the East in large numbers had made their way to the West. Groups of Syrian merchants were found in all the major cities of Italy, Gaul, Spain, and Germany before the Germanic migrations, during, and after.[56] Italy was the major recipient of this Oriental influence. When the seat of government in Italy moved from Rome to Ravenna in the fifth century, that town attracted a number of Eastern bishops, Greeks, Syrians, and Copts. As Dalton points out, the economic relationship established through the ports of Classis and Aquileia with the Eastern Mediterranean coast at this time led to the introduction of many Eastern elements into Ravennate art (58).

Monastic culture played a major role in the Orientalization of the West from the fifth century. For example, Cassiodorus, minister of Theodoric and founder of two religious houses in southern Italy, lived for a time at Ravenna and was familiar with the Syrian monastic circles of Nisibis, home of St. Ephrem. As Werner argues, "he sought to introduce their [Syrian] religious teachings into his own country and probably imported...illuminated manuscripts of a Copto-Syriac character" (17). Syriac books were found in the sixth-century Italy; for example, the famous Gospels of Rossano are still extant. Werner thinks that Northumbrian manuscripts were influenced by Cassiodoran theology and Copto-Syriac iconographic types (17). Oriental influence in Rome can be guaged by the fact that between 685 and 741 five Popes were Syrian and four were Greek. The Roman monasteries also contained large number of Syrian monks.[57] It was to this Orientalized Italy that the English bishops and churchmen of the seventh century went.

Gaul also felt significant Oriental influence during the same period as Italy. Gregory of Tours speaks of the presence of "Syrian" bishops in several Frankish towns.[58] From the fourth century on, many Gallic monasteries housed Syrian and Coptic monks; for example, Leguge near Poitiers, founded by St. Martin, and Lerins, founded in 410 by St. Honorius. It was at Lerins that a semi-eremetical monastic life style was introduced from Egypt; St. Patrick was trained at Lerins, which probably served as a conduit for Oriental elements to Ireland (Werner 19). John Cassian, the founder of St. Victor at Marseilles, was trained in Bethlehem and lived as a monk among Antonines at Thebaid in Egypt. Cassian wrote a discussion of Coptic monastic life in his Collation of Monks and patterned life at St. Victor after Coptic monasticism.[59] Indeed, as Dalton puts it, "In the fifth and sixth centuries Gallic monasticism was clearly Egyptian, both in theory and practice" (88).

In short, Europe and the British Isles were part of the mainstream of cultural life of the East-West world. The Anglo-Saxons traveled far and wide and brought back books, languages, art, and other cultural goods from the East through Gaul and Spain. It was not one-way traffic; the Anglo-Saxons gave as much as they received from Europe to Europe, but not necessarily to the Eastern world, which apparently gave more than it received in return. Just as the Visigothic writer Isidore was popular in England and Ireland, so were the works of the Englishman Bede in Spain and the rest of Europe. The educational activities of Alcuin in the Frankish kingdom and missionary work of Boniface in Germany are just a few shining examples of this cross-cultural enterprise that made the British Isles an integral part of the East-West commonwealth of belletristic tradition.

NOTES

1. J. Higget, "Prestige Grave-goods and the Pagan Anglo-Saxon Economy," B.A. Dissertation, University of Leeds, cited by C. J. Arnold, *An Archaeology of the Early Anglo-Saxon Kingdoms* (London, 1980), pp. 51-2.

2. See Beckwith, *Ivory Carvings in Early Mediaeval England* (London, 1972).

3. W. A. Oddy, *Aspects of Early Metallurgy* (London, 1980), pp. 129-34.

4. E. T. Leeds, Anglo-Saxon Exports: A Criticism," *Antiquarian Journal* 33 (1953): 208-10; see also Richard Hodges, *The Anglo-Saxon Achievement* (Ithaca, 1989), pp. 68 ff.

5. For Procopius' view of Britain, see E. A. Thompson, "Procopius on Brittia and Britannia," *Classical Quarterly*, 30 (1980), 498-507. M. G. Fulford, "Byzantium and Britain: A Mediterranean Perspective on Post-Roman Mediterranean Imports in Western Britain and Ireland," *Medieval Archaeology* 33 (1989): 1-6; K. K. Dark, *Civitas to Kingdom: British Political Continuity 300-800* (Leicester, 1994), p. 209.

6. Cuthbert's Letter on the death of Bede in *Bede's Ecclesiastical History of the English People*, eds. B. Colgrave and R. A. B. Mynors (Oxford, 1969).

7. See I. Wood, "The End of Roman Britain: Continental Evidence and Parallels," in *Gildas: New Approaches*, eds. Lapidge and Dumville, pp. 1-25; cited by Dark, p. 211.

8. Charles Thomas, *The Early Christian Archaeology of North Britain* (Oxford, 1971), p. 23.

9. Charles Thomas, "Imported Late-Roman Mediterranean Pottery in Ireland and Western Britain: Chronologies and Implications," *Proceedings of the Royal Irish Academy* 76 (1976): 245-55, esp. 245, 247, 253.

10. See III; 27, II: 26, IV: 13, V: 9, V; 10 - 12.

11. See O. Cróinin, "Rath Melsigi, Willibrord, and the Earliest Echternach Manuscripts," *Peritia* 3 (1984): 17-49.

12. See Marina Smyth, *Understanding the Universe in Seventh-Century Ireland* (Woodbridge, 1996), pp. 1-36.

13. The name is written as two words in the two earliest manuscripts of the Bede's History; See O. Arngart, *The Leningrad Bede* (Copenhagen, 1952), f. 74r; see Cróinin, pp. 17-49).

14. A. Hamilton Thompson, ed., *Bede: His Life, Times, and Writings* (Oxford, 1935), pp. 263-66.

15. J. N. Biraden and J. Le Goff, "La Peste dans le haut Moyen Age," *Annales* 24 (1969): 1484-1510.

16. Wilfrid J. Moore, *The Saxon Pilgrims to Rome and the Schola Saxonum* (Freiburg, 1937).

17. See Karl Hauck, *Das Katschen von Auzon* (Munich, 1970).

18. See Pierre Riche, *Education and Culture in the Barbarian West: Sixth through Eighth Centuries*; trans. J. J. Contreni (Columbia, 1976), p. 368.

19. Thomas D. Kendrick, *Anglo-Saxon Art to A.D. 900* (London, 1938), pp. 62-68.

20. Aldhelm, *Epistola, MGH,AA,* XV: 476-77.

21. Alcuin, *Versus,* lines 1433-1545; MGH, PAC, I: 201-4.

22. Bede, *Super Parabolas Salomonis,* II, 20; PL 91: 997.

23. Council of Cloveshoe, 6, in A. W. Haddan and W. Stubbs, eds., *Councils and Ecclesiastical Documents Relating to Great Britain and Ireland* (Oxford, 1869-78), III: 364; see Riche, p. 394.

24. Council of Cloveshoe, 10; Bede, *HE,* V, 13; *Vita Alcuini,* 2; PL 100:93. Most lay brothers and nuns continued to recite the psalms and prayers in religious communities in Latin without having received any formal education in the fundamentals of the Latin language. Even priests and monks who knew Latin had only a rudimentary knowledge of the language even when they continued to say Mass in Latin and recite the breviary in Latin. Such is the case with most Muslims who recite the Qur'an, especially in non-Arabic countries. I know as a matter of fact that such was the case of the Syrian monks and priests in the Syro-Malabar Church of Kerala, where they used to recite the breviary in Syriac without really knowing the language. Since the 1960s they no longer say mass nor recite the breviary in Syriac!

25. HE V: 13: "I thought I ought to tell this story [of the thane who refused to repent even after reading about his misdeeds in the devil's book] simply…for the benefit of those who read and hear it."

26. For preliminary work, see J. D. A. Ogilvy, *Books Known to the English 597-1066* (Cambridge, 1967) and Michael Lapidge, "Surviving Booklists from Anglo-Saxon England," in *Learning and Literature in Anglo-Saxon England,* eds. M. Lapidge and H. Gneuss (Cambridge, 1985), pp. 33-90.

27. Mary Catherine Bodden, "The Preservation and Transmission of Greek in Early England," in *Sources of Anglo-Saxon Culture,* ed. Paul Szarmach (Kalamazoo, 1986), p. 56: "We have preserved to us over a thousand manuscripts known to be of Anglo-Saxon provenance or use or ownership. Surprisingly enough, however, of these thousand manuscripts, apart from the Gospels, Psalter, the works of Prudentius, Gregory, Bede, Aldhelm, Alfred and Aelfric, remarkably few of the remaining manuscripts preserve more than one or two copies of individual texts. The situation limits dramatically the field for study of the transmission of texts."

28. *HE,* II: 13; see note by Colgrave and Mynors, *Bede's Ecclesiastical History,* pp. 182-3.

29. For a commentary on the booklist, see Peter Goldman, *Alcuin: The Bishops, Kings, and Saints of York* (Oxford, 1982), pp. 122-7.; Lapidge, pp. 46-49.

30. See Patrizia Lendinara, "The World of Anglo-Saxon Learning," in Malcolm Godden and Michael Lapidge, eds. *Cambridge Companion to Old English Literature* (Cambridge, 1991), pp. 263-80.

31. Mario Esposito, "On the New Edition of the *Opera Sancti Columbani*," in *Irish Books and learning in Mediaeval Europe*, ed. Michael Lapidge (1961), p, 195.

32. Ogilvy, p. 251; M. J. B. Allen and D. G. Calder, *Sources and Analogues of Old English Poetry* (Cambridge, 1976), pp. 84-93; Patrick Sims-Williams, "Thoughts on Ephrem the Syrian in Anglo-Saxon England," in *Learning and Literature in Anglo-Saxon England*, eds. Lapidge and Gneuss, pp. 205-226. Though Thomas H. Bestul ("Ephraim the Syrian and Old English Poetry," *Anglia* 99 (1981): 1-24) thinks that Ephrem was not the direct source of any Old English literary text, in view of the many manuscripts and library-catalogue entries found on the Continent as well as on account the presence of one Ephrem-manuscript in pre-Conquest England, it is likely that Ephrem was known in England also. See Helmut Gneuss, "A Preliminary List of Manuscripts Written or Owned in England up to 1100," *Anglo-Saxon England* 9 (1981): 1-60, at 33 (no. 510).

33. Peter Goolden, ed. *The Old English Apollonius of Tyre* (London, 1958).

34. In the original Greek version of St. Christopher, which comes from the sixth century, *Reprobos*, the Lycian king, is a cannibal with a dog's head. The legend seems to be based on the story of Prince Sutasoma of the Buddhist Jataka stories. I think the Greek *Reprobos* is a variation of the Syriac *Rabrab* ("the greatest").

35. Kenneth Sisam, *Studies in the History of Old English Literature* (Oxford, 1953), pp. 65-96.

36. See J. E. Cross and Thomas D. Hill, eds. *The Prose Solomon and Saturn and Adrian and Ritheus* (Toronto, 1982).

37. See Sebastian Brock, "The Syriac Background," in *Archbishop Theodore*, ed. Michael Lapidge (Cambridge, 1995), pp. 30-52.

38. The following chapters will dwell more at length on these issues.

39. Nils Aberg, *The Anglo-Saxons in England during the Early Centuries after the Invasion* (New York, 1975), p. 172.

40. John Leyerle, "The Interlace Structure of *Beowulf*," *University of Toronto Quarterly* 3 (1967-68): 3.

41. John Leyerle, 1-17.

42. Ronald Murphy, *The Heliand* (New York, 1992), pp. 221-30.

43. *Bedae Opera Historica*, trans. J. E. King (London, 1930), II: 404-7.

44. O. M. Dalton, *Byzantine Art and Archeology* (New York, 1961), p. 8.

45. See J. N. Hillgarth, "The East, Visigothic Spain, and the Irish," *Studia Patristica* 4 (1959): 442-56.

46. J. N. Hillgarth, "Old Ireland and Visigothic Spain," in *Old Ireland*, ed. Robert McNally (New York, 1965), pp. 200-27.

47. D. Meehan, ed. *Adamnan's De Locis Sanctis* (Dublin, 1958), pp. 6-11.

48. Edmund Bishop in *The Book of Cerne*, ed., A. B. Kuypers (Cambridge, 1902), pp. 277-83. The Book of Cerne was in part copied from an eighth-century Northumbrian collection.

49. C. W. Jones, *Bedae Opera de Temporibus* (Cambridge, 1940), pp. 75-77.

50. J. N. Hillgarth, "The East, Visigothic Spain, and the Irish," *Studia Patristica* 4 (1961): 454.

51. Andrew Breeze, "The Transmission of Aldhelm's Writings in Early Medieval Spain," *Anglo-Saxon England* 21 (1992): 5-22; The reference to Apostle James and Spain is found in Aldhelm's *Carmina ecclesiastica*, IV.iv. M. Winterbottom, "Aldhelm's Prose Style and its Origins," *ASE* 6 (1977), 39-76, notes possible stylistic links between Spain and England. Lapidge and Herren, *Aldhelm: the Prose Works*, p. 187, n.7, indicates a probable connection between Julian of Toledo and Hadrian of Canterbury.

52. C. M. Sage, *Paul Albar of Cordova* (Washington, D.C. 1943), pp. 199-200: "Inde secum librum Ciuitatis beatissimi Augustini et Eneidos Uergilii siue Jubenalis metricos itidem libros atque Flacci saturata poemata seu Porfirii depincta opuscula uel Aldhelmi epigrammatum opera necnon et Abieni Fabule metrice Ymnorum catholicorum fulgida carmina cum multa minutissimarum causarum ingenia ex sanctis questionibus congregata."

53. *Proceedings of the Soc. Ant.*, 17, p. 606; cited in Martin S. Werner, "Coptic elements in the Book of Durrow," (Unpublished M.A. Dissertation at New York University, Institute of Fine Arts, 1957), p. 34.

54. J. Anderson, *Scotland in Early Christian Times* (Edinburgh, 1882); cited by Martin Werner, p. 34.

55. J. F. Kenny, *The Sources of the Early History of Ireland* (New York, 1929), p. 159.

56. L. Bréhier, "Les colonies d'Orientaux en Occident au commencement du moyen âge," *Byzantinische Zeitschrift*, 12 (1903): 2.

57. Dalton, p. 59; Santa Maria in Cosmedin and Santa Saba were founded by monks from Jerusalem in the sixth century. St. Georgio in Velabro and St. Lucien de Renatis were also very Orientalized after the seventh century (Werner 176).

58. Werner, p. 18.

59. Jean Kelso, "Coptic Sources of Irish Art "(thesis, IFA, 1940), p. 52; cited by Werner, p. 19.

CHAPTER SEVEN

Anglo-Saxon Preaching:
Apocalypse and Antichrist

In the earliest biographies of Buddha, unlike in popular Buddhism, eschatological thought stops short of life after death except for the statement that Buddha has entered nirvana, about the nature of which Buddha always refused to speculate just as he refused to speculate on the nature of God and the soul. The four visions of Buddha—of old age, disease, death, and the ascetic—dwell on the inevitability of the death of the individual, of the necessity of reordering life, and of the elimination of suffering. However, popular Buddhism of the Mahayana branch, as we have seen in chapter one, dwells on the joys of afterlife and the details of suffering in hells. If we consider the conservative tradition of early Christian religion as reflected in the synoptic Gospels, it is very much similar to conservative Buddhism in its approach to the questions of the nature of God, the soul, and afterlife. However, later Christian theology, beginning with the Book of Apocalypse loves to dwell on the themes of post-mortem Judgment and afterlife—reward and punishment—not only of the individual but also of humankind and the cosmos.

Anglo-Saxon writers faithfully record and redefine traditional Christian eschatological thinking in the cultural context of the end of the first millennium of the Christian Era, which they had to confront. Anglo-Saxon religious poetry and sermon literature more or less faithfully continue to propound the classical teachings of the Western and Eastern Christian writers; on the other hand, the secular *Beowulf* forges a provocative alliance of Christian religion, historical apocalypticism, political propaganda, and Germanic revisionism. While the latter view is the subject matter of chapter eight, the present chapter will discuss apocalyptic thought in Anglo-Saxon preaching.

Millennium and Doomsday

Needful to repeat that ideas and images of the end of the world were very much alive in the tenth century all over Europe just as they were in the early centuries of the Common Era. The folk traditions included a belief also in the millennium underscored by Apocalypse 20, which was reinforced by the classical view that the world would come to its predicted end with the completion of six thousand years from the time of creation, corresponding to the six days of creation—as claimed in the anonymous second-century Epistle of Barnabas and later by Lactantius (c. 317), or a thousand years after the reign of Christ and the saints, when Satan would be loosed from his captivity. But the questions when the world began and when the reign of the saints would start still remained unresolved. The idea of the seventh day when Christ would descend to reign for a thousand years also captivated popular imagination. Nonetheless, the fear of the end of the world was always at the back of Christian consciousness, and this fear of the end of the world was reinforced by the predicted commonplace signs of the end times like wars, plagues, famine, earthquakes, etc. Of course, Church leaders like Gregory the Great, Augustine, Gregory of Tours, Adso, Bede, and others warned against a literal interpretation of the signs of times and against the fixing of an exact date for the end of the world and the reign of Antichrist. Regardless of such preaching, fear of impending doom continued to haunt the imagination of preachers and faithful then, as now, as we are moving toward the end of the second millennium. The temptation to interpret the ever-present phenomena of natural disasters and wars as the ones prophesied by Christ as the signs of end times was very strong. As for plausible dates for the end of the world, one popular date seems to have been the year 1000; for instance, Emperor Otto III apparently rushed to Rome on the eve the year 1000 to await the return of the Lord, according to one report![1] Otto probably went to Rome to celebrate the duration of the world along with his famous contemporary Pope Sylvester II who rejected the millennial end of the world.[2] The year 1033 (1000 years after the death of Christ) or 1065 (since Christ died supposedly on March 25, the first time Good Friday and Annunciation could coincide was the year 1065) were also attractive dates, and pilgrims flocked to Jerusalem to await the end there.[3] However, there is much ambivalence as to the medieval perception on the exact date of the end of the world. Henri Focillon writes:

> We are faced with a paradoxical situation: for the middle of the tenth century and all through the eleventh, we possess either compelling proof, or else significant traces, of the belief in the world's end; for the years immediately preceding before the year 1000 and for that year itself we no longer have any. The decisive moment, it would seem, left people indifferent. (62)

The fundamental reason for this ambiguity is the issue of computation and chronology. When Lactantius used the chronology of the Christian chronicler Sextus Julius Africanus (third century), he counted 5500 years from the creation of the world to the birth of Christ; thus the year 6000 would coincide roughly with A.D. 500. But the world did not end in the year 500. The sixth century introduced another computation—the chronology of Abbot Dionysius Exiguus of Rome, who in 525 composed his *Liber de Paschate*, an Easter table, at the request of Bishop Petronius. He preferred to indicate the years from the incarnation of Christ.[4] Thus Dionysius substituted the Christian for the Diocletian era and started the new era in 753 *ab urbe condita*. The crucial question with regard to the millennium is simply this: How popular was the new Dionysian era in the minds of the officials and in the imagination of the common people? The first official document which carries Dionysius' era was a capitulary of Carloman in 742; about the same time it began to be used in French private documents and in Germany in the ninth century. Only in 876 did the imperial documents start using the new era. The Popes began to use it with John XIII (965-72), but only with Pope Eugenius IV in 1431 has the Dionysian era been used regularly. All this means the year 1000 was not yet a significant historico-eschatological landmark all over Europe or in the minds of the ordinary people who continued to compute time or other markers like births and deaths in families. In the Byzantine world, the Dionysian era began to be used only in the sixteenth century, after the fall of Consantinople.[5] In Russia, Peter the Great introduced the new era in 1700. No wonder, then, that there was no universal expectation for the coming of Christ in the year 1000 for the simple reason that the Dionysian era had not received universal acceptance by the year 1000.

Therefore, on account of the uncertainty of various era computations, we find only scattered outbreaks of the apprehension of the end of the world approaching in the year 1000. The eleventh-century French chronicler Raoul Glaber can attest only to some rumblings around the year 1000 and after. He notes the incidence of signs and prodigies: "These things aforesaid befell more frequently than usual in all parts of the world about the thousandth year after the birth of Our Lord and Savior."[6] Glaber continues:

> After the manifold signs and prodigies which came to pass in the world, some
> earlier and some later, about the thousandth year from Our Lord's birth, it is
> certain that there were many careful and sagacious men who foretold other
> prodigies as great when the thousandth year from His Passion should draw
> nigh. (IV,1;Coulton 6)

The increasing economic activity and construction programs of the time
seem to indicate that people paid little attention to an impending doom:
"On the threshold of the aforesaid thousandth year, some two or three
years after it, it befell almost throughout the world, but especially in
Italy and Gaul, that the fabrics of churches were rebuilt, although many
of these were still seemly and needed no such care" (III,4,13; Coulton
3). Henri Pirenne notices the first symptoms of commercial renaissance at the beginning of the eleventh century.[7]

The medieval myth of the year 1000 seems actually to be a renaissance legend attributed by those "enlightened" moderns on "simple-
minded" medieval people, beginning with Cardinal Baronius (early
seventeenth century), who wrote:

> A new century starts. The first year after the thousandth one begins....By vain
> assertion of some people it was announced as the last year of the world, or
> nearly so: in that year the man of sin, son of perdition called Antichrist, should
> be revealed. This was promulgated in Gaul, first predicted in Paris and then
> proclaimed over the world; it was credited by many; indeed, the simpler ones
> accepted it with fear; to more educated people it seemed unacceptable.[8]

The eighteenth-century English historian William Robertson (1721-
1793) goes further and rhapsodizes:

> The thousand years, mentioned by St.John (XX,2,3,4), were supposed to be
> accomplished, and the end of the world to be at hand. A general consterna-
> tion seized mankind; many relinquished their possessions; and, abandoning
> their friends and families, hurried with precipitation to the Holy Land, where
> they imagined that Christ would quickly appear to judge the world.[9]

The upshot of this confusion is simply that the year 1000 as such did
not evoke any massive religious and political upheaval either in Europe
or in England, though some preachers might have occasionally dwelt
on the theme for moral instruction. It seems that the general population, then as now, paid more attention to personal eschatology rather
than to political and cosmic eschatology.

Doom

It appears that eschatological ideas such as the notions of the end of
the world and Last Judgment were more important than the date of

these events for medieval writers probably because the official Church consistently discouraged speculations on the exact day and hour as Christ himself reportedly did so: "Of that day or that hour no one knows, not even the angels in heaven, nor the Son, but only the Father. Take heed, watch; for you do not know when the time will come..." (Mark 13: 32-33). Such is the case with early English works dealing with eschatology: Doom (Judgment) rather than the Day of the Doom was what they were primarily concerned with.

A. Doomsday Poems

One prominent eschatological theme of several Anglo-Saxon works is doomsday. Early editors called the poems *Descent into Hell, Judgment Day I, Judgment Day II*, and *Christ III* Christian Judgment Day poetry. As the excellent study of Graham Caie shows, these poems are

> not primarily concerned with narrating the biblical and apocryphal accounts of the Apocalypse and Judgment.... Instead, the poetry uses metaphors of the Apocalypse and Judgment Day themes...as a vehicle to convey a moral truth that the moment of apocalypse or revelation and the judgment of man on each deed is ever present, and that man's dom, 'glory' is established by a lifetime of such favourable judgments.[10]

These poems, like homilies, are parenetic or didactic works and not records of the apocalyptic events of Doomsday celebrated in homilies. One important point to be noted about *Christ III* is that the ultimate source of this poem is Oriental, the Latin translation of the sermon "The Day of Judgment" by the Syrian Church Father Ephrem.[11]

Eschatology is also an implicit theme in the Old English biblical paraphrases (*Genesis, Exodus, Judith*, etc.) as well as in hagiographies (*Guthlac, Juliana, Elene*, etc.); these poems are highly didactical in the sense that they are designed to lead readers/hearers to a life which will be judged worthy of reward on Doomsday. As for Cynewulf's interest in eschatology, Norman Hinton and Roberta Box Bosse write:

> Even a cursory scrutiny of the four signed poems (*Juliana*, The *Fates of the Apostles, Christ* and *Elene*) reveals at least one striking departure from normal Anglo-Saxon poetic practice, and, further, a commonality of thematic interest which may suggest that, throughout his career, Cynewulf was possessed of an evolving interest in apocalyptic materials, particularly the Second Coming.[12]

Concern with last things is also implicit in the elegies *The Wanderer* and *The Seafarer*. Martin Green sees the apocalypticism of these elegies not as a focus on a future phenomenon but as judgment present here and now; he writes:

"The hour is coming and now is": although it is found in the least apocalyptic
of all the Gospels, no phrase more aptly sums up the apocalyptic sense of the
urgent present than this one. The paradoxical language of this formulation
establishes a link between the "now" of the present with the "then" of the
future; and since the future expectation is one which has been anticipated
through history, the present is linked also with the "then" of the past. This
linking is what Kermode calls concord—the present is brought into significant relationship with the past and future. Looked at another way, the paradox
transforms the apocalyptic moment, a moment in which the past and future
are left to impinge relentlessly, and, perhaps more important, a moment when
the future is felt to be fulfilled in the present.[13]

The Seafarer views the life in the world as exile after which one
returns to heaven by renouncing earthly values and meditates on the
"last things" and rues on his exile from God, who is the real lord of the
thane. Though The Wanderer is not explicitly eschatological, the poet
reflects on the transitory nature of life on earth through the use of the
ubi sunt motif.

Critics find that the apocalyptic vision informs also The Dream of
the Rood. J. V. Fleming sees the whole poem reverberating with
eschatological themes. He writes:

The controlling themes of The Dream of the Rood are eschatological. All the
"last things" are there: the death of Christ, spiritual crucifixion and the impending Doom, the Heaven to which the Dreamer aspires and the Hell spoiled
by Christ. These points have been prepared for from the opening lines of the
poem.[14]

Patton, Lee, Finnegan, and Brzezinski also see the Last Judgment and
Harrowing of Hell playing a significant thematic function in the poem.[15]
Significantly, Richard Payne has demonstrated that the poem has borrowed motifs on the approach of the Last Judgment from traditional
depictions of the last days such as that by Syrian Ephrem.[16] Payne
writes:

It should be noted...that the Last Judgment scene, which became so stan-
dardized in Romanesque and Gothic art, was portrayed in several different
forms in the earlier Middle Ages. In Anglo-Saxon England, subject as it was to
artistic influences from Irish, Gaulish, South Italic, Byzantine, and perhaps
even Coptic sources, we should not necessarily expect the scene that was later
to become standard to be the only form or even the dominant form of the
scene in use. (330)

Many of the details of the Last Judgment theme, as the study of
Georg Voss shows, were derived from the sermons of St. Ephrem, who
Voss considered to be important in establishing the conventional ico-
nography of the Last Judgment in the early Middle Ages.[17] Cook had

noted earlier a close connection between Ephrem and *Christ III*.[18] Payne adds:

> From the fear and terror in the assembled multitude of all creation, to the domination of the scene by the "sign of the Son of Man," with its dual appearance as terrifying and gloriously illuminating, the Old English description is obviously in the tradition established by Ephraem. (332)

The Old English poem "Soul and Body," which is a dialogue between the soul and body during or after death, is another eschatological work with Eastern undertones. Louise Dudley's study shows the connection between the body-and-soul theme and Egyptian thought.[19] The Egyptian works are the visions associated with the fourth-century Egyptian monk Macarius and *The Apocalypse of Paul*, which was popular in both East and West in the Middle Ages.[20] One vision of St. Macarius, summarized, is as follows: Once the saint, traveling through the desert in the company of two angels, encounters a corpse. The saint closes his nose on account the foul odor of the corpse while the angels do the same. Then the angels explain to Macarius the diverse fates of both good and wicked souls. They tell him that they closed their nose only on account of the foul smell emanating from the sinful deeds of the soul, that the soul is terrified by the envoys of God at death, and that the soul's only source of support is its good deeds. The angels also tell the saint that the soul tarries on earth for the first forty days after death and that only on the fortieth day is the soul sent to heaven or earth (Moffat 28). What is remarkable about the forty-day waiting period of the soul is that this notion is derived from Zoroastrian or Persian eschatology.[21]

The most eschatological of all English poems is *Beowulf,* which is the subject of the following chapter. The rest of this chapter, however, focuses primarily on the apocalyptic tradition found in the homilies.

B. Doomsday Sermons

There exist a number of Anglo-Saxon tenth-century sermons of considerable apocalyptic interest and importance. Milton McC. Gatch reminds us:

> It is only in Old English that we are presented with a substantial body of writings [of vernacular preaching] which are not only reasonably close to the main intellectual developments of the tenth and eleventh centuries but also responsive to peculiar local traditions.[22]

What is remarkable about Anglo-Saxon eschatological thought is that it is not all *semper idem* and that it does not slavishly follow the spiritual reading of the Apocalypse popularized by Augustine and Bede, in spite

of the commonplace observation that Anglo-Saxon theology is mainly
derivative in doctrine, pastoral in approach, and practical in the application of inherited teaching and in the devising of effective ecclesiastical
administrations.   Gatch notes:

> Contradictions [within various] homilies are discernible in the treatment of
> the destiny of the soul between death and Doomsday. The strength of the
> primitive tradition which stressed the apocalyptic expectation of the last times
> is surprising. There is also considerable attention to the fate of the soul—the
> convention of the address of the soul to the body and material based on the
> apocryphal and, in some respects, heterodox *Visio Pauli* are prominent, for
> example. But these materials are confused, and sometimes incompatible pic-
> tures are presented. I believe this is evidence that doctrines concerning im-
> mortality in the terms later made normative by the schoolmen had not been
> fully defined in the sources of the Anglo-Saxon homilists or by the homilists
> themselves and that they neither recognized this situation as a methodological
> problem nor needed to settle it. Neither of these conclusions is particularly
> surprising in the light of the general characteristics of Western theology in the
> Early Middle Ages.[23]

The eschatological homilies come in several collections. The Vercelli
collection, preserved in a north Italian library, is dated at the turn of the
tenth and eleventh centuries and the Blickling collection comes from
the latter half of the tenth century.[24]   The sermon collection of Abbot
Aelfric of Eynsham and Archbishop Wulfstan of York were written c.
990-1020.[25]

1. The Vercelli Homilies

Eschatology is a major concern of the homilist; he talks about death
and life almost in one breath. Death is not just an event that takes place
once and for all; it is a state of being which is the opposite of life. Just as
there are three stages in life for the righteous, there are three stages in
death for the sinner:

> The books mention three deaths: The first death is found here on earth of the
> one overwhelmed by sin. The second death is the later separation of the soul
> and body. The third death is the life of the sinful soul in hell, where no one
> may praise glorify the Creator on account of the terrible pain the damned
> endure. Just as there are three deaths for the sinners, there are three lives for
> the righteous. The first stage of life is the life in the body; the second stage of
> life is the life in the splendor of God; the third stage takes place in the coming
> world with all the saints (Homily IX).

The homilist dwells at length on the pains and pangs involved in
death and the joys of eternal life. A life of sin is living death; further,
death is separation; it is parting from friends, from all inhabitants of the

middle earth, and from all the joys of the earth. The sinner will begin to experience five forms of suffering—old age, death, burial in the grave, becoming food for worms, and hell torments. These five images seem to be an adaptation of the visions (sickness, old age, death, ascetic) of Sidhartha Gautama Buddha retold in the hagiography of Barlaam and Josaphat, a work popular all over Western and Eastern Europe.

The homilist says that the torments of hell are so far beyond the comprehension of human imagination that not even seven individuals endowed with the gift of tongues—of two-hundred-and-seventy languages multiplied by seven—will be able to describe the intensity and extent of hell's torments even if they are given the span of eternity to do so. Rather than recalling the images of the suffering of Hephaestus or of Loki, the homilist prefers to use an image found in Indian mythology to illustrate the nature of suffering in hell. In hell the sinner will be hung from a tree with head downwards and feet upright for seven thousand years. This image is borrowed from the Indian story of the Vedic Seer (Maharshi) Agastya. Once this sage was given a vision of his ancestors suffering in hell, suspended by their heels hanging from the branches of trees because the sage had not produced a son who would make offerings for the redemption of the dead from hell. According to the Indian epic and puranic tradition, the sage went on to create a Pandora-like beauty from all the pretty things of the earth and married her after having her (Lopamudra) to be born as a princess.[26] Blickling Homily XVI also uses the same image found in *Visio Pauli*, which seems to have been used by the *Beowulf*-poet in lines 1359-1417.[27] The homily also indicates that it is the devil who discloses all these mysteries of hell to an anchorite—a tradition that goes back to the Egyptian monachism of the *Vitae Patrum* of the Thebaid.[28]

Homily VIII is a Last Judgment sermon, which dwells on sin and damnation with Christ speaking to the sinners by dismissing them to eternal fire but beckoning the elect to eternal rest. The Rogation-tide sermons, XI, XII, and XIII are also calls to repentance and conversion, reminding the faithful of the transitoriness of this world.

Homily XV is the most important of Vercelli's eschatological sermons. Being also a paraphrase of *The Apocalypse of Thomas*, it opens with a discussion of the signs of the last times in answer to Thomas's query about the coming of Antichrist. As the homilist paraphrases *The Apocalypse of Thomas*, he gives details of the years that will precede the final week of the end of the world, which the apocryphal work provides. The homilist enumerates the signs of the last times like hunger,

war, discord among nations, hatred and envy among rulers, priests, bishops, and popes. The clergy will become tainted with all kinds of sins
and wickedness, with monasteries in disarray. Then a series of rulers
will appear. Two ealdormen, under whom there will be famine and
civil war, will be exiled. An Antichrist-like king will appear and order
that golden images be set up in churches and worshipped, leading to
the martyrdom of saints, especially of the famed ones, who are probably
Elijah and Enoch. Afterwards, a great king will arise from the east and
establish order and prosperity in the land. He will be followed by
another king, an emperor, from the south; he will trade gold for oil and
wheat in his commercial transactions with much financial loss to the
empire in his wars with Rome. Then there will arise Antichrist—the
homilist does not mention him by name—in royal appearance with
famine and destruction in tow. Famine and strife will follow him to the
land of Canaan and Babylon. Then stars will fall from heaven and the
sun and moon will fail to shine; darkness will rule once again the face
of the earth. Such are the signs of the days preceding the week of the
coming of Antichrist. Then he describes the events that happen during
the seven days of the Final Week, which will culminate on the Sunday
of the General Judgment. During the judgment scene, the Lord will
grant a portion of the human race into the protection of Blessed Virgin
Mary, Archangel Michael, and St. Peter, as they intercede for their salvation—elements not found in the Apocalypse of Thomas. Finally he
will dispatch the sinners on his left into eternal fire and the saints on
the right into the everlasting joys of heaven.

Remarkably, this homily departs from the traditional Western spiritualist interpretation of the Apocalypse popularized by Augustine and
Bede. Instead, the homilist draws information from apocryphal sources
and the Eastern apocalyptic tradition of the Sibylline oracles of Baalbek,
Pseudo-Ephrem, and the Syriac Pseudo-Methodius, as discussed earlier in chapter three.[29]

2. The Blickling Homilies

The ninth-century homiliary called *Blickling Homilies* contains sermons appropriate for eighteen events of the church calendar. As far as
eschatology is concerned, the Paschal Homily (No. VII) and Homily X
("The End of This World is Near") are the important sermons in the
collection.

The main eschatological premise of the homilist is that the end of
the world is near because of the presence of the signs of the times

predicted in the Bible:

> May we then see and know and very readily understand that the end of this
> world is very near; and many calamities have appeared and crimes and woes are
> greatly multiplied; and we from day to day hear of monstrous plagues and
> strange deaths throughout the country, which have come upon us, and we
> often perceive that nation riseth against nation, and we see unfortunate wars
> caused by iniquitous deeds; and we hear very frequently of the death of men
> of rank whose life was dear to men, and whose life appeared fair and beautiful
> and pleasant; so we are also informed of various diseases in many places of the
> world, and of increasing famines□.... These tokens that I have just related
> concerning this world's tribulations and calamities are such as Christ himself
> mentioned to his disciples, that all these things should happen before the end
> of this world.[30]

Homily XI states that all the signs mentioned in the Gospel have
been fulfilled except the coming of Antichrist (Morris 117), which is
mysterious and undatable. He relies, as does the Vercelli homilist, on
The Apocalypse of Thomas to describe the events of the end times as
heaven, earth, and sea shall pass away:

> And six days before this day various marvellous tokens shall befall each day.
> On the first day, at mid-day, a great lamentation of all creatures shall take place,
> and men shall hear a great noise in heaven as of an army being gathered
> together and set in array there. Then shall ascend a great bloody cloud from
> the north and cover all this heaven; and after the cloud shall come lightning
> and thunder all day. And in the evening there shall rain a bloody rain. On the
> following day there shall be heard in the heavens a great sound of the arraying
> of armies; and earth shall be moved out of her place, and heaven shall be open
> at one quarter—in the east...and heaven shall fall to the four ends of the earth;
> and all the earth shall be overwhelmed with darkness at the eleventh hour of
> the day.... On the third day the earth on the north and east parts will speak to
> one another, and the deep will rage and will devour the earth...and a great
> earthquake shall happen on that day.... On the fifth day at nine the heaven
> will burst asunder from the east unto the west quarter; and then all angel-kind
> shall look through the aperture on mankind.... On the sixth day before the
> third hour from the four ends of the earth all the world shall then be filled
> with accursed spirits, who will endeavour to take great spoil of men's souls, *as
> Antichrist previously did.* And *when he [Antichrist] cometh* then will he
> threaten to send those souls into eternal punishments who will not obey him.
> And then at last he himself shall be driven into everlasting woe. Then [on the
> seventh day] Saint Michael the Archangel will command the four trumpets to
> be blown at these four quarters of the earth and will raise up all bodies from
> the dead....All must rise again then, and go forth to the Doom. (Morris 90-94)

Though the Blickling homilist uses graphic details borrowed from
The Apocalypse of Thomas, he seems to be rather Augustinian in his
approach without tying historical events and historical rulers to apoca-

lyptic events and Antichrist. His orientation is primarily pastoral. The
fire-and-brimstone sermon is a call to repentance and conversion:

> Wherefore we must now consider, the while we may and can, our soul's need,
> lest we lose this opportune time and desire to repent when we are no longer
> able. Let us be humble and merciful and charitable, and let us put away and
> banish from our hearts deceit, leasings, and envy, and let us have a right mind
> towards other men. (94)

Whereas the Vercelli homilist talks about the efficacy of the interces-
sion of Mary, Michael, and Peter in the redemption of sinners on the
Last Judgment scene, the Blickling homilist says that prayers of inter-
cession will be of no avail on that last day, but faceless justice alone will
prevail then:

> For God himself shall then take no heed of any man's penitence, and no
> intercession shall avail us there; but he will then be more relentless and re-
> morseless than any wild beast, or than any anger might ever be.... He himself
> shall merit and obtain relentless and harsh justice, as it is written concerning
> such, 'The man who now judgeth the poor without mercy shall hereafter be
> doomed to stern justice.' (94)

The Blickling homilist also shows familiarity with Eastern apocalypses,
where two Antichrists or rather two comings of Antichrist are noted
(see italicized phrases in the citation above). Antichrist first comes as a
precursor of the signs; then he reappears on the seventh day as the
leader of the band with whom St. Michael and his army fight. The
homilist's knowledge of and access to Eastern texts and tradition is further supported by a reference in the Michaelmas homily (XVI), where
the preacher uses *Visio Pauli* (mentioned above in the Vercelli section),
which is ultimately derived from the Indian tradition.

This homilist conveys a sense of the imminence of the end since we
are living in the sixth age, which will be followed by the Sabbath of rest,
which is eternal rather than a specified period of a thousand years (Gatch
129). The homilist does not speculate on the exact time of the end; he
simply says that since the end is near, we must be ready for the judgment when it comes.

3. Aelfric

Aelfric, abbot of Eynsham and the most important English theologian of the tenth century, composed two series of *Catholic Homilies*
(980-991), each of which contains forty occasional homilies or sermons
designed for the liturgical year.[31]

A powerful theme of some of Aelfric's sermons is eschatology. In the

Homily for the Second Sunday after the Epiphany (second series), Aelfric compares the six water jars of the marriage scene at Cana to the six ages of the world: from Adam to Noah, from Noah to Abraham, from Abraham to David, from David to the Babylonian Captivity, from the Babylonian Captivity to the incarnation of Christ, from the incarnation to the coming of Antichrist. The seventh age of the reign of the saints does not follow but rather runs parallel to the six ages, like the earthly city and heavenly city of St. Augustine. That means the Church is the present fulfillment of the prophecy on the millennial reign of the saints, but the final fulfillment that follows the world's harvest time is to be realized in the eighth age, which follows the general resurrection and endures for ever. He writes:

> So the sixth age of this world reaches from Christ to the day of doom which no man knows but the Lord himself. A seventh age is that which runs on together with these six ages, from the righteous Abel to the end of the world, not of men living here but of souls departed for the other life; there they rejoice in expectation of eternal life after their resurrection; we must all rise again with sound bodies to meet our Lord. The eighth age is that one everlasting day after our resurrection, when we shall reign with God in everlasting happiness both of soul and body; of that day there shall be no end, and then the saints shall shine as the sun does now.[32]

One may wonder whether there is any connection whatsoever between millennarism and Aelfric's preaching, given the fact that the latter part of the tenth century was, according to some historians, a period of some apocalyptic expectation.[33] There seems to be some connection between the year 1000 and Aelfric's eschatological preaching since the impending end of the world is one of the themes of his preaching. Joseph Traherne thinks that both Aelfric and Wulfstan, "saw evidence of the last times in current events transpiring on either side of the year 1000."[34] Aelfric announces in the Preface of his *Catholic Homilies*: "I presumed...to undertake this task,...because men have need of good instruction, especially at this time, which is the ending of this world, and there will be many calamities among mankind before the end (I:3). He goes on to say rather explicitly in his sermon for the Second Sunday in Advent:

The Lord said, "There shall be signs in the sun, and in the moon, and in the stars, and on earth there shall be affliction of nations," etc. Some of these signs we have seen accomplished, some we fear are to come. Verily in these new days nations have arisen against nations, and their affliction on earth has happened greater than we in old books read. Oft an earthquake in diverse places has overthrown many cities, as it hap-

pened in the days of the emperor Tiberius, that thirteen cities fell through
an earthquake. With pestilence and with hunger we are frequently
afflicted, but we have not yet seen manifest signs in the sun, and in the
moon, and in stars.... The minglings of the sea, and the sound of the
waves have not yet unusually happened, but when many of the before-
said signs have been fulfilled, there is no doubt that the few which are
remaining will also be fulfilled (Thorpe 609-11). Aelfric tries to interpret the Viking attacks at the end of tenth century in terms of God's will
and the end of the world in his homily called "On the Prayer of Moses"
(*De Oratione Moysi*) begun after 995 (Skeat xiii); he writes:

> There will be many misfortunes at the end of this world, but everyone must
> bear his lot patiently, so that he does not sin against God by complaining and
> earn punishment for his love of this world. This time is last and the ending of
> this world, and people will be made evil towards each other, and as a result
> father will fight with his own son and brother with his brother, to their own
> destruction.[35]

Malcolm Godden thinks that the text is not definitive and that Aelfric
interprets Viking raids "as a divine punishment for English attacks on
the monastic movement occurring since the time of Edgar, presumably
in the reign of Ethelred himself" (135). Whether Aelfric associates Viking raids with the end times or not, there is a sense urgency and a
sense of awareness of end times in his sermon, which is an adaptation
of a homily of Gregory the Great. He writes:

> My brethren, set the remembrance of this day before your eyes, and whatso-
> ever now appears to be trouble, it shall all be mitigated in comparison with it.
> Correct your lives, and change your conduct, punish your evil deeds with
> weeping, withstand the temptations of the devil; eschew evil and do good,
> and you will be by so much the more secure at the advent of the eternal Judge,
> as you now with terror anticipate his severity. The Prophet said that the great
> day of God is very near at hand and very swift. Though there were yet another
> thousand years to that day, it would not be long; for whatsoever ends is short
> and quick, and will be as it had never been, when it is ended. But though it
> were long to that day, as it is not, yet will our time not be long, and at our
> ending it will be adjudged to us whether we in rest or in torment shall await
> the common doom. Let us, therefore, profit by the time which God has given
> us and merit the everlasting life with him who lives and reigns for ever and
> ever.[36]

Aelfric displays considerably more knowledge about the tradition
of Antichrist, both Western and Eastern, than the Vercelli and Blickling
homilists. Aelfric calls Antichrist devil incarnate, who will, with his
minions, turn the faithful away from Christ to his lies; in order to ac-
complish this, he will even perform miracles:

[Antichrist] is man and true devil, as our Saviour is truly man and God in one person. And the visible devil shall then work innumerable miracles, say that he himself is God, and will compel mankind to his heresy; but his time will not be long, for God's anger will destroy him, and this world will afterwards be ended. Christ our Lord healed the weak and diseased, and the devil, who is called Antichrist, which is interpreted, Opposition-Christ, weakens and enfeebles the healthy and heals no one from diseases save those whom he himself had previously injured. (Thorpe I: 6)

Aelfric refers to the tradition that Enoch and Elijah will return to combat Antichrist (Thorpe II:100). Citing 2 Thessalonians 2:7-8 and Jerome's commentary on the passage, he repeats the Eastern notion that Antichrist will not come as long as the Roman emperor is in power and that after the departure of the emperor Antichrist will be slain by the power of Christ.[37] In his sermon on the Day of the Judgment, Aelfric refers to the numerous miracles performed by Antichrist's disciples, to his reign in God's temple and to his claim that he is God, to his persecution of the faithful in those evil days, and to his rule over mankind lasting 42 months.[38]

Though Aelfric's sermons do not give a full treatment on the life and times of Antichrist and of the last judgment, they emphasize five aspects of the end times: the suddenness of the coming of the last times, the need to be ready, the signs of the last times, the end of the reign of Antichrist, and the final triumph of Christ. In fact, many of his sermons contain enough information to conclude that the abbot was well aware of the various traditions of eschatology discussed in his times; further, one gets the impression that the theologian was careful not to deviate from the path of orthodoxy.

4. Wulfstan

Archbishop Wulfstan (d. 1023), the other great Anglo-Saxon homilist, has much more to say than Abbot Aelfric on eschatology and Antichrist, which was a theological preoccupation of Wulfstan at the beginning of his career, though toward the end of his life he had modified his theme somewhat.

Like his contemporary, Abbot Aelfric who influenced his career, Archbishop Wulfstan lived through the same crises. Like Aelfric, he too viewed the end of the world and the coming of Antichrist as imminent. Besides his famous sermon *Sermo Lupi ad Anglos* on this theme, Wulfstan also wrote a sequence of five eschatological sermons dating from around the year 1000.[39]

Wulfstan develops the Antichrist theme in *de Antichristo*, which appears in two versions, Latin and Old English. Wulfstan says that the ministers of Antichrist are already at work, that the hour of Antichrist's coming is at hand, and that priests should prepare the faithful to face the challenges of the end times. An interesting point to note here is that Wulfstan translates the Latin *Antichristus* into *Godes withersaca*, which for Aelfric is *thwyrlic crist* (*contrarius Christo*).[40]

Wulfstan develops the Antichrist theme more at length in his sermon *de Temporibus Antichristi*. Though he begins the sermon, as usual, with the commonplace parenetic salutation "leofan men" (my dear people), the tract is more theological than homiletic. He warns the audience to beware that the terrible time of Antichrist is at hand. He describes Antichrist as the devil in human form; just as Christ is true God and true man, Antichrist is true devil and man. God will permit Antichrist to reign for two reasons: one, to find out those who will follow the devil through committing sins, two to glorify the elect who will resist the temptations of the devil. In the contest for the souls, the devil will perform signs and wonders. Those who are deceived and follow the devil will go to hell, while those who purge themselves of sin will inherit eternal life. Wulfstan ends the tract with a call to conversion.

The archbishop seems to have dropped the Antichrist theme from his later eschatological sermons and replaced them by more general eschatological references. This change of language signals a change in Wulfstan's thinking after the year 1000 had come and gone. The case in point is his famous *Sermo Lupi ad Anglos*, written in 1014 and surviving in several versions.[41]

The sermon begins with a reference to Antichrist and seems to envision the present times as far removed from Antichrist: "My dear people, know well the truth: this world is moving at a fast pace to its foreordained end. The longer we live, the worse it gets. Before the coming of Antichrist it will get still worse. Indeed, the future of the entire world appears grim and dreadful." Clearly, the central theme of this sermon is contained in this opening sentence: As the moral fabric of mankind deteriorates, so does the physical well-being of the world; physical deterioration follows moral deterioration, and at the apogee of moral depravity Antichrist's reign will be ushered in. Stephanie Hollis, who makes a significant contribution to the study of the *Sermo Lupi*, writes: "Antichrist's reign is presented not as the ultimate horror foreshadowed by manifold tribulations but as the climax of a progressive growth of afflictions which is proportionate to the increasing quantity of sin."[42]

Wulfstan knows that, according to the Christian tradition, the coming of Antichrist is inevitable simply on account of the increase in human sinfulness. He also suggests that Antichrist's coming can be delayed or postponed with the decrease of human sinfulness. Of course, Wulfstan does not spell out this position, which can only be inferred from his premises—a position native to pre-Christian Germanic thought, as we shall see later. The implied reasoning is fairly simple. Sin and Antichrist's coming are related; the greater the number of sins, the faster the coming of Antichrist. If Antichrist hasn't come around the year 1000, it is a sign that sinfulness is on the decline. The less we sin, the slower is Antichrist's coming. Hollis continues:

> If, however, punishments accrue in proportion to the sins of man, the reign of Antichrist may also be postponed by a diminution of man's sins. It follows from this that the fulfillment of the prophecies of the last days is contingent upon the actions of mankind. There is therefore a remedy. (179)

The remedy is repentance and reform of life, which can alter the course of human history. The final chapter of the sermon is a call to conversion:

> It is extremely imperative that we examine our conduct and seek forgiveness from God. Let us do what is necessary: return to righteousness and refrain from wrong-doing and atone sincerely for our past sins. Let us love God and observe His Laws and fulfill the baptismal vows undertaken by us and/or the promises made for us by our sponsors.

Wulfstan suggests that if sin can hasten the coming of Antichrist's reign then repentance can slow down the inevitable process. We may even conclude that the *Sermo Lupi* sums up Wulfstan's views on the last days. It is possible that Wulfstan changed his views on impending doom after the failed eschatological expectation of the year 1000, or his quasi-secular office as legislator and archbishop which required of him the maintenance of law and order for the preservation of the social fabric made him temper his older eschatological fervor (Gatch 114). Wulfstan was probably afraid that misguided application of Antichrist references to political figures like the Danish kings of England could land him in trouble with authorities. Naturally, he did not want to antagonize King Cnut for whom he worked. No wonder, then, that Antichrist ceased to be central to Wulfstan's preaching—see the entire English text of three of Wulfstan's apocalyptic sermons in the Appendix.

In conclusion, ecclesiastical preaching tends to be more doctrinaire and less freewheeling in the sense that priests, being official spokesmen of established Church doctrines, as a rule, abhor the introduction of pagan or pre-Christian themes into their preaching unless it is for the purpose of rebuttal of heretics. Such is obviously the case with the Anglo-Saxon homilists. They make hardly any references to pagan Germanic apocalyptic thinking in their sermons. But literature and art are exceptions to this rule of orthodoxy, as we shall see in chapters nine and ten.

NOTES

1. B. Gebhart, *Handbuch der deutschen Geschichte* (Stuttgart, 1954), I: 206; see Henri Focillon, *The Year 1000*, trans. F.D.Wieck (New York, 1969), 39-72; G. L. Burr, "The year 1000 and the Antecedents of the Crusades," American *Historical Review* 6 (1901): 429-39; R. J. Menner, *The Poetical Dialogues of Solomon and Saturn* (New York, 1941), pp. 14-15; A Vasiliev, "Medieval Ideas of the End of the World: West and East, *Byzantion*, American Series, 2 (1942/3): 462-502—I am indebted to this article for some ideas developed in this chapter.

2. Vasiliev, p. 484.

3. See Ernst Wadstein, *Die eschatalogische Ideengruppe* (Leipzig, 1896); Dorothy Bethuram, *Homilies of Wulfstan* (Oxford, 1967), p. 279.

4. Dionysius Exiguus, *Liber de Paschate, praefatio*, PL 67:487; see also Jülicher, *Dionysius Exiguus*, in Pauly-Wissowa, *Real-Encyclopedie der classischen Altertumswissenschaft*, V (1905): 998-9.

5. S. F. Rühl, *Chronologie der Mittelalters und der Neuszeit* (Berlin, 1897), p. 129; 197-200.

6. Raoul Glaber, *Historiae*, II.6.12; see English translation in C. G. Coulton, *Life in the Middle Ages* (New York, 1931), p. 3.

7. See H. Pirenne, *Medieval Cities: Their Origin and the Revival of Trade* (Princeton, 1925), pp. 79-80

8. Baronius, *Annales ecclesiastici*, XVI (Lucca, 1644), 410 (under 1001); ed. Barri-Ducis, XVI (1869), p. 386; cited by Vasiliev, pp. 480-1; Baronius sources were Sigebert and Glaber, both of whom had only a limited historical perspective on account of their limited resources.

9. William Robertson, *The History of the Reign of the Emperor Charles V...* (New York, 1836), p. 16; Vasiliev, p. 481. Nineteenth-century historians like Plaine, Rosiere, Roy, and von Eicken reacted to the claims of earlier historians and dubbed their theory as myths and legends; see Vasiliev, pp. 483-4, for details.

10. Graham D. Caie, *The Judgment Day Theme in Old English Poetry* (Copenhagen, 1976), p. 4.

11. See M. J. B. Allen and D. G. Calder, *Sources and Analogues of Old English Poetry* (Cambridge, 1976), pp. 84-93.

12. Norman D. Hinton and Roberta Box Bosse, "Cynewulf and the Apocalyptic Vision," *Neophilologus* 74 (1990): 279. The Cynewulfian runic acrostic's (FWULCYN) location in the margin of F48r, opposite Vercelli homily 15, a homily which describes the last days of the world, suggests that a reader of the homily and

Cynewulf's *Fates* and *Elene* was struck by thematic resemblance between the homilist and Cynewulf and put Cynewulf's signature there, argue Hinton and Bosse (283).

13. Martin Green, "Man, Time, and Apocalypse in *The Wanderer, The Seafarer,* and *Beowulf," JEGP,* 74 (1975): 505.

14. J.V. Fleming, " *The Dream of the Rood* and Anglo-Saxon Monasticism," *Traditio,* 22 (1966): 70.

15. Fay Patton, "Structure and meaning in *The Dream of the Rood,*" *English Studies,* 49 (1968), 394 ff.; Robert Finnegan, " *The Gospel of Nicodemus* and *The Dream of the Rood* 48b-156," *Neuphilologische Mitteilungen* 84 (1983): 338-43; N. A. Lee, "The Unity of *The Dream of the Rood,*" *Neophilologus,* 56 (1972): 478 ff.; Monica Brzezinski, "The Harrowing of Hell, the Last Judgment, and *The Dream of the Rood,*" *NM* 89 (1988): 252-265.

16. Richard C. Payne, "Convention and Originality in the Vision Framework of *The Dream of the Rood,*" *Modern Philology* 73 (1976): 334-41.

17. Georg Voss, *Das jüngste Gericht in der bildenden Kunst des frühen Mittelalters* (Leipzig, 1884); See Ephraem, "De Caritate: Et in Secundum Adventum Domini Nostri Jesu Christi," ed. Josephus Assemani, 2 (Rome, 1743)" 21-13; "Sermo in Adventum Domini," *Ibid.,* 3; cited by Payne, p. 331.

18. A. S. Cook, *The Christ of Cynewulf* (Boston, 1900), pp. 189-90.

19. Louise Dudley, *The Egyptian Elements in the Legend of Soul and Body* (Baltimore, 1911).

20. Se Douglas Moffat, *The Old English Soul and Body* (Woodbridge, 1990), pp. 28-31.

21. See chapter one.

22. Milton McC. Gatch, *Preaching and Theology in Anglo-Saxon England* (Toronto, 1977), p. 7.

23. Milton McC. Gatch, *Preaching and Theology in Anglo-Saxon England* (Toronto, 1977), p. 8.

24. N. R. Ker, *Catalogue of Manuscripts Containing Anglo-Saxon* (Oxford, 1957)' R. Morris, ed., *The Blickling Homilies* (London, 1967); Max Förster, *Die Vercelli Homilien: 1- VIII Homilie* (Darmstadt, 1964); Paul Szarmach, *Vercelli Homilies IX-XXIII* (Toronto, 1981); Celia Sisam, *The Vercelli Book* (London, 1976). The best study of the eschatology of the Vercelli and Blickling collections is Milton McC. Gatch's "Eschatology in the Anonymous Old English Homilies," *Traditio* 21 (1965): 117-165; I am indebted to this study for many of the remarks and observations that follow.

25. John C. Pope, ed., *Homilies of Aelfric: A Supplementary Collection,* 2 vols. (London, 1967); Dorothy Bethuram, *The Homilies of Wulfstan* (Oxford, 1952).

26. See Benjamin Walter, *Hindu World,* (London, 1968), I: 10-11; Margaret and James Stutley, *Harper's Encyclopedia of Hinduism* (New York: 1977), p. 4.

27. R. Morris had noted this connection long ago in his edition of the *Blickling Homilies.*

28. As Paul Szarmach reminds us, there is no Latin source for this homily (3).

29. See J.K. Elliott, *The Apocryphal New Testament* (Oxford, 1993), pp. 646-9, for the eighth-century Verona fragment of *The Apocalypse of Thomas*, which is based on the Sibylline Oracles of Eastern provenance. For an interesting study of this problem, see also Paul J. Alexander, *The Oracle of Baalbek: The Tiburtine Sibyl in Greek Dress* (Washington, 1867); James Charlesworth, *The Old Testament Pseudepigrapha* (New York, 1983), I: 452-67; W. Bousset, pp. 121 ff. and McGinn, *Antichrist*, pp. 87-97.

30. *Blickling Homilies*, trans, Morris, pp. 106-8.

31. Benjamin Thorpe, ed. *The Homilies of the Anglo-Saxon Church: The First Part, containing the Sermones Catholici or Homilies of Aelfric*, I (London, 1844). I use this text and translation in this book. Malcolm Godden, ed., *Aelfric's Catholic Homilies: the Second Series* (London, 1979); *Aelfric's Lives of Saints*, ed. W.W. Skeat (London, 1881-1900, reprinted as two volumes in 1966). For an excellent treatment of Aelfric's homilies, see Milton McC. Gatch, *Preaching and Theology in Anglo-Saxon England* (Toronto, 1977).

32. *Heptateuch*, lines 1185-94; Gatch, pp. 78, 222.

33. Jules Roy, *L'an mil: Formation de la légende de l'an mil: état de la France de l'an 950 à 1050* (Paris, 1885). Abbo of Fleury says that he had witnessed an instance of apocalyptic outburst in 995: "When I was a young man, I heard a sermon about the end of the world preached before the people in the cathedral of Paris. According to this, as soon as the number of a thousand years was completed, Antichrist would come and the last judgment would follow in a brief time. I opposed this sermon with what force I could from passages in the Gospels, the Apocalypse, and the Book of Daniel" (*PL* 139:471; McGinn, *Visions of the End*, p. 89).

34. Joseph B Traherne, "Fatalism and the Millennium," *Cambridge Companion to Old English Literature*, eds. Malcolm Godden and Michael Lapidge (Cambridge, 1991), p. 168.

35. Skeat, xiii: 290-9.

36. *II in Adventum*, Thorpe, I: 618.

37. Pope 38;13; Aelfric changes the "breath" of Christ of Pseudo-Methodius to "thurh Cristes miht on hys tocyme."

38. See the entire sermon "*Sermo de Die Iudicii*" in Gatch, 590-612.

39. See Dorothy Bethuram, *The Homilies of Wulfstan* (Oxford, 1957); the sermons are numbered i-v.

40. For a comparative study of the Latin and Old English versions, see Gatch, pp. 106-8.

41. Dorothy Whitelock, *ed., Sermo Lupi ad Anglos* (New York, 1966).

42. Stephanie Hollis, "The Thematic Structure of the *Sermo Lupi*," *Anglo-Saxon England* 6 (1977)" 178.

CHAPTER EIGHT

The Road to Valhalla: Germanic Apocalypses

Look at the names of the days of the week (presumably names of planets) in the English language: Monday, Tuesday, Wednesday, Thursday, Friday, and Saturday. While the names of the first six days are of Germanic origin, Saturday is of Roman origin. Now the very name Woden in *Wednesday* raises a curious issue. Is Woden himself a newcomer as a planet in the English language? There are no literary records for Woden before the eighth century, whereas there is a planet called *budha/budhan* in the Indian tradition as the Germanic word *tungol* (meaning "the moon") appears as *tingol* in the Dravidian languages of South India. One wonders whether Woden as a planet is derived from the ancient Indian tradition. I just raised the issue of the linguistic purity of the names of the days of the week to address the more complex problem of the ethnic purity of European apocalyptic tradition.

As noted earlier, no apocalyptic tradition is ethnically pure in its origins and development; that is, there is no such thing as pure Jewish apocalypticism, pure Hindu apocalypticism, pure Christian apocalypticism, or pure Anglo-Saxon apocalypticism. Further, purity is not a result of virginal conception though it can be a byproduct of immaculate conception as in the case of the Virgin Mary born of Joachim and Anne, as Roman Catholic tradition holds; that is, purity is compatible with mixed ancestry. Which means, early English apocalypticism, while it can maintain its own purity of identity, is born of mixed ancestry. This so-called Anglo-Saxon ancestry is undoubtedly Christian as we have demonstrated above; nonetheless, it is radically Indo-European (pagan), profoundly Germanic, and developmentally Christian with many traces of Eastern influences.

Though no literary texts of Germanic eschatological teaching exist in pre-Christian England and the rest of Germania, there survives some genuine medieval Germanic apocalyptic literature of the Christian times especially in Iceland.

The Old High German apocalyptic *Muspilli*-fragment of the eighth/ninth century (preserved in a hand of c. 870) is thoroughly Christian in content; it describes the eschatological strife between Elijah and Antichrist, the anthropomorphic dragon, the Serpent of the tribe of Dan, and Elijah's triumph over his enemy:

> I heard good men of this world declare that Antichrist would fight with Elijah. The wicked one is armed; then battle between them shall begin. The champions are so mighty, the cause is so great. Elijah fights for eternal life—he means to strengthen the realm of the righteous; in this he who holds the heavens shall help him. Antichrist stands for the old fiend, for Satan, who will bring him to perdition, since on that battlefield he shall fall and there be vanquished. But many men of God believe that Elijah shall be destroyed (*arunartit*—"injured"?) in that war. When Elijah's blood drips on the earth, the mountains shall break into flame, no tree will be left standing, none on earth, rivers will run dry, marshes be sucked up, the sky will smoulder in the blaze—the moon will fall, Middle Garth will burn, no stone will stand; then Judgement Day will come upon the land, come with fire to punish mankind. Then no kinsman can help another before that *Muspilli*. When the broad wet earth is all consumed, and fire and wind sweep it all away, where will be then the territory man fought over with his kinsmen? That territory is burnt away, the soul stands afflicted, knows not how to make atonement—and goes to Judgement.[1]

As Hermann Schneider argues, there is little Germanic paganism to be discovered in the fight between Elijah and Antichrist.[2] Rather, the poem reflects knowledge and awareness of Eastern apocalyptic literature, where only we find the idea of Elijah as the military opponent of Antichrist, namely, in *The Apocalypse of Elijah,* written in Greek in Coptic Egypt. According to this work, Elijah and Enoch will appear before Antichrist, the son of lawlessness, and denounce him. Thereupon Antichrist or "the Shameless One" will fight them for seven days; they will be dead for three days, and rise on the fourth day. The Eastern tradition of Pseudo-Methodius and Pseudo-Ephrem identifies the two witnesses of Apocalypse 11 as Elijah and Enoch. According to Pseudo-Ephrem:

> God, seeing the human race endangered and wavering under the breath of the frightful Dragon, sends them a consoling exhortation through His servants the prophets Enoch and Elijah; and when these just ones shall appear, they shall indeed confound their adversary, the Serpent, with his cunning, and

bring back the faithful elect to God.[3]

Bousset traces this tradition through other Eastern writers like Pseudo-Hippolytus, the Syriac Apocalypse of Peter, the Ethiopic Apocalypse of Peter, Ireneus, Tertullian, and Hippolytus (206). What Tertullian says in his *de Anima* is interesting here: "Enoch and Elijah were translated, nor were they found dead, but their death deferred, though they are reserved to die, that they might extinguish Antichrist in their blood."[4]

It seems that the *Muspilli*-poet decided to deviate from the twin tradition of Enoch and Elijah to the Jewish and Gospel tradition of the single witness Elijah (Malachi 4:1), a tradition found also in the Sibylline literature (II:187), Justin and Lactantius, while Commodian hesitates between one and two witnesses. Such a difference of view indicates the writer's awareness of the diverse Antichrist-traditions found in the early Church and later Middle Ages. While the *Muspilli*-poet is satisfied with just one witness, the *Beowulf*-poet resorts to two witnesses in the persons of Beowulf and Wiglaf who together battle against the dragon-Antichrist as did Enoch and Elijah.

The most important "pagan" Germanic document of the last times— of the end of the world and its future regeneration—which describes the *ragnarøk* (the fall of the ruling powers) is the *Voluspa*.[5] This tenth-century poem is found in the Old Norse collection known as the *Elder Edda*.[6] It contains within its sixty-some stanzas a series of visions by a Sibyl-like *volva* (wise woman) who, at the bidding of God Othin, who is always eager for knowledge, describes creation (20 stanzas), the rise of the gods, and their war with the Vanir (stanza 21); then she turns to prophesy the final doom of the gods or *ragnarøk* (18 stanzas).

First, there will be the great winter (*fimbulvetr*), which is to last for years with no summer in between. During this time brothers will slay brothers, and suffering and turmoil will stalk the earth. With earthquakes and an eclipse of the sun, the mighty serpent of the sea will rise, causing flooding on earth. The ship *naglfar*, made from the uncut nails of the dead, will ferry the giants, and Surt will arrive on land over the Rainbow Bridge to storm Asgard, the home of the gods. The armies of the gods and the giants will meet on Vigrid plain for the final battle. In the battle, all the gods will die along with their adversaries: Fenris-Wolf will swallow Othin; Thor will slay the Midgard Serpent; Othin's son Vidarr will kill the Wolf in retaliation; Thor will finally succumb to the Serpent's venom. She also tells of the Valkyries ("choosers of the slain" or "Wish-maidens") who bring slain warriors to Valhalla to aid Othin and the other gods, of the death of the beautiful Baldr through the wicked wiles of Loki, and of Surt's destruction of heaven and earth when "fire leaps up as high as heaven itself" (31-58).

It is not all over yet; destruction is followed by reconstruction: two members of the human race will escape cosmic conflagration by surviving on morning dew in order to procreate a new race of men and women, and a new earth will arise from the sea, signaling the arrival of a new age with the return of Baldr:

> Now do I see   the earth anew
> Rise all green   from the waves again;
> The cataracts fall,   and the eagle flies,
> And fish he catches   beneath the cliffs.
>
> The gods in Ithavoll   meet together,
> Of the terrible girdler   of earth they talk,
> And the mighty past   they call to mind,
> And the ancient runes   of the Ruler of Gods.
>
> In wondrous beauty   once again
> Shall the golden tables   stand mid the grass,
> Which the gods had owned   in the days of old.
> ....
> Then fields unsowed   bear ripened fruit,
> All grow better,   and Baldr comes back;
> Baldr and Hoth dwell   in Hropt's battle-hall,
> And the mighty gods: would you know yet more?
> ....
> More fair than the sun,   a hall I see
> Roofed with gold,   on Gimle it stands;
> There shall the righteous   rulers dwell,
> And happiness ever   there shall they have. (stanzas 59-64)

The final stanzas on new heaven and new earth have created much dissension among scholars.   Earlier scholars like Finnur Jonsson and Müllenhof steadfastly maintain that *Voluspa* is a pagan poem, whereas most recent critics see evidences of Christian coloring derived from the Book of Apocalypse in the last stanzas (Bellows 2). Tolkien favors the pagan interpretation of the poem by reading the poem as a celebration of absolute resistance without hope in the face of the triumph of the monsters of chaos over the gods of order.[7] The given logic of this argumentation is that, since paganism does not offer hope and whereas Christianity offers the hope of eternal life, the last lines must be a Christian interpolation. Ursula Dronke correctly objects to the pessimistic pagan interpretation of the *Voluspa* by arguing for the integrity of the text as it stands: "Chaos and Unreason—the monsters—do not win;

they destroy what is ripe for destruction, a decaying and tainted world, but a world whose defenders have sufficient strength to destroy their destroyers. Absolute resistance there is—but there is no lack of hope" (303). The point simply is that heathen or Indo-European mythology has survived in the *Voluspa*, which was composed at the end of the tenth century when Norway and Iceland were still pagan or still not yet converted to Christianity. This poem attempts to give a coherent account, shaped by Indo-European or/and Germanic mythology. As Ursula Dronke puts it, "The poet of *Voluspa* has selected and organized, according to a logical linking of his own, the myths of the gods within the temporal framework of the world's birth and death" (308).

The Norse Sibyl's conception of eschatology is not necessarily Christian in inspiration but rather profoundly Germanic or Indo-European. The *Voluspa*-poet's apocalyptic view simply corresponds to the Indian conception of the world's ages; for example, the defeat of gods by demons and destruction of the old world and recreation of the new cosmos; in other words, the return of Baldr is not just a plagiarism of the resurrection of Christ and the rise of the new world a copycat of the Christian book of Apocalypse. As Dronke argues, "when the poet of *Voluspa* composed his drama of the world and of the gods from creation to destruction and renewal, he found ethical substance for this drama already inherent in his native mythology" (310-11).

Let me point out a few close parallels between the Germanic apocalypticism and Eastern Indo-European apocalypticism. The Germanic *fimbulvetr* of the end times corresponds to the Zoroastrian myth of the terrible winter preceding Doomsday, during which time some humans and animals will find shelter in Yima's bosom.[8] Similarly the Germanic bifrost Bridge is akin to the Persian Chinvat Bridge, and the motif of the ship made of nails of the dead corresponds to the Zoroastrian belief that fingernails should be consecrated to the divine bird Askozushta lest they be used by evil forces.[9] Most importantly, the Germanic views on the mortality of the gods as well as the deemphasis on the immortality of the individual humans and emphasis on the survival of both the races of gods and humans show closer parallels to Indo-European or Indian thought than to Christian theology.

A significant difference between the *Voluspa*'s eschatology and Christian apocalypticism is that while the Christians pray daily "Thy kingdom come" and for the Second Coming of Christ "Come, Lord Jesus" (Apocalypse 22:20), Othin tries to postpone the inevitable end even though Othin, the All-Father, himself is subject to destiny. Of course,

Othin appears in mythology as the god of the dead and as the god of battle, but he is also the god of wisdom who is aware of his own mortality. Yet he is always acting in such a way as to foil the designs of the Grey Wolf (Fenrir). In the *Hakonarmal*, Othin answers to the question why he allows noble kings to die in battle: "The Grey Wolf watches the abodes of the Gods," in the sense his power is ineffective often against that of Fenrir.[10] While Othin continues to gather valiant warriors in Valhalla, he often travels, as hero Odysseus or the biblical John the Baptist or Jesus Christ of harrowing-of-hell fame did once, to the underworld realm of Hel to pry into the future by consulting the gods and the deceased as in the poem *Baldrs Draumnr*. Further, the heroic image of the suffering, Christ-like Othin hanging on a tree to win wisdom (mastery of runes) and of the generous image of the one willing to sell one eye to Mimir for the sake of wisdom, and of the daring questor of wisdom in *Vafthrudnismal* depict him as one trying to avert or at least postpone the inevitable doom of the gods and humans and demons. In short, Germanic mythology holds out the proposition that wisdom is the antidote to fatalism: "Struggle wisely whatever the outcome may be." It is this kind of heroic resistance that Ker and Tolkien talk about.

The mixedness of the Anglo-Saxon ancestry of apocalypticism or its hybridity reveals itself particularly in *Beowulf* and the Gosforth Cross. Native Germanic myths seem to have left their markable traces in these two works of art.

There are two points worth bearing in mind as we discuss the mixed ancestry of the mythological traditions or works of art. One, just as one parent alone cannot explain the birth of a child, one source alone cannot explain adequately the creation of a work of art. Germanic mythology or Christian apocalypticism in insular solitude is incapable of explaining the apocalypticism of *Beowulf* or of the Gosforth Cross. As for *Beowulf*, it is worth repeating Charles Donahue:

> Tolkien saw clearly that the poem must be interpreted in terms of both the Christian elements and non-Christian elements. It is precisely the relationship of the two that gives the poem its peculiar power. Older critics were wrong when they tried to extract the pagan core, the poetic heart of the poem from the bungling addition of Christian scribes. More recent critics are also wrong when they try to find the "thoroughgoing Christian interpretation" [Huppé] called for by advocates of Christian allegorical interpretation.[11]

Two, Christian apocalypticism with its Eastern versions does complement the so-called pagan aspect of *Beowulf* and of the Gosforth Cross.[12]

The point I would like to emphasize is simply that non-Christian Germanic apocalypticism alone is insufficient to account for *Beowulf*s eschatological thought.[13] *A pari*, it is equally undeniable that pagan Germanic and/or Indo-European apocalyptic thought is also discernible in the poem. For example, Thor's battle with the World-Serpent is comparable to Beowulf's fight with the dragon, for in both "a hero in defence of his people kills a marauding dragon and himself dies in the fight" (Dronke 313). Thor is overwhelmed by the Serpent's poison as is Beowulf. Though it may appear that Thor has no helpers in the *Voluspa*, his sons return to fresh sanctuaries, bearing their father's hammer (*Vafthrudnismal* 51)" (315). The young helper (Wiglaf) who appears in *Beowulf* is paralleled by the avenging son of Othin, who plunges his sword into the heart of the Wolf. The *Voluspa* gives two more instances of the mutual slaying of god and monster in the fights between Tyr and the hound of Hel and of Heimdallr and Loki. Dronke also shows that the Indo-European tradition itself bears a strong resemblance to this episode; for example, in the Indian tradition found in the *Mahabharata*, the Vedic winner Indra, who fights the Serpent Vrtra, also suffers death and discomfiture at least temporarily, as in the case of Jesus (315).[14] On the other hand, the Christian Book of Apocalypse, as we shall see later, offers more striking parallels to the demonic beasts of *Beowulf*, where we find a beast of the land and a beast of the sea as in the Apocalypse; as John Niles suggests, Grendel is associated chiefly with the surface of the earth, while his mother keeps to the depths of the mere.[15] In addition, there are the signs of Doom found in both works; Risden, for example, has found ninety-four instances of the signs of Doom in *Beowulf* (67). Summarily, the Christian poet of *Beowulf* tries to imagine the pagan mythology in his Christian apocalyptic vision.

Apart from the *Beowulf*-poem, the most striking example of religious syncretism in Anglo-Saxon apocalyptic thinking is found in the mid-tenth-century Gosforth Cross in Cumberland, England.[16] While most scholars agree on the source of the motifs carved on the cross, they disagree in the interpretation of the motifs. Some view them exclusively as pagan; others see them exclusively as Christian; yet a few critics see them as both pagan and Christian. Risden finds in the cross "a syncretism of Christian and northern Germanic culture" (1).

There is no doubt that the crucifixion on the east side is explicitly a Christian scene, but the other carvings on the cross are based on the Norse accounts of *ragnrøk*. Hilda Davidson writes:

There seems little doubt that the scenes on the cross at Gosforth in Cumberland have been based on an account of Ragnarok closely resembling that given in *Voluspa* and Snorri. Here monsters struggle in bonds; a woman holds a bowl beside a bound figure, suggesting Sigyn and Loki; a figure battles with a monster, holding open its jaws with hand and foot, precisely as Vidar was said to do when he slew the wolf that had swallowed Odin. In addition we have a figure with a horn, and a warrior riding into battle. So many separate points of resemblance seem to establish the fact that the artist was working on a series of scenes deliberately grouped together. All these scenes were capable of a Christian as well as a heathen interpretation, and as there is a crucifixion scene on the other side of the cross, there is no doubt that it was erected as a Christian monument. (207)[17]

As Davidson reminds us, there are other grave stones at Gosforth as well as a Swedish rune-stone at Skarpaler, besides Saxo Grammticus' *Gesta Danorum* (VIII.262), that suggest that *ragnarøk* was a traditional theme in Germanic thinking and preaching and writing (208).

The Gosforth Cross as well as in *Beowulf* can be viewed as a juxtaposition of Christian and non-Christian apocalypses, each illuminating the other. This diptych-like portrayal seems to suggest that the Anglo-Saxons could have interpreted Germanic apocalypse as type and Christian apocalypse as anti-type, the former adumbrating the latter and finding its fulfillment therein. Or, as Risden would put it, "by making use of eschatological imagery, the sculptor has created a kind of parable for the understanding of Christian mysteries without derogating its Norse analogues" (3). I see Christian and non-Christian apocalypses rather as fuzzy sets, like East and West, leaking into each other, as I shall show in my concluding essay on fuzzy literature.

NOTES

1. W. Braune and K. Helm, *Althochdeutsches Lesebuch* (1949), p. 75; it is possible to identify Elijah with the god of thunder (Thor) because Elijah was carried off to heaven in a fiery chariot; see J. Grimm, *Teutonic Mythology* (1883-88), I: 173 ff. I am indebted to the studies of Ursula Dronke, "*Beowulf* and *Ragnarok*," *Saga-Book of the Viking Society for Northern Research*, 17 (1961): 302-25 and Edward L. Risden, *Beasts of Time: Apocalyptic Beowulf* (New York, 1994). See translation of *Muspilli* in Dronke, p. 318.

2. Hermann Schneider, "Muspilli," *Zeitschrift für Altertum* 73 (1936): 1 ff.

3. Cited by Bousset, *The Antichrist Legend*, p. 204.

4. Cited by Bousset, p. 206-7.

5. Often *ragnarok* is confused with the word *røkker* ("twilight") as in the German *Götterdammerung* (Twilight of the gods).

6. *The Poetic Edda*, trans. Henry Adams Bellows (Princeton, 1936), pp. 1-27; Snorri Sturluson, *The Prose Edda*, trans. A. G. Brodeur (New York, 1916), pp. 77-84.

At the beginning of the *Codex Regius* collection stands the *Voluspa*, the most important of all Eddic poems. Another version can be found in the fourteenth-century *Hauksbok*, and many stanzas are included in the *Prose Edda* of Snorri Sturluson.

7. J. R. R. Tolkien, "*Beowulf* the Monsters and the Critics," *Proceedings of the British Academy*, 22 (1936): 245 ff.

8. R. C. Zaehner, *The Dawn and Twilight of Zoroastrianism* (London, 1961), p. 135.

9. Hilda Ellis Davidson, *Gods and Myths of Northern Europe* (Baltimore, 1964), pp. 204-7.

10. Hilda Ellis Davidson, *The Lost Beliefs of Northern Europe* (London, 1993), p. 76.

11. Charles Donahue, "Social Function and Literary Value in *Beowulf*," *Epics in Medieval Society: Aesthetic and Moral Values*, ed. Harald Scholler (Tübingen, 1977), pp. 387-8.

12. Next chapter discusses the Eastern dimensions of the Christian apocalypticism of *Beowulf* in greater detail.

13. The works of Tolkien, Ursula Dronke, and Edward Risden are worth recommending. Since many other scholars also have dwelt at length on Germanic apocalypticism in *Beowulf*, I shall be necessarily very brief on *Beowulf* except to reaffirm that *Beowulf* contains many native Germanic and Indo-European apocalyptic elements.

14. For a good account of the correspondences between Thor and Indra, see G. Turville-Petre, *Myth and Religion of the North* (New York, 1964), pp. 75 ff.

15. John Niles, *Beowulf: The Poem and Its Tradition* (Cambridge, 1983), p. 10.

16. See the excellent article of Edward Risden, "The Gosforth Cross Narrative and *Beowulf*," *Proceedings of the Medieval Association of the Midwest* 3 (1995) 1-14.

17. See K. Berg, "The Gosforth Cross," *Journal of the Warburg and Courtland Institutes* 21 (1958): 27 ff, where one can find excellent illustrations.

CHAPTER NINE

Beowulf: Apocalypse and Antichrist

About seventy years ago, S. J. Crawford, talking about the monsters of the sea and land populating the Apocalypse, observed: "I am somewhat surprised that we have not already had an article with the title '*Beowulf* and the Apocalypse.'"1 The main reason no such study appeared until recently is simply that scholars were too preoccupied with reading *Beowulf* as a pagan Germanic poem or as a poem shaped almost exclusively by the Western Latin intellectual traditions dominated by St. Augustine and his disciples or that they were trying to avoid these two extremes. I view this very absence of agreement and agon as an invitation to open the critical window ("wind's eye") wider because there is more light and heat out there in the oft-wintry world of scholarship for rereading and revisioning the fading lines of the English poem, which must continue to remain an open text: *Tolle et lege* ("Take and read"), as St. Augustine would urge us to do.

The Old English epic *Beowulf* composed in its present form around the tenth or early eleventh century has been the subject of much criticism, interpretation, and controversy.2 Early critics of the nineteenth and early twentieth century viewed the poem primarily as a pagan work with Christian interpolations. In the second half of the twentieth century the critical pendulum has swung in the opposite direction of Christian interpretation, according to which the poem is a thoroughly Christian work with pagan residues. Critics find that the Christianity of the poem is nonetheless a Euro-centric Christianity or Western Christianity derived from the teachings of the Western Fathers of the Church, (Augustine, Ambrose, Jerome, and Gregory), erroneously called "the Founders of the Middle Ages" (Haskins) as though there were no other eminent personalities figuring in this foundation myth! In such a conceptual framework we are faced with

opposites as though one excludes the other, as though Western Christianity is antithetical to Eastern Christendom, as though paganism is the impla-
cable foe of Christianity. The traditional response to Alcuin's famous rhetorical question: "*Quid Hinieldus cum Christo*? (What has Ingeld to do
with Christ?")—a paraphrase of Tertullian's "What has Athens to do with
Jerusalem?"—is "Nothing." Wrong. The answer should be, "Everything."
Christianity is Western as well as Eastern; Western literary tradition is thoroughly Eastern in origin and development. Christianity itself is a religion
which has derived its mythology and cult not only from the Roman pagan
world but also from the Eastern religions of Judaism, Gnosticism, Buddhism, and Hinduism. I have shown the extent of such intercultural dependence in the development of eschatological thought in the first chapter.
In this chapter I shall show that the Anglo-Saxons' jewel in the crown,
Beowulf, has an Eastern aura and dimension.[3]

Though we are often reluctant to admit it, literary interpretation is based
on the critical assumptions the reader brings to a literary text. As James Earl
puts it, "In literary criticism everything depends upon the assumptions we
bring to the text. Some of these are imprinted deeply in our characters and
in our cultures, and some are the result of intellectual struggle and insights."[4]
As for me, my literary hermeneutics to a great extent consists of the principles of "fuzzy literature," as explained in the conclusion, which recognize
the presence of opposites in a text and eschew reductionism while celebrating Nils Bohr's motto *Contraria sunt complementaria*. It means that
in the case of *Beowulf* the poem does not have to be purely pagan or purely
Christian, oral folklore or written literature, Western or Eastern. It is all this
and more. By avoiding the scylla of narrow ethnic interpretations and the
charybdis of total subjectivity in interpretation, I follow the middle-road
critical principle that *Beowulf* is also an apocalyptic work with ideas, inspiration, and motifs drawn from Germanic paganism, Latin Christianity, Eastern thought, and Byzantine apocalypses. The fact that the poem was composed—written or copied or recited—around the apocalyptic year 1000
may perhaps have something to do with the apocalyptic character of the
book, which is a tragic tale of doom and disaster though not devoid of
hope, the last survivor in Pandora's Box.

Earlier critics were more fascinated with historical aspects, folkloric elements, structural analyses, moral vision, and the mythological dimensions
of the poem than with the poem's apocalypticism. The first great student of
the poem, the Danish Grundtvig, though he did not like the poem's mix-
ing of history and folktale, its lack of unity, and its many digressions, sees the
moral vision or "higher meaning" of the poem as the universal theme of

the struggle of good against evil.[5] Writing around the turn of the century, W. P. Ker disapproved of the poet's use of folktales but praised the poet's dignified style:"It is too simple. Yet the three chief episodes are well wrought and well diversified....The great beauty...is in its dignity of style."[6] From the middle of the nineteenth century to about World War II, during the heydays of philological scholarship, the poem was taught in colleges in England, North America, Australia, and India primarily as a linguistic, cultural, and historical document, which J. R. R. Tolkien thought were the wrong reasons for studying the poem. Tolkien says:

> Nearly all the censure, and most of the praise, that has been bestowed on *The Beowulf* has been due either to the belief that it was something that it was not—for example, primitive, pagan, Teutonic, an allegory (political or mythical), or, most often, an epic; or to disappointment at the discovery that it was itself and not something that the scholar would have liked better—for example, a heathen heroic lay, a history of Sweden, a manual of Germanic antiquities, or a Nordic *Summa Theologica*.[7]

Tolkien's Gollancz Lecture to the British Academy in 1936 was a turning point in *Beowulf* criticism; all subsequent criticism, especially the present one, is only a footnote or appendix to Tolkien's seminal study. Tolkien called for a re-evaluation, appreciation, and criticism of the poem on its own terms. Against the detractors of the structural unity of the poem, he states:

> The general design of the poet is not only defensible; it is, I think, admirable....For *Beowulf* was not designed to tell the tale of Hygelac's fall, or for that matter to give the whole biography of Beowulf, still less to write the history of the Geatish kingdom and its downfall. But it used knowledge of these things for its own purpose—to give that sense of perspective, of antiquity with a greater and yet darker antiquity behind. These things are mainly on the outer edges or in the background because they belong there, if they are to function in this way. But in the centre we have an heroic figure of enlarged proportions." (85)

Tolkien sees in the *static* structure of the poem, since "the poem was not meant to advance" (81), a balance, an opposition between beginnings and endings, rising and setting, youth and age, first achievement and final death (81). As such, the poem is not a narrative epic but an elegy:"It is an heroic-elegiac poem; and in a sense all its 3136 lines are the prelude to a dirge" (85). Tolkien places the monsters—Grendel, Grendel's mother, and the dragon—alongside Beowulf in the center of the poem: "I would suggest...that the monsters are not an inexplicable blunder of taste; they are essential, fundamentally allied to the underlying ideas of the poem" (68). Tolkien sees the monsters as adversaries of God and powers of evil, "mortal denizens of the material world, in it and of it" (69). He sees Grendel as "an ogre, a physical monster, whose main function is hostility to humanity (and its frail efforts at order and art upon earth" (91); Tolkien also admits that Grendel "approaches to a *devil*, though he is not yet a true devil" (89). Tolkien prefers to view the monsters as mortal beings, inhabiting the real world and symbolizing the forces of evil. He seems to have a problem with Grendel's mother, who "becomes a marginalized woman" (Clark 10), because, as Clark argues, "Grendel's mother spoils the lyric balance of ends and beginnings....Worse still, the poet's explicit representation of Grendel's mother (and the dragon) seems morally neutral" (Clark 10).[8]

Tolkien sees the *Beowulf*-poet as an English Christian author at home in the Christian traditions and in the pagan Germanic lore, though the poet suppresses specific references to the Christian deity as well as the old gods (71-72). The poet cleverly fuses various traditions, and Tolkien sees "the key to the fusion-point of imagination that produced this poem lies...in those very references to Cain" (68). As I shall show later, the references to Cain leads to Islam and Antichrist, Islam and Apocalypse, which is the key to the deeper understanding and appreciation of the poem.

Tolkien's view of the Christian authorship of the poem was anticipated by Blackburn and Klaeber and later supported by a large number of critics.[9] By 1922, Fr. Klaeber had already talked about "the Christian coloring" of *Beowulf.* "The presentation of the story material in Beowulf has been influenced, to a considerable extent, by ideas derived from Christianity."[10] He argued for "the transformation of old heathen elements in accordance with Christian thought" (xlix). He concludes:

> We might even feel inclined to recognize features of the Christian Savior in the destroyer of hellish fiends, the warrior brave and gentle, blameless in thought and word, the king that dies for his people. Though delicately kept in the background, such a Christian interpretation of the story could not but give added strength and tone to the entire poem. It helps to explain one of the great puzzles of our epic. (li)

Klaeber is right: A Christian apocalyptic interpretation of the monster fights as the battles of Christ with with the Antichrist-like hellish fiends explains the great puzzle of *Beowulf.* In fact, the apocalyptic tone displayed by the poet in his references to creation, destruction, and regeneration is the hallmark of *Beowulf.* The poet, who announces the creation of the world through the symbolic building of Heorot, laments the destruction of the great hall (lines 81-85) and later ends the poem with the death of the hero and of his nation. This eschatology of *Beowulf,* however, is not purely and simply Christian with the revelation of a new heavenly Hierusalem/Heorot at the end. The poet's eschatology is historical apocalypticism with a veneer of Germanic speculation as outlined in the *Voluspa*. As James Earl would put it, "We might be tempted to say…that Beowulf's eschatology is essentially northern and not Christian; but there are…Christian components to it. Beowulf takes the myth of the eschaton from native belief and historicizes it the way Christianity does" (48).

Earl is right in suggesting that the historical pattern employed by the poet is similar to Augustine's presentation of the fall of Rome, Gildas' story of the fall of Britain, and Wulfstan's analysis of the fall of England. I shall show that the poet incorporates not the fall of Rome and of Britain but also the fall of Europe to Islam through the use apocalyptic imagery. As Margaret E. Goldsmith avers:

> The poet was concerned with the minds and hearts of men *sub specie aeternitatis*, and only secondarily with wars and banquets and feats of swimming. One of the strongest reasons for this belief is the extraordinary way in which the poet has avoided writing an epic about a martial hero.[11]

Goldsmith's excellent perception of *Beowulf* as an allegory goes beyond Tolkien's reading of the monsters of the poem as symbolizing evil. She argues that the three fights in *Beowulf* allegorically represent humankind's battle against the sins of cupidity and pride but that Beowulf, not being a Christ figure, was guilty of cupidity for the dragon's gold.[12] Thus, Goldsmith interprets the poem primarily as a moral allegory, which makes sense like Kaske's ethical paradigm of *sapientia et fortitudo* (wisdom and courage) in the character of hero Beowulf.[13] Remarkably, both Kaske and Goldsmith acknowledge the presence of the eschatological idea of the transience of life and wealth and honor in the poem but subordinate the apocalyptic motif to moral allegory.

For good reasons, Charles Donahue dislikes Goldsmith's slightly negative view of Beowulf as a flawed hero; for him the pre-Christian, pagan Beowulf is a Christ-figure, *figura Christi*, who dies in the state of grace.[14] Donahue draws some significant parallels between Christ and Beowulf, especially both as *faege* (fated to die) and giving farewell speeches, and with a companion—Wiglaf with Beowulf and Apostle John with Jesus—at the end. His conclusion is worth citing:

> Our poet…liked diptychs, and he left his audience with a pair of images, Beowulf at the dragon's barrow on one side of the diptych, Jesus on Calvary, on the other. In the confrontation of these images he found the ultimate reconciliation between his *pietas* towards the doomed kings of his native past and his loyalty to a new faith (116).

Donahue's confrontation of the contrasting images of Christ and Beowulf does not go beyond the deaths of these two figures. In fact, the poet seems

to present a diptych of the slain Beowulf the dragon-slayer and of Christ
agnus quasi-occisus (the sacrificed lamb) overcoming the dragon of the
Apocalypse. These two figures are also alike in the cosmic apocalyptic conflict; the conflict itself, as mentioned above, between Christ and Antichrist
is not only eschatological but also historical, as the earlier exegesis of the
Book of Apocalypse has shown. The *Beowulf*-poet, in effect, gives historical applications of the universal conflict in allegorical fashion.

Allegory is, therefore, the key to the interpretation of this poem, and
allegory simply means saying one thing to mean other things. So, when
the poet talks about the pagan king Beowulf or a pagan god by the name of
Beowulf, he also means Christ the king and the Lord. The one meaning or
literary figure without being wholly co-extensive and coterminous with
the other does not contradict the other but rather complements it while
retaining opposition as *contrarium*.[15] For example, the moral meaning of
the poem so ably elucidated by Tolkien and Goldsmith or the literal meaning of a vampire story contained in the folkloric antecedents of the poem
or the historical meaning of Germanic kings and tribes at war with one
another does not in any way prevent either the poet from presenting allegorical and anagogical meanings or the reader from perceiving them. The
extremely allusive poet of *Beowulf*, without contradicting himself, has left
enough traces in the form of images, for example, in the poem to lead
readers to the discovery of the presence of allegorical and anagogical meanings, as co-existence of opposites, leading the readers to the discovery of
fascinating and tantalizing new syntheses.

The apocalyptic reading of *Beowulf* is one such fascinating synthesis.
The apocalyptic elements of *Beowulf* can be grouped into three: (1)
eschatological themes, (2) artistic techniques of apocalyptic composition,
(3) apocalyptic monsters of the poem as historical entities.

Eschatological Themes

Eschatology is about end. We can view the end of the individual as
death, the end of society as its disintegration, and the end of the world as
consummation by fire or water. As Edward Risden's study indicates, we
find a tripartite apocalypticism in *Beowulf*: societal apocalypse, personal
apocalypse, and cosmic apocalypse. He writes:

> In *Beowulf*, I find three levels of apocalypticism: (1) societal—*Beowulf*
> presages a society's collapse and enslavement; (2) personal—*Beowulf* is largely
> about death and how to meet it; (3) cosmological—*Beowulf* metaphori-
> cally prefigures the end of the world and seeks partly to direct the reader's
> attention to imminence of the end.[16]

The prologue of the poem deals with the deaths of Scyld Scefing and his son Beowulf and then the succession of kings and their deaths, indicating that death is inevitable and that all human beings are fated to die. As the poet puts it, "Then at his destined hour Scyld departed, still full of vigor, to pass into the keeping of the Lord" (26-27); his death is followed by the death of his son Beowulf I, and then by the death of his son Healfdene, and so on. Some deaths are peaceful, but others violent; some die by fire, others in battle; some by treachery and others fratricidally, and yet others in the violent clutches of Grendel, Grendel's mother, and the dragon. Grendel kills, but he dies in shame and disgrace; Grendel's mother also kills, but she, too, dies ignominiously. In three passages—lament of the last survivor (2247-66), the father's lament (2444-62), and Hrothgar's speech (1700-84)—the poet explicitly reminds his hearers of the inevitability of death. For example, Hrothgar exhorts:

> O renowned champion, now for a little while your might is at its full glory; yet soon it will come to pass that sickness or the sword's edge will strip you of your strength; or it will be the embrace of fire, or the surge of the flood, or the bite of a blade or the flight of a spear, or fearsome old age; or else the clear light of your eyes will fade and grow dim; presently it will come about that death shall overpower you, O warrior. (1761-68)

In one sense, the poem is the celebration of death culminating in the death of the two great adversaries—Christ-like Beowulf and the Antichrist-like dragon. As Risden puts it, "*Beowulf* as a whole becomes a *memento mori*" (93).[17] *Beowulf*, however, celebrates not only death but also life after death. Evil-doers go to fiery hell, while the righteous enjoy happiness after death; for example, Heremod (1709-22), Unferth (581-9), and Grendel (809-24) suffer torments in hell, whereas Scyld goes into the Lord's protection (27) and Hrethel finds Divine light (2469-70).

Apocalypses talk about the end not only of individuals but also of human societies. Empires come and go; heroic societies come into existence and then disappear into oblivion. Kingdoms fall sometimes due to external aggression but often due to internal strife. The poet waxes eloquently about the end of the Scylding dynasty caused by internal rivalries and of the Geatish royal family. After the death of Beowulf, the Geats would find themselves unable to hold off their enemies. The poet implies that with the death of the hero king, society itself will fall into chaos. For instance, the poet's lament bears out this perception:

> O earth, guard now what earls have owned, now that heroes cannot! Indeed, it was from you that noble men once won it. Death in the fray, that fierce destroyer of life, has carried off every single man of my race, and they

have forsaken this life and seen the last of the joys of the hall. I have none to bear the sword, none to burnish the gold-plated flagon or the precious drinking-vessel; the flower of the host has passed swiftly away. The hard helm must be bereft of its plates and golden ornament; the burnishers whose task it was to polish the vizored helm are now sleeping in death. So too the warlike mail-coat which, amid the crashing of shields, endured the slash of steel blades in battle, will crumble away along with the warrior; nor can the ringed corselet travel far and wide with the war-leader, or be at the hero's side. There comes no delight from the harp, no mirth from the wood that brought good cheer, nor does the good hawk swoop through the hall, nor the swift steed stamp in the courtyard. Deadly slaughter has carried away many of the race of the living! (2247-66)[18]

No wonder that many past critics stress the symbolic value of the death of Beowulf as presaging the passing away of civilization.[19]

Another apocalyptic theme that haunts *Beowulf* is its indirect preoccupation with the end of the world. Nowhere does the poet directly refer to the end of the world, but he alludes to it several times inasmuch as "he implies a consistent cosmological (or anagogical) metaphor, though not a full-blown allegory, as part of his apocalyptic technique" (Risden 109).

Risden shows that references to the Signs of Doom or the traditional fifteen biblical signs associated with the coming of Antichrist in end times, as listed, for example, in *de quindecim signis* of Pseudo-Bede, abound in *Beowulf*.[20] The desolation and burning of Heorot caused by Grendel's depredations and by wars and the cremation of Beowulf at the end of the poem are the prime signs of end times and symbols of cosmic conflagration in the poem. The poet depicts the two episodes as Jesus describes the destruction of Jerusalem and lists the signs of the last times. Jesus says:

> O Jerusalem, Jerusalem, killing the prophets and stoning those those who are sent to you!... Behold, your house is forsaken and desolate....You see all these [buildings of the Temple], do you not? Truly, I say to you, there will not be left here one stone upon another, that will not be thrown down [The Romans set fire to the temple and destroyed it without a stone upon another in 70 CE]. And you will hear of wars and rumors of wars; see that you are not alarmed; for this must take place, but the end is not yet. For nation will rise against nation, and kingdom against kingdom, and there will be famines and earthquakes....And then they will deliver you up to tribulation and put you to death; and you will be hated by all nations for my name's sake. And many will fall away, and betray one another, and hate one another. And many false prophets will arise and lead many astray.... But he who endures to the end will be saved.... So when you see the abomination of desolation spoken of by the prophet Daniel standing in the holy place..., then let those who are in Judea will flee to the mountains.... And if those days had not been shortened, no human being would be saved. (Matthew 23:37-24:22)

The *Beowulf*-poet's description of Rome-like Grendel's destruction of Heorot (a pun on Hierusalem) and the attendant incidents resemble very much the persecution of the Jews and the Roman destruction of Jerusalem described in the Gospels. The powerful and tyrannic Grendel terrorized the Danes and reigned in Heorot without resistance from the Danes who fled the hall:

> This creature, cut off from grace, grim and greedy, fierce and fell, at once set to work and seized thirty thanes from their couches....Too fierce was that strife, too relentless and long-lasting.... He again wrought more murderous havoc, more violent and bloody deeds and felt no remorse; he was too deeply rooted in such ways. It was not hard now to find a man seeking elsewhere for some resting place farther afield or some bed among the outbuildings.... From that time onwards, whoever escaped the foe kept himself at a safe distance for the future. Thus did Grendel make himself master and wage a wrongful war against them all, single-handedly, until that finest of halls stood empty. This went on a long time; for twelve year's space...Grendel had waged war on Hrothgar, pursuing through many seasons his spiteful hatred with violent and bloody deeds, a conflict which had no end. (120-54)

The long passage cited above indirectly describes the Roman persecution of the Jewish people and their predatory attacks on Jerusalem. As a result, the Danes left Heorot and sought refuge elsewhere as the Jewish people did during the siege of Jerusalem. The following description of Grendel's entry into the hall and the use of fire metaphor seem to describe the Roman attack on the Holy Temple and its destruction by fire:

> Grendel came, making his way to the building, an attacker bereft of all joys. The door gave way at once, though held by fire-forged bars, when he touched it with open palm; then, with his mind set on havoc, he thrust back the doors of the building, for fury was rising in him. Next, the fiend swiftly set his foot upon the bright-hued floor and advanced with wrathful heart; from his eyes there flashed an ugly gleam, much like a flame. Inside the building he saw many a warrior, a friendly company of young warlike kinsmen sleeping together. At this his heart laughed within him, for the fearsome monster meant, before day came, to tear the life out of the body of every single one of them, now that the chance of a lavish feast had come his way. (720-35)

The Roman allusion of the poet in this section is found in Wealhtheow's appearance in Heorot (612 ff) since *Wealh* means not only Welsh but also foreign and Roman. Following Helen Damico's argument that Wealhtheow is a valkyrie-figure who appears in end times in in *Voluspa* (stanza 30), one may find here a poetic pun, another eschatological allusion.[21]

Two other apocalyptic signs found in *Beowulf* are interesting; they are references to widespread apostasy and the appearance of the false prophet. According to the predictions of Jesus, during the eschatological times many faithful will fall away from the true faith and false messiahs and prophets will try to seduce them: "Take heed that no one lead you astray. For many will come in my name and say, 'I am the Christ,' and they will lead many astray" (Matthew 24: 4-5). Some of the Danes became apostates, like the followers of Antichrist during the end times:

> At times they viewed holy sacrifices to honor the shrines of idols and prayed aloud that the Destroyer of the Souls [devil] might render them aid against the calamities of their nation. Such was their custom; such was the hope of the apostate. It was towards hell that they turned their minds; they ignored God, the Judge of deeds [at the Last Judgment]; they ignored the Lord God; they preferred not to worship the Heavenly Father, the God of glory. Woe unto those who through evil deeds must lose their souls in the expanse of eternal fire without the hope of any respite. (175-86)

In the Apocalypse an associate of Antichrist is the false prophet (19:20); he is very much like Unferth, who prophesies that Beowulf will fail in his undertaking against Grendel (525-8). Both of them end up in hell; the false prophet is thrown into hell with Antichrist: "These two were thrown alive into the lake of fire that burns with brimstone" (19:20) just as Grendel and Unferth were also cast into hell.

The end of the world is foreshadowed in two passages in *Beowulf:* in the reference to the destruction of Heorot by fire and in the cremation of Beowulf. The high hall of Heorot goes up in flames only much later, symbolizing the end of the world: "There stood that lofty towering hall with its broad horns; yet it was for swirling flames of war and for destroying fire that it waited" (81-3).

It is more logical than arbitrary to place the cremation of Beowulf at the end of the poem. The sad funeral scene of Beowulf is a vivid portrayal of last days of the world:

> Then the Geatish people made ready a funeral pile for him on that spot—no petty one, but one hung around with helms and battle-shields and bright corslets, as had been his request. Then in the midst of it the lamenting warriors laid the renowned prince their beloved lord. The fighters then began to kindle the greatest of funeral fire upon that crag; woodsmoke rose up, black above the blaze, and roaring of flames was mingled with wailing, while the swirling winds fell still, until fire had split his bony frame and lay hot about his heart. With cheerless spirits they mourned the killing of their lord, a heavy grief to them. Also a Geatish woman, with her hair bound up, in her sorrow and care sang again and again a funeral chant, saying she sorely dreaded that she would know days of mourning, and a time of great slaughter and terror among the host, with humiliation and captivity. Heaven swallowed up the smoke. (3137-55)[22]

While fire and smoke filled the skies, the retainers of the king cried their hearts out in grief and sang the late king's praises; they also left behind countless treasures in the barrow of the dragon. This passage is reminiscent of the fall of Babylon in fire and smoke, with her treasures laid waste in an hour (18:17), wailed over by merchants of the earth but celebrated by the visionary of the Book of Apocalypse (18:2-24).

One often gets the impression that Beowulf is devoid of the sense of hope in regeneration and recreation which the biblical book of Apocalypse exudes in the following verses:

> Then I saw a new heaven and new earth; for the first earth has passed away, and the sea was no more. And I saw the holy city, new Jerusalem, coming down out of heaven from God, prepared as a bride adorned for her husband; and I heard a great voice from the throne saying, "Behold, the dwelling of God is with men. He will dwell with them, and they shall be his people, and God Himself will be with them." (21:1-2)

Even though the English poem does not use the same language, it offers an interesting alternative in the memorial shelter built by the Wederas on the headland [Hronesnaes]. This building is like a lighthouse-like beacon of hope for seafarers as in the Apocalypse, where "by its light [of the Heavenly City] shall the nations walk" (21:24); it does not take a millennium to build it but ten days—10 seems to be a deliberate parallel to 1000—; it is a dwelling for hero Beowulf in order to be with his people; this house, which is built on a hill as Jerusalem is built on Mount Zion, is adorned with treasures, jewels, and rich trappings, somewhat like a well-adorned spouse, the heavenly Jerusalem, that the Apocalypse is talking about; the poet's references to fire reminds us of the destruction of Jerusalem by fire and to wall reminds us of the Apocalypse's description of the wall (Apoc. 21:12) of the Heavenly Jerusalem; it exists on earth and is made by human hands. Obviously, the poet interprets the Apocalypse and invents his own heaven on earth made of human hands for human beings struggling in the sea of life as pilgrims and wayfarers—like human beings caught in the sea of *samsara* (cycle of rebirths) of the Hindu tradition. The poet seems to suggest that, while alive, we build our castles of hopes here on earth and not elsewhere. In other words, he implies that we humans should build the new heaven and new earth on the middle earth by our own hands until the end of the world. In fact, the poet has already mentioned this point earlier in the passage where Hrothgar gives orders that "Heorot be again bedecked inside by human hands; there were many, both men and women, who made ready the banquet-chamber, the hall for the guests" (991-4). This is how the poet unfolds his existential vision of life after death for the survivors on earth:

> Then the people of the Wederas built a shelter on the headland; it was high
> and broad and could be seen far and wide by those who travel the waves. In
> ten days they had built up this memorial to a man bold in combat; they
> raised a wall round what the fire had left, the worthiest that men of deep
> knowledge could devise. In this barrow they placed armrings and jewels,
> and all the rich trappings which men intent upon strife had taken from the
> hoard; they left this wealth of earls for the earth to guard, laying the gold in
> the ground, where it still exists, and now, as before, is set apart from the use of
> men. (3156-68)

The values and good deeds that make a person worthy of fame and
glory both on earth and in heaven are deeds of valor, loyalty to liege lord,
gentleness, graciousness, kindness, and eagerness to win fame:

> Then round the burial mound rode men brave in battle, sons of high-born
> men, *twelve* in all; they wished to lament their sorrow and mourn for their
> king, to utter a lay and to speak of this man. They praised his heroism and
> proclaimed the excellence of his deeds of valor, for it is fitting that a man
> should thus honor his liege lord by his words and show him heartfelt love
> when his spirit has been taken from his body. Thus did men of the Geats, his
> own hearth-companions, bewail the fall of their lord; they said that among
> all the kings in this world he had been the gentlest of men and the most
> gracious, the most kindly to his people, and the most eager to win renown.
> (3169-82)

The poet's use of the symbolic number of twelve in the passage above
recalls the apocalypse's use of the same symbolic number for the twelve
tribes of Israel, and for the twelve Apostles:

> And in the spirit he carried me away to a great, high mountain, and showed
> me the holy city Jerusalem coming down out of heaven from God, having
> the glory of God, its radiance like a most rare jewel, like a jasper, clear as
> crystal. It had a great, high wall, with twelve gates, and at the gates twelve
> angels, and on the gates the names of the twelve tribes of the sons of Israel. . . .
> And the wall of the city had twelve foundations, and on them the twelve
> names of the twelve apostles of the Lamb. (21:10-14)

Thus the visionary author of *Beowulf*, while reflecting on the themes of
the Book of Apocalypse, gives a secular twist to them and uses several artistic devices borrowed from the biblical Apocalypse.

Apocalyptic Techniques

The biblical Apocalypse uses the literary devices of repetition of formulas like " I saw" and "I heard," intercalations, recapitulations, interlocking,
digressions, and ring compositions, as explained in chapter two. That the
Beowulf-author also uses similar techniques suggests that he is probably
trying to imitate the apocalyptic style in his writing of *Beowulf*, which is

not an oral formulaic poem at all.[23] Some of the techniques are the use of formulas, prophecy-cum-history, intercalation, recapitulation, the use of numbers, and chiasmus (ring composition); because of space restrictions, I shall discuss these only briefly.[24]

Use of Formulas

As in the Apocalypse, there are in *Beowulf* so many instances of the use of formulas—especially of "I heard" (from *gehyran*) in lines 38, 62, 273, 582, 1197, 1346, 2163, 2172, and "I learned" (from *gefrignan*) in 74, 575, 776, 837, 1011, 1027, 1196, 1955, 2484, 2685, 2694, 2752, 2773, and 2837.[25] Most people tend to associate repetition of phrases and formulas with oral composition and extempory singers of tales and to think that lettered poetry is not formulaic. The formula-laden, visionary biblical Apocalypse, on the other hand, is a written text, as we know from chapter 1:11: "Write what you see in a book and send it to the seven churches." Without getting into the mine field of theories of and controversies on oral formulaic composition, let me simply suggest from the evidence of apocalyptic literature that formulaic composition is quite compatible with literary poetry. I further suggest that the English poet has probably used the repetition of formulas to create a visionary poem after the model of the biblical Apocalypse.

Prophecy and History

The Apocalypse was, and is still, considered a prophetic book as the book itself states explicitly: "The revelation of Jesus Christ, which God gave to him to show his servants things which must shortly come to pass" (1:1). The author also identifies his words as "words of prophecy" (1:2; 22:18,19). Most readers then, as now, interpreted the eschatological prophecies of the Apocalypse not simply as the message of God but as the foretelling of future events taking place in end times. In other words, prophecy is history. As we have seen before, interpreters had been and are still busy unravelling the mysterious threads of prophetic statements in the Apocalypse and trying to apply them to past, present, and future events. As for *Beowulf*, there is the unfulfilled false prophecy of Unferth; and the fulfilled, half-fulfilled and to-be-fulfilled prophecies about wars and uprisings pronounced by the last survivor in lines 2910-3006; and the Sibyl-like Geatish woman's prophecy that there would be "days of mourning, and a time of great slaughter and terror among the host, with humiliation and captivity" (3150-55). The most important prophetico-historical dimension of the poem is tied up with the allegory of the beasts of the poem—I shall develop this point below.

Intercalation with Digressions

Intercalation is a technique of connecting two related episodes with a digression, as explained earlier; for example, in Apocalypse chapter 8:1-2, the seven angels with the trumpets are introduced but a heavenly liturgy (8:3-5) intervenes before they can blow the trumpets and start the plagues in 8:6.[26] The well-known digressions of *Beowulf,* like the Finn episode (1063-1160) and the story of Modthryth (1925-62), function in the poem as examples of the technique of intercalation. The scop in Beowulf brings about some such digressions. Risden gives the following example:

> An example occurs when the poet interrupts Grendel's approach to Heorot with comments on the creature's heritage, the brood of Cain (ll.100-14), before continuing with Grendel's murderous attack. This intercalation accounts for the presence of monsters in the world. (74)

These intercalations are "tinged with doom foreshadowing violence...and a strongly apocalyptic sentiment (Risden 74-5). It is the method of intercalation that gives a chiasmic or ring or envelope structure to the poem. Lack of the understanding of the method of intercalation is one of the obstacles to the correct understanding of *Beowulf* since literary critics are trained to divide a text into sections which follow one upon another in logical linear fashion. The author of Beowulf does not divide the text into sections or parts but joins units together by interweaving them through the method of intercalation as the author of the Apocalypse does. It is very important to identify the links or joints in this type of structure.[27] Much more work remains to be done in this area.

Recapitulation

Recapitulation means literally "repetition." It does not mean always a summary or concise review, as the word is supposed to mean today. This ancient literary device could simply be the exact repetition of a story or the restating of an idea slightly differently in any place in the narrative or poetry.[28] The biblical practice of recapitulation is quite obvious in the Psalms, in which the second half-line, as a rule, restates what the first half-line has already stated; for example,

> The heavens are telling the glory of God; and firmament proclaims his handiwork. Day unto day pours forth speech, and night to night declares knowledge. There is no speech, nor are there words; their voice is not heard. Yet their voice goes out through all the earth, and their words to the end of the world. (Ps. 19:1-4)

The author of the Apocalypse makes frequent use of this device especially in the case of the monsters and the dragon. The visionary sees two
beasts, the harlot, and a dragon, which are all repetitions of the same concept, which is the Roman Empire. By using the metaphors and prophecies
borrowed from Daniel, the author of the Apocalypse incorporates the Old
testament type and its anti-type of fulfillment in end times. He repeats the
same theme with many variations, emphasizing not only similarity but also
antithesis. For example, the dragon or Antichrist is like Christ the Lamb of
God and Christ the warrior, but the dragon/Antichrist is also opposed to
the slain Lamb of God and Christ, the ultimate victor. F. C. Burkitt says,
"According to the terminology of Tyconius a 'recapitulation' is made when
a Biblical writer is speaking of the type and the anti-type, the promise and
fulfillment."[29] In other words, type and anti-type are not diametrically opposed to each other and cancel each other but rather complement each
other like the two sides of the coin; one is not given without the other.

The *Beowulf*-poet, as Hugh Keenan brilliantly demonstrates, makes frequent use of the device of recapitulation, which involves not only repetition but also fulfillment. For example, in *Beowulf*, there are two creation
stories and two judgments; Scyld creates a tribe of Danes and thereafter
there is the biblical story of creation; that is, as God created heaven and
earth, Scyld created the Danish nation; likewise, Cain's banishment parallels Heremod's banishment. In the end, there is a judgment on Beowulf,
who is saved, whereas his tribe, in the words of the messenger, is doomed
(122). Earlier, hero Scyld is entrusted to the waters of the sea, while Beowulf
is consigned to the flames; Scyld is associated with the beginning, whereas
Beowulf is associated with the end. As Fitela fights with a dragon and kills
it, so does Beowulf; kinsmen play a role in both stories; Fitela survives, but
Beowulf does not; Fitela's sword is effective, but Beowulf's isn't.[30] Hero
Beowulf's harrowing of Grendel's netherworld lair is reminiscent of Christ's
own harrowing of hell. Above all, Beowulf's victory over Grendel in the
first part of the poem foreshadows Beowulf's eschatological victory over
the dragon. In all these instances the poet uses the technique of recapitulation effectively with variation recalling secular as well as Old Testament
types and biblical anti-types.[31]

Use of Numbers

We have noted earlier the careful use of numbers in the Book of Apocalypse. Besides the twofold revelations, two ecstasies, and twelve tribes, we
find the number seven—seven candles, seven churches, seven angels, seven
trumpets, seven bowls of wrath, and seven seals. Then there is the mysteri-

ous number 666 standing for the devil or Antichrist. The *Beowulf*-poet is
also preoccupied with numerical structures. Hrothgar rules for fifty years
as Grendel's mother lives in the underwater lair for fifty years, and the dragon
is fifty feet long. Grendel kills thirty men in the first attack and carries away
fifteen bodies. Beowulf leads a group of fifteen men to Heorot. Beowulf
has the strength of thirty men; he carries thirty suits of armor from the
battle scene. The number twelve is also important: Beowulf takes twelve
men with him to fight the dragon and twelve warriors circumambulate
Beowulf's grave—almost in accordance with traditional Indian customs—
, while Grendel reigns in Heorot for twelve years. The millennial number
1000 is applied to the period of time the dragon guards the buried treasure.
Isn't it fascinating that the name of Grendel appears on line 666 of the
poem? My intention here is only to allude to the poet's familiarity with
the Apocalypse-author's use of numbers and not develop the idea. The poet's
fascination with numerical structures is the subject matter of the scholarly
studies of Thomas Hart and David Howlett.[32]

Allegory

Allegory, or a deeper meaning other than the literal, underlies the Apocalypse. Readers have never failed to recognize this deeper meaning
(*hyponoia*); that is, the Apocalypse contains more than what is said on the
literal level. The moral message of the story, as can be gleaned from Hrothgar's
sermon, is easy and obvious: "Pride goes before a fall." The Augustinian
interpretation of the Apocalypse is the best example of this kind of reading.
But the interpretation that places stress on prophecy and history seeks out a
deeper meaning in the work by relying on the literary and historical contexts of the book. The images of beasts and the dragon have always been
seen and interpreted in that way. As for *Beowulf*, too, the search for the
deeper meaning has always led to the search for allegorical meanings, as we
shall see below. Particularly, this issue is relevant to the poem since the poet
introduces the figures of Cain and Abel about whom Philo, the archpriest
of allegorical interpretation, has written extensively. In the beginning of
his book *On the Birth of Abel and the Sacrifices Offered by Him and by
His Brother Cain*, Philo writes:

> In case these unfamiliar terms may cause perplexity to many, I will attempt
> to give as clear an account as I can of the underlying philosophical thought.
> It is a fact there are two opposite contending views of life, one which as-
> cribes all things to the mind as our master, whether we are using our reason
> or our senses, in motion or at rest, the other which follows God, whose
> handiwork it believes itself to be. The first of these views is figured by Cain
> who is called Possession, because he thinks he possesses all things, the sec-

ond by Abel, whose name means "one who refers (all things) to God." Now both these views or conceptions lie in the womb of the single soul.[33]

The Philonesque preoccupation with allegory and history seems to be a hallmark of the poetic art of *Beowulf,* as we shall see in more detail in the following pages.[34]

Chiasmus/Ring Composition

We have already seen in chapter three that the Johannine Apocalypse follows the ring structure of compositional method, in which the prologue is contrasted against the epilogue in decremental contrast and repetition as a b c d c′ b′ a′. This type of chiasmic structure is found also in *Beowulf,* as the studies of A. C. Bartlett, Constance B. Hieatt, J. O. Beaty, David R. Howlett, John Niles, and H. Ward Tonsfeldt have clearly demonstrated.[35]

In this type of composition, the series revolves around a single kernel, which we can call *media res* as in the classical phrase *in medias res.* The author first establishes or determines or marks off this "middle piece" as in a tic-tac game and then looks for the pieces at each end and then moves centripetally by alternating the arrangement of the pieces. As for the Apocalypse, we have seen that the central episode is that of the small prophetic scroll (10:1-11), which the seer eats from the hand of the angel, and he is told, "You must again prophesy about many peoples and nations and tongues and kings (10:11). In *Beowulf* it is the passage found in lines 1677-97, the episode of the decorated hilt of the melted sword that Beowulf retrieved from Grendel's cave after he had defeated Grendel's mother and harrowed the lair. The engraved sword-hilt is similar to the small scroll of the Apocalypse. The hilt told the story of the past and held the secrets of the future in runic script:

> Then the golden hilt, the work of giants of yore, was given into the hand of the aged warrior, the grey-haired leader in battle. Thus after the fall of the devils, this work made by wondrous craftsmen passed into the possession of the Danish lord. When the savage-hearted creature, guilty of murder, the adversary of God [*Godes andsaca*—Antichrist] and his mother, too, had forsaken this world, it passed into the power of the noblest of all earthly kings from sea to sea, and of all who have shared out their wealth in the realm of Denmark. Then Hrothgar spoke, after he examined the hilt, the ancient heirloom. There was engraved on it the origin of that strife after which the flood and the gushing waters had struck down the giant race, who had brought that peril upon themselves. Also, by means of runic letters on foil of shining gold, it was rightly marked down, set forth and recorded, for whom that sword had first been wrought.... (1677-96)

As the hilt tells the story of the flood and the destruction of the race of the ancient giants on the literal level, it also allegorically alludes to the fall of the Roman Empire and the passing of power into the hands of the Germanic people, to the triumph of Germania over the Roman Empire, to the first victory over Antichrist at his first appearance.[36]

The following diagram will give a rough idea of the way the poet created his poem chiasmically, with the golden-hilt episode (D) as the capstone event.

A   B   C   D   C'   B'   A'

The poet conceived the poem in his mind probably in the linear pattern given above. He could have then composed each segment episodically and centrifugally. The resulting schema would look like this:

	a. Scyld's creation
	b. Scyld' funeral
A	c. History of the Danes
	d. Hrothgar's order to build Heorot
B	Night attack
C	Second Fight
D	The hilt episode
C'	Dragon's attack
B'	Beowulf's fight with the dragon
	a' Beowulf's order to build the barrow
	b' History of Geats after Beowulf
A'	c' Beowulf's funeral
	d' Re-creation

I have given here only a bare skeleton of the structural framework of the poem according to the principle of ring composition just to indicate that the Book of Apocalypse and *Beowulf* are very much alike in their compositional technique. Since other scholars have already shown in greater detail various ring-structural patterns of the poem, I shall not belabor the point any further.[37]

Where did the *Beowulf*-poet learn the techniques of such symmetrical tectonic composition? David Howlett suggests: "The author of *Beowulf* may have learned the art of symmetrical composition from the works of Vergil."[38] In view of the English poet's familiarity with the Book of Apocalypse, it is reasonable to suggest that the Apocalypse may also have contributed to the poet's use of tectonic structure in the Old English poem.

Monsters as Historical Allegories

The monsters of *Beowulf* are related not only archetypically but also genetically to the monsters of Apocalypse. As the apocalyptic monsters are historical and allegorical, so are the Beowulfian monsters. Martin Green is willing to admit that Grendel "fits the paradigm of the apocalyptic beasts in general terms. He is the enemy of men and God (*godes andsaca*); he is associated with apostasy.... In other words, like apocalyptic beasts, Grendel becomes a physical projection of the world in a state of imminent collapse; and it is this level of symbolism that gives to Beowulf's battle against him its intensity and urgency."[39] Green, however, refuses to dwell on the allegorical element of the apocalyptic beasts and instead talks about them as symbols and archetypes. Margaret Goldsmith, who also links the Beowulfian monsters to the beasts of the Apocalypse, sees rather only the moral sense of the patristic tradition which associates the dragon to concupiscence. In general, most critics, following the lead of Tolkien, view Grendel as an elemental force of evil unleashed on an orderly universe, which forces of order and good overcome. But the question is how and why the monsters are forces of evil and adversaries of God.

Grendel, indeed, is an archetype of evil and malevolence and a figure of the devil. Grendel is all that because he is also an allegory in the context of Germanic political history and the apocalyptic context. If he is a historical allegory—I refrain from calling Grendel an individual person—, then he must be identifiable by a referent in a literary text and in historical time. Further, if he is an apocalyptic allegory, he should be identifiable, at least partially, with the denizens of the Apocalypse.

The Beowulfian monsters in their physical and moral and allegorical nature are patterned after the monsters of the Book of Apocalypse. In other words, their textual existence is derived, to a great extent, from the Apocalypse, and they are human and demonic at the same time—far be it from me to deny the genealogical literary descent of these monsters from the Irish, Nordic, Latin, and other traditions.[40] Let me show how similar are the Beowulfian monsters to the apocalyptic monsters.

Grendel is not just a cannibalistic, misanthropic animal; he has anthropomorphic characteristics like Antichrist. On three occasions Grendel is referred to as a man (*wer* 105, 352; *rinc* 720; *guma* (1682); as Lars Malmberg (241-3) points out, Grendel is not just an ordinary human enemy who engages in honest combat to redress a right violated; he rules in Heorot where he has no rights; he does not care to follow the Germanic law of *wergild*, which implies that he follows some other law code. Grendel's mother is also human; as the poet says, she draws her sword and strikes

Beowulf (515 ff).

Grendel is associated with the devil, as Greenfield has suggested, on account of the formulaic link between him and the other exiled devils.[41] Like the devil, Grendel bears God's anger and is Antichrist or *godes andsaca* (786, 1682). There are ten occurrences of *godes andsaca* in Old English poetry, and six of these refer to Lucifer and his fellow demons (Malmberg 241-242).

Other epithets of Grendel that make him demonic are *feond mancynnes* (164, 1276) and *ealdgewinna* (1776). These two expressions are literal translations of Latin phrases for the devil: *hostis humani generis*, which in *Vespasian Psalter* becomes *feond mennesces cynnes* (13.4) and *hostis antiquus* (Malmberg 242). The reference to Grendel as *helle hæfta(n)* (785), as captive in hell, is the English translation for the Latin *captivus inferni* found in the seventh *Blickling Homily*, which is another important demonic characteristic pertinent to the apocalyptic tradition, where the beast is a captive in hell. Further, the poet's clear identification of Grendel as a spirit from hell (*helle gæst* 1274) and as *wergan gæstes* (1747)—translation of *malignus spiritus* —[42] tells us more about the demonic dimensions of this apocalyptic monster. As Malmberg (243) suggests, we must talk about Grendel not simply as a hellish fiend but as a fiend in hell (*feond on helle*) (101). Most readers also readily recognize that the account of Grendel's lair is similar to the description of hell in the seventeenth (XVI) *Blickling Homily*, which is based on the visionary apocalyptic work of *Visio Pauli*.

Though the netherworldly personality of Grendel as a demonic or Antichrist figure would place him in the biblical world from the time of the Fall of the Angels, during the time of creation, during the time of Adam and Cain, during the time of the Noachic Flood, and to the end of the world, the physicality of Grendel places him at a certain place on the Continent and point in time; the numerous historical references and allusions place Grendel not only in the specific land of Europe, in the land of the Danes, but also in a specific historical time. Heusler, Klaeber, and others place the dates of Hrothgar, Halga, Hrothulf, and the other historical figures of the epic in the fifth century, the period of Germanic migrations in Europe (Klaeber, *Beowulf*, xxxi). At least one of the events mentioned in the poem, the disastrous Frankish raid of Hygelac, is considered by most historians, since the days of Grundtvig, as a real event taking place in the sixth century (Klaeber, xlv). According to R.W. Chambers, Grundtvig's identification of Chochilaicus with Hygelac "is the most important discovery ever made in the study of *Beowulf*, and the foundation of our belief in the historic character of its episodes."[43]

In the fifth century, Antichrist was still operating under the assumed name of Grendel, the murderous enemy of the Germanic nations. The major sinister power, the evil force, that threatened the existence of the Germanic nations in the fifth century was imperial Rome; it was not the Huns, for they were already a remnant at that time and somewhat friendly, though still treacherous, toward the Germanic nations—that is what *Hunferth* and *Hunlafing* seem to indicate. I feel like suggesting here that *Beowulf* is like the thirteenth-century *Nibelungenlied*. The latter historicized in epic form the conflicts among the Germanic tribes and the Huns without much deep emotional involvement. I would go further and stake the claim that the Old Norse *Volsungasaga* is also like *Beowulf,* in the sense that it, too, allegorizes the conflict between Rome and the Germanic nations; in this saga, for instance, Sigurd's (Siegfried's) killing of the she-wolf—in *Beowulf,* Sigurd kills a dragon—allegorizes the victory of Germania over Rome which is represented by the she-wolf that suckled Romulus and Remus. I do not imply that the Old English poet and the other German writers were trying to give vent to their hatred toward Rome or the Huns when they wrote these epics; they were rather like Virgil when he wrote the *Aeneid;* Virgil does not display any strong animosity toward the Greeks in his epic. In other words, poets could write national epics on ancient conflicts without being emotionally involved or without taking sides in the conflict or without having to admit that emotional conflict was still important at the time they wrote their poems. Therefore, it is not necessary to establish the absurd thesis that the Old English poet was still smarting under Roman persecution when he wrote the poem about the conflict between Germania and Roma in the tenth century!

Was it feasible for the Old English poet to portray Rome as Antichrist, as the diabolical, apocalyptic, cannibalistic, vampirish, detestable, abominable, hellish, satanic fiend Grendel? It is impossible for us who tend to identify Rome with Virgil, Livy, Horace, Ovid, and Gregory the Great to talk about Rome as the great Satan. But the Germanic peoples could talk about imperial Rome and her blood-thirsty legions that destroyed the Jerusalem Temple, that executed Jesus Christ, that massacred countless innocents, that traded in blond English boys in the Roman market place as hideous and devilish. The Romans robbed the Germanic peoples of their land, destroyed their homes, killed their men, just as Grendel did, over a period of some four hundred years. It is important to point out that there are a few allusions to the language and culture of Rome in the poem. Dorothy Whitelock had already called our attention to the poet's use of *gigant*-giant (113, 1562, 1690—a Latin loan-word), *candel* (1572—Latin *candela*), *forscrifan* (106—from the Latin *proscribere*, and most significantly to the word *non* (1600)—from the Latin word *nona* meaning church service at the ninth hour (5-6). Then there is the common word *beor* as in *beor-scealc* ("beer-drinker," 1240), *beorsele* ("beer hall," 482, 492, 1094); *beor* is not a native Germanic word even though it is a popular Germanic drink; it is a sixth-century monastic loan word from the Vulgar Latin *biber*. Interestingly, the poet even uses the Latin word *recte* and *rihte* in line 2110. The Roman roads are mentioned in *stræt wæs stanfah* ("The highway gleamed with bright stones, 320); the hall of Hrothgar (724-25) has the tessellated floor of the Roman buildings, according to Klaeber, Gummere, and Stanley (Thundy, "Meaning" 19). Grendel, as the Romans desecrated the Temple of Jerusalem, would also trample Heorot, Antichrist-like, underfoot. Beowulf, like Christ or like the Last Emperor, would later cleanse the temple; Grendel's grasp in Heorot, even though it was placed there by Beowulf himself (830-36), is ironically like the abomination of desolation set up by the Romans in the Jerusalem Temple (Matt 14: 15).

Rome as an Allegory of Evil in Early Christianity

Did the poet have any literary precedent to portray Rome as the apocalyptic monster? The answer is yes.[44]

In the literary tradition of historical apocalypticism, which the Christian author of *Beowulf* inherited, Rome is presented as a hideous apocalyptic monster and as Antichrist—morally and literally-physically.

It is true that St. Paul presents Rome in a favorable light and exhorts Christians to give Rome her due because political rulers receive their authority from God (Rom. 12-13). St. Paul would also counsel the Christians: "Bless those who persecute you" (Rom. 12: 14); the implication is that God in His turn will prosecute the persecutor to avenge the persecuted (Rom. 12: 19). However, as we have noted before, other contemporary Jewish and Christian writings (1 Peter, 2 Esdras, and the Book of Sibylline Oracles) present Rome in a negative light. The most anti-Roman Christian text is the Book of Apocalypse. It is the moral and theological view of this Christian text that underlies the *Beowulf*-poet's portrayal of Grendelkin as images of the sub-human, demonic Roman Empire as well as his ethics of the desire for vengeance on one's enemies.

Obviously, Beowulf's desire to avenge the death of his kinsmen does not conform to the spirit of the Sermon on the Mount, where Christians are urged not only to avoid murder but also anger (Matt. 5: 21-26). Neither *Beowulf* nor the Book of Apocalypse shows the Old Testament Ezra's concern for the multitude which will be damned (2 Esdras 7: 45-48, 62-69).

Rather, the Christian Apocalypse entreats God to avenge the blood of the saints (6:9-11). The angel over the waters does not preach and practice non-violence but the law of revenge or vindication. The author says that those who shed the blood of the saints and prophets will be given blood to drink, because "they deserve it!" (16:4-7). Grendel's drinking of blood and eating of human flesh is to be seen as punishment in the light of this passage; this act makes Grendel look detestable and deserving of punishment like Rome, the Prostitute of the Apocalypse, for she is portrayed as drunk with the blood of the saints and prophets and of all who have been slain on the earth (17:16; 18:24). The poet also gloats over the fall of these fiends, especially when he gives all the gory details of the battle between her and Beowulf (1534-89). All this makes sense if we bear in mind that the entire story is told in the spirit of the Christian work of Apocalypse. Further, Grendel's mother is patterned after the prostitute of the Apocalypse who was made naked and defenseless, her flesh burned up and devoured by fire. Indeed, all this happened, as in *Beowulf,* to fulfill God's purpose (17:17).

Is the prostitute of the Apocalypse an allegory of Rome? Jewish and Christian apocalyptic writings assimilate Rome, the destroyer of Jerusalem, to Babylon, the early destroyer of the Holy City. In chapter 16, God makes Babylon "drink the cup of the fury of his wrath" (16:19); in chapter 17, the city of Rome is personified as a prostitute with whom the kings of the earth have prostituted themselves (17:1-2); she is clothed in gold and surrounded by a treasure and holds a golden cup (17:4). In *Beowulf,* the poet transfers the treasure and golden cup to the dragon, though there is reference to treasures in Grendel's abode as well—incidentally, Beowulf did not take any treasures, except the hilt of the melted sword, from Grendel's house; like Beowulf, Alaric did not plunder Rome and take treasures away with him. The inference that the prostitute is Rome can be seen from facts that she is seated on seven hills (17:9) and that she has dominion over the kings of the earth (17:18), as mentioned earlier in chapter three.

As in *Beowulf,* the prostitute of the Apocalypse is found in the company of a beast, which also represents Rome (17:10-11), and the beast's ten horns represent ten Roman emperors; in other words, the Book of Apocalypse allegorizes Rome in several ways: as the beast from the sea, as the beast from the earth, as the ten horns of the beast, and as the prostitute. Obviously, there is no one-to-one correspondence between image and reality in the biblical work; rather, it seems that the biblical author is employing different allegories to represent the same reality in order to achieve a more intense effect. I suggest that it is the same technique that the author of *Beowulf* is employing in the poem: he, too, uses the allegories of Grendel, Grendel's dam, and the dragon to signify the Roman empire.

The following similarities between *Beowulf* and Apocalypse are also worth mentioning:

The apocalyptic beast, or Antichrist, is allowed to exercise power for a certain period of time (42 months—13:5), and Grendel for twelve years (147); Rome, the beast, and Antichrist enjoyed universal power and divine worship: "Over every tribe and people and tongue and nation" (13:7); "all who dwell on earth worship the "beast" (13:8); likewise, Grendel is associated with divine honors in the sense that the Danes "vowed holy sacrifices to honor the shrines of idols and prayed aloud that the Destroyer of Souls might render them aid against the calamities of their nation. Such was their custom; such was the hope of the heathen" (175-79). That the Germanic peoples in Grendel faced a human force or an imperial power is evident in the following passage: "Grendel had long waged war on Hrothgar...a conflict which had no end. No peace did he wish with any man of the Danish host, nor was he willing to...offer blood-money in settlement; nor need any counsellors there expect compensation in bright gold from the slayer's hand" (151-58). In chapter 19, the apocalyptic beast is captured after the battle between him and the Word of God by the armies of heaven; the beast is then thrown alive into the lake of fire (19:20); likewise, when Grendel is dispatched to his fiery lake abode (*fyr on flode*, 1366), he is alive. In both works, the monsters are identified with Satan/Antichrist (12-13); in both works there is also reference to an interregnum: In *Beowulf*, there is the period of prosperity between the death of Grendel and the start of the attacks of the dragon while in the Apocalypse there is the anticipation of the messianic millennium (20:1-6). In both works, after the introductory part we find three acts: (1) the first Act of the eschatological drama (5:1-11:4): the events which introduce the decisive struggle between God and Satan; in *Beowulf*, it is the Beowulf-Grendel struggle; (2) the second act of the eschatological drama: the decisive struggle between God and Satan for the possession of "the kingdom of this world" (11:15 - 20:15); in *Beowulf*, it is the battle between Beowulf and Grendel's mother; (3) the third act of the eschatological drama (21:1 - 22:5): it is the establishment of the eternal kingdom of God with the Heavenly Jerusalem as its center upon a new earth; in *Beowulf*, it is the battle between Beowulf and the dragon. In the biblical work, there are two accounts of the fall of Satan (12:9-12; 20:2-3); *Beowulf* also recounts the twin fall of the Roman empire in the stories of the defeat of Grendel and his mother. In the Apocalypse, "one of the beast's ten heads seemed to have a mortal wound" (13:3); Grendel also receives a mortal wound in the Old English poem.

The Beowulfian identification of the Grendelkin with the apocalyptic beasts, Antichrist, and Rome finds support not only in the Book of Apocalypse but also in the early medieval exegeses of the Apocalypse. Briefly recapitulated from chapter three, the anti-Roman reading of the Apocalypse was fairly well known among Christian exegetes. For example, Ireneus (second half of the second century) sees the Roman empire in the Beast of the Sea of the Apocalypse, without mentioning Rome by name; however, he attributes the mysterious number 666, which indicates the name of the Beast, to *Latinus* since the Latins currently hold imperial power (*Adversus Haereses* 5.30.3). Hippolytus of Rome (third century) does not hesitate to identify unequivocally the beast of Daniel with Rome (*Refutation of Heresies* 25, 28, 33); later on, he referred to the Second Beast of the Apocalypse 13 as Antichrist, who would be a Roman emperor (49). Like Ireneus, Hippolytus, too, thought that the number 666 stands for *Latinus* (50). The Latin Christian poet Commodian, enraged by the persecution of the Christians by imperial Rome, became a convinced chiliast (*Instructions* i. 44) and wrote a fervent anti-Roman poem in the tradition of the Book of the Apocalypse. He taught that there would be two Antichrists—a revived Nero in the West who would be killed by the final Antichrist arising from Persia (*Song of the Two Peoples* 933-935; McGinn 23). The Latin Church Father Tertullian, who himself was persecuted, had no hesitation whatsoever in calling Rome a devil and the Babylon of the Apocalypse (*Adversus Judaeos* 94; Paschoud 49). The Latin Fathers—Cyprian, Victorinus, and Lactantius—who, too, were persecuted, saw one of the caesars as Antichrist and Rome as the prostitute of the Apocalypse (Paschoud 55-57). The Latin version of the fifth-century apocryphal work, *Testament of the Lord*, after enumerating the recognizable physiognomical signs of Antichrist, ends with the statement" Dexius [Emperor Decius] erit nomen Antichristi" which statement seems to refer to the mid-third-century persecuting emperor Decius.[45]

The anti-Roman attitude of the early Christian writers, as mentioned before in chapter three, underwent a significant change with the conversion of Constantine and the Christianization of the empire in the fourth century. Eusebius of Caesarea, Jerome, and Augustine rejected the anti-Roman interpretation of the biblical Apocalypse. Augustine, for instance, without denying the theological veracity of the coming of the Antichrist, refused to calculate the time of the advent of the Antichrist or to read the signs of the final consummation; he understood apocalyptic symbolism in terms of the constant struggle between the forces of good and evil within the Church in every age. Hence the prophecies of the Apocalypse do not refer to any particular catastrophe but to the end of all history, and the time of that no one can know (McGinn 26-27).

Mainline Christianity since the time of Augustine has officially taught the Augustinian interpretation of the Apocalypse. This does not mean that all medieval writers necessarily rejected the anti-Roman interpretation of the Book of Apocalypse. For instance, Beatus of Lièbana's influential eighth-century Commentary of the Apocalypse identified the Apocalyptic beasts with Rome (VI:7). This implies that all medieval Christian writers did not follow the Augustinian interpretation the Apocalypse. Even the staunch Augustinian Bede refers to Rome as Antichrist in his exegesis of Matt. 24:19: Woe to you, women with children."[46] Most of them probably could not overtly proclaim their anti-Roman interpretation of Apocalypse for fear of official censure since Church authorities in Rome could easily misinterpret anti-imperial statements and sentiments as anti-papal/anti-ecclesiastical statements and sentiments; so poets had to exercise caution and employ ambiguous expressions when they treated controversial topics.

The Dragon: Cain's Seed, Heretics, and Islam

Tolkien suggested a link between *Beowulf* and Islam when he said:

> The monsters are not an inexplicable blunder of taste; they are essential, fundamentally allied to the underlying ideas of the poem, which give it its lofty tone and high seriousness. The key to the fusion-point of imagination that produced this poem lies, therefore, in those very references to Cain which have often been used as a stick to beat an ass—taken as an evident sign (were any needed) of the muddled heads of early Anglo-Saxons. They could not, it was said, keep Scandinavian bogies and the Scriptures separate in their puzzled brains. The New Testament was beyond their comprehension. (68)

Tolkien is right: The Anglo-Saxons and the English poet deserve better treatment from us simply because they were smarter than many of their critics. As for the Cain-reference, Tolkien could have said instead of Cain *Cham* because that is the manuscript reading in line 107. Cham's/Ham's sons are Muslim Arabs from Egypt and Moorish marauders or Moorish Vikings from Africa, who invaded Europe in the eighth century. For example, the *Cronica Mozarabica* of 754 from Spain uses the following names for Muslims: *Arabes, Sarracini, multitudo Ismahelitarum,* and *Mauri* (when referring to the Berbers who made up the bulk of forces that invaded Spain); very remarkably the annalist prefers *Gothi* and *Franci* for Christians.[47] Understanding the image of the dragon is the key that unlocks the door of the dragon's barrow where the secret of Islam lies buried.

In the Book of Apocalypse, Rome/Antichrist is represented by several allegories: the beast of the land, the beast from the sea, the harlot, Babylon, and the dragon. The *Beowulf*-poet also manipulates the dragon allegory to represent Rome (the first Antichrist or Antichrist's first coming), but his dragon represents Antichrist (the second Antichrist or Antichrist's second appearance), who is more than Rome in the latter part of the poem.

There is increasing consensus among critics—against Tolkien's views—that the dragon is "a different sort of creature from the Grendel tribe" (Gang 6) and that among the innumerable dragon stories "there is probably not one which we can declare to be really identical with that of *Beowulf*" (Chambers 97). Of course, nobody denies that the dragon is like the Germanic worm that dwells in a barrow and guards treasure. The dragon, unlike, Grendel, has no ancestry, no companion; he is a venomous foe (*attorsceatha*, 2839) and is the enemy of the Geatish nation (*theodsceatha*, 2278, 2688); therefore, a confrontation is bound to take place between the shepherd of the kingdom (*rices herde*, 3080) and the kingdom's enemy, who is mindful of past enmity (*fæhtha gemyndig*, 2689). Therefore, Beowulf is obliged to take up arms against the dragon to defend his country and to avenge his fallen comrades: "With his live coals the fiery dragon had utterly destroyed all the coastline and nation's impregnable fortress, the stronghold of that region; the warlike king, the prince of the Wederas, planned to take revenge on him for this" (2333-36). The dragon's attacks, indeed, are like the attacks of Grendel on Heorot, like the attacks of the Romans against Jerusalem, and like Antichrist's attacks against the believers.

The dragon also, like Grendel, hates the Geats and humbles them (2318-19); he too harms the Geats and even destroys the royal hall of Beowulf (2325-26), while Grendel is not allowed to approach Hrothgar's *gifstol* (168-169). The dragon, like Grendel (166-167), is also a ruler of the land only during dark nights (2210-11). Though remarkably, Grendel is called heathen (852, 986)—appropriate for pagan Rome, the dragon is not called "heathen" specifically by the poet, or guards.[48] The dragon is more like the heresy of Islam.

Seed of Cain and Heretics

The poet disguises Antichrist as the dragon and links it with Cain's/ Cham's kin who are connected with Islam the latter-day Antichrist. The controversial passage on Cham/Cain in *Beowulf* reads:

> The unhappy man [Grendel] occupied the dwelling of the monsters a while after the Creator had condemned him [to live] among Cham's kin. The eternal Lord avenged that murder, because he [Cain] slew Abel. He [Cain] rejoiced not in that feud, but the Creator banished him far from mankind for that crime. Thence arose all monstrous births, ogres, and elves and spirits

from hell; likewise, the giants that strove against God for a long time; for this he gave them their reward. (104-14)[49]

The poet seems to be deliberately playing an onomastic game here. He is playing *Cham* with *Cain*. It makes sense. According to medieval tradition, the Arabs are considered descendants of Cham, and Muslims are heretics; and as heretics Muslims are also the seed of Cain.[50]

In the biblical tradition, Ham (Cham) is the son of Noah, brother of Shem and Japheth. Cham's descendants are Cush (Ethiopia), Egypt (Misri), Arabia, Canaan (Palestine), and (the rest of) Africa (Gen. 10:6). Egypt is called "the land of Cham" (Ps. 78:51; 105:23, 27; 106:22); Palestine was for centuries part of Egypt since it was often under Egyptian control.

Though Cain, in general, is accredited to be the patriarch of biblical monsters, Alcuin, who knew about Muslims, preferred to use Cham for Cain when he talked about the birth of the giants resulting from the union of the daughters of men with the sons of God referred to in the books of Genesis and Enoch. Alcuin probably did so because of the belief that all humans died during the flood including all the giants. He could also draw from tradition that Cham was a spiritual progeny of Cain, the ancestor of all giants, as evident from Irish traditions.[51] In that sense, Cham could be considered to be a son of Cain. It is also possible that Alcuin inherited a confusion of the names of *Cainus* and *Chamus*, which confusion is evidenced in the Old English *Salomon and Saturn*, where to the question who made the first plow, the answer is Cham, son of Noah, whereas the answer should have been Cain.[52] Alcuin writes:

> When men began to multiply on the face of the earth, the daughters were born to them, the sons of God saw the daughters of men were fair, and they took to wife such of them as they chose.... Scripture chose to call the progeny of Cham daughters of men and the children of Seth sons of God. The former were unchaste on account of Noah's curse on Cham; the latter were religious by virtue of ancestral (Adam's) blessing;...but, after the sons of Seth, overcome by lust for the daughters of Cham married them, from such a union men of great stature who prided themselves of their immense strength, whom Scripture calls Giants, were born.[53]

The poet, I think, is deliberately merging Cham into Cain and into Cain's theological tradition, which incorporates heretics into Cain's kin, the typical brood of monsters and giants. It is this tradition that prevails in the depiction of Muslim opponents of Christian warriors with gigantic stature, flaming eyes, cannibalism, and a knowledge of sorcery—traits shared by Grendel and the dragon—in the later *Chansons de geste*.[54] Though the common tradition equates the monsters with Cain's seed, another tradition equates them with Cham's kin. Since there exists considerable literature on the monsters as Cain's kin, I shall not belabor the point.[55] What is, however, less known but important to note here is that heretics were also called Cain's seed and that Muslims, because they were considered heretics, were also classified as Cain's seed in the Middle Ages.

Though it is possible exegetically to derive Grendel and the dragon from Cain, the poet seems to repudiate a literal reading by stating that the giant race perished in the Deluge (1687-97).[56] Only an allegorical reading can save us from the danger of falling into literalism, which would compel us to postulate an ante-diluvian date for the events of the poem. The poet implies that Grendel and the dragon are allegorical figures who could have lived before the Flood and after the Flood; they could even be living today. D. W. Robertson makes this point very clearly:

> Figuratively, the generation of Cain is simply the generation of the unjust to which all those governed by cupidity belong. They are monsters because they have distorted or destroyed the Image of God within themselves. Babylon…traditionally began with Cain, and it is maintained on earth by his generation…. Thus Grendel is the type of the militant heretic or worldly man.[57]

Marie Padgett Hamilton also makes a similar observation She writes:

> In identifying the Grendel family with "the race of Cain," the poet, I take it, is merely employing a metaphor for the society of reprobates, which is tersely contained in St. Guthlac's condemnation of his fiendish tempters: *Vae vobis, filii tenebrarum, semen Cain!*"[58]

Hamilton also points out, in support of her views, that Bede in his *Commentary on Genesis*, chapters 4 and 5, presents Abel as a type of Christ, Christ on the cross, Christian martyrs, and the elect, whereas Cain is the type of those who persecute the just and are shut out from the grace of God and from the faith and hope of the elect.[59]

Actually, this perception of the heretics as seed of Cain comes down from Patristic writings, which use the term "seed of Cain" to designate heretics. For instance, Tertullian in his *Praescriptio* against heretics (ch. 33) says that besides the Nicolaitans of Apoc. 2:6,15 and Acts 6:5, "There are even now another sort of Nicolaitans; they are called Cainites." In *De Baptismo*, he talks about "the viper of the Cainite heresy…who has carried away a great number with her most venomous doctrines, making it her aim to destroy baptism."[60] Ireneus says that some heretics glorify Cain:

> Others again say that Cain was from the superior power and confess Esau and Korah and the Sodomites…as their kinsmen. They were attacked by the creator [*hystera*—the womb], but they suffered no ill. For Sophia snatched what belonged to her away from them to herself. This Judas the traitor

knew very well, and he alone of all the apostles recognized the truth and accomplished the mystery of the betrayal....They say they cannot be saved unless they experience every thing...every sinful...action....And this is the perfect "knowledge," to enter without fear into such operations, which it is not lawful even to name.[61]

Pseudo-Tertullian also refers to the Cainites: "They glorify Cain, as if conceived by some potent power. Abel was conceived and brought forth by an inferior power and was therefore found to be inferior" (*Haereses* 2; Pearson 98).

Some Gnostic treatises develop the idea that Cain is a superior power. In *TheApocryphon ofJohn*, Ialdabaoth, the First Archon begotten by Sophia, brings forth twelve "powers' (zodiacal constellations), and Cain is the name of the sixth power" (Pearson 99). The source of Cain's power lies in his supernatural origin; in some Jewish and Gnostic traditions, he is the son of Eve and the devil (Sammael).

Through some heavy word-play, Gnostic writers develop the idea that Cain is teacher and beast. He is teacher because he is born of Eve (*Hawa*); he is the teacher of life (*hayye*) because Eve is the mother of all the living; because Cain is from Hawa, he is also called *hewiya* (serpent). The Gnostic treatise *On the Origin of the World* states:

> The Hebrews call Eve the mother of Life, namely, the female instructor of life. Her offspring is the creature that is lord. Afterwards, the authorities called him "Beast," so that it might lead astray their modelled creatures. The interpretation of "the beast" is "the instructor." For it was found to be the wisest of all beings. Now, Eve is the first virgin, the one who without a husband bore her first offspring. It is she who served as her own midwife. (Pearson 101)

Partially, it is this Gnostic tradition that has seeped down into the Apocalypse, wherein the Beast is worshipped with the overlay of the Roman conception of emperor-worship because the Beast, the Antichrist figure, appears also as instructor and as seducer of mankind.

On the contrary, it should also be emphasized here that in the vast majority of Gnostic and Jewish and Christian texts Cain is portrayed in a negative light, and the seed of Cain is a general designation for heretics. That is how the Epistle of Jude addresses Heretic Gnostics: "Woe to them! For they walk in the way of Cain" (11) because Cain is the progenitor and prototype of theological heresy. In the Alexandrian Judaism of Philo, Cain's race is associated with "impious and atheistic opinion," whereas Seth (not Abel) is the "seed of human virtue," and all virtuous people are by implication the "seed of Seth."[62] Pearson concludes: "By the first century at the latest, there is an established Jewish tradition that assigns to Cain the role of the first heretic. All subsequent heretics are of his (spiritual) lineage, his *genos*"(105).

The figure of Cain as the patriarch of heretics persisted throughout the Middle Ages. The seed of Cain appears as *Caines cynne* in *Beowulf*, as *Kaymes kunrede* in *Kyng Alisauder* (1933), as *Kaym kin* in *Havelok the Dane* (2045), as *Kaymes kyn* in *Ywaine and Gawin* (589), and *kyndrede of Caym* in *Piers Plowman* (486).[63] As Hamilton suggests, "These analogies, which obviously cannot result from the influence of *Beowulf*...point to a common tradition, compounded of European giant-lore and Christian doctrine" (318).

As for *Beowulf*, the race of Grendel, which includes the dragon, belongs to the race of Cain who is the archheretic. Just as the Beast leads Christians astray from the worship of the true God in the Apocalypse, Grendel leads the Danes astray because they refuse to acknowledge the true God and worship false gods. These Danes are heretics. In the context of the Apocalypse's condemnation of emperor worship, the heresy of Rome is tied closely to that of emperor worship, as noted in chapter two.

The Dragon and the Heresy of Islam

Does the dragon, like Grendel, belong to the heretic race of Cain? What kind of heresy is the dragon associated with?

The English poet says that from Cain sprang all unholy broods—ogres and elves and revenants and even the giants who strove against God (111-4). Though the dragon is not mentioned specifically, he belongs to the unholy brood of Cain. In his *Moralia on Job*, Gregory says: "'I was a brother to dragon and a companion ostriches.' What is there denoted by 'dragons' but the life of malicious men?... He refuses to be Abel whom the evil of Cain does not distress" (20:39).[64] Most likely, the idea of the dragon as the devil in monster form comes from the Apocalypse, which derives it from Genesis, where the devil tried to seduce Eve by assuming the form of a serpent. Gregory associates the image of the dragon with Cain, when he says that Cain succumbed to the fire of the dragon Leviathan when he murdered Abel (*Moralia* 34:38).[65] The dragon, being a member of the race of Cain, thus stands also for heresy.

The dragon of *Beowulf* represents the heresy of Islam with the figure of Muhammed as Antichrist. It was John of Damascus (d. 749) who first called Islam a heresy in his catalogue of heresies.[66] In the following century (857), the Spanish Eulogius declared: "He [Muhammed] teaches with his blasphemous mouth that Christ is the Word of God, and Spirit of God, and indeed a great prophet, but bestowed with none of the power of God."[67] The same Eulogius connects Muhammed's errors with those of Arius who denied the divinity of Christ, and Muhammed is a heresiarch in Eulogius' eyes:

> Of all the authors of heresy since the Ascension, this unfortunate one, form-ing a sect of novel superstition at the instigation of the devil, diverged most widely from the assembly of the holy church, defaming the authority of the ancient law, spurning the visions of the prophets, trampling the truth of the holy gospel, and detesting the doctrine of the apostles.[68]

Beatus of Lièbana, though characteristically silent about Islam in his fa-mous Commentary on the Apocalypse, seems to refer to the heresy of the Muslim ruler of the province of Bishop Elipandus in *Adversus Elipandum* by suggesting that "the prince of the land be put away completely from your [Elipandus'] lands for promoting schism and heresy."[69]

There is much behind this sort of passionate condemnation of Islam as heresy in Spain.

Between 850 and 859, the Muslim rulers of Cordoba put to death some fifty Christians for blasphemy, for alleging that Muhammed was a false christ.[70] Eulogius and Paul Alvarus, outraged by the turn of events, inter-preted the signs of the times as a fulfillment of biblical prophecies on the end of the world. The Book of Daniel was the focal text of the apologists:

> Thus he said: "As for the fourth beast, there shall be a fourth kingdom on earth, which shall be different from all the kingdoms, and it shall devour the whole earth and trample it down, and break it to pieces. As for the ten horns, out of this kingdom ten kings shall arise, and another shall arise after them; he shall be different from the former ones, and shall put down three kings. He shall speak words against the Most High and shall wear out the saints of the Most High and shall think to change the times and the law; and they shall be given into his hand for a time, two times, and half a time." (7:23-25)

Alvarus and Eulogius interpreted this passage as follows:

The fourth beast was the Roman Empire, following the empires of the Assyrians, Persians, and Greeks. The ten horns were the barbarian invaders who had destroyed the Roman Empire. The one that arose after them is the army of Muhammed which triumphed over the Greeks, Franks, and Goths. Islam would flourish for three and a half periods of seventy years each, giving 245 years all told. From the year 854 of his writing to the year 1000, the space is 246, making it evident that the end was very close.[71]

By this time, in 848 at the monastery of Leyre, Eulogius discovered a spurious life Muhammed, which gave the year of his death as 666, the num-ber of the Beast of the Apocalypse (13:18).[72] In 883, an anonymous Oviedan cleric edited the *Cronica Profetica*, which gives a convenient interpreta-tion of Ezekiel 39 by stating that the Visigothic state, called the biblical

Gog, would take revenge on the Ishmaelites after 170 years (884), after the Muslim invasion of Spain:

> That the Saracens were going to possess the land of the Goths was stated in the book of the Prophet Ezekiel: "You, son of man, turn your face against Israel, and say to him: I have made you the strongest among the peoples and you have multiplied.... And you will enter the land of Gog easily and you will fell Gog with your sword.... Even so, since you abandon the Lord your God, so I will deliver you into the hands of Gog.... As you did to Gog, thus will I do to you. Once you have possessed them in slavery for 170 years, Gog will repay you, even as you had done. *Explanatio:* Gog is certainly the people of the Goths.... Gog signified Spain under the domination of the Goths.[73]

Paul Alvarus in his *Indiculus* (26, 30) applies the description of Leviathan and Behemoth found in Job 40 and 41 to Antichrist Muhammed. Leviathan's breathing of fire and smoke—as in the case of the fire-breathing dragon of *Beowulf*—symbolizes the persecution of the Christians of Cordoba (Wolf 98).

Though Beatus generally gives the Augustinian interpretation in his famous *Commentary on the Apocalypse*, he says on Apocalypse 7:4 that there are only fourteen years to complete the sixth millennium. He attacked Elipandus as an Antichrist for teaching the heresy of Adoptionism, which taught that Christ was only a man before his adoption as the Son of God. Elipandus counter-attacked Beatus for teaching the imminence of the end in a letter to the bishops of Gaul in 793, wherein he compared Beatus with the heretic Migetius in a case of prophecy unfulfilled:

> Beatus prophesied the end of the world to Hordonius of Liébana in the presence of the people during the Easter Vigil so that they became terrified and crazed. They took no food that night and are said to have fasted until the ninth hour on Sunday. Then Hordonius, when he felt afflicted with hunger, is said to have addressed the people, "Let's eat and drink, so that if we die at least we'll be fed."[74]

In 1954, Menendez Pidal suggested that the imagery of the tenth-century Beatus Commentaries identified Islam with Antichrist and prophesied the defeat of the Muslims; Peter Klein finds Christian-Muslim conflict in the illustration of the Killing of the Two Witnesses of Apocalypse 11:7-10.[75] The scene included a siege of Jerusalem labeled as "Antichrist overthrows the city of Jerusalem" (*antichristus civitatem hierusalem subvertit*)— the image is evocative of the damage done to Heorot by Grendel and the damage done by the dragon to the realm of Beowulf. Klein sees the combination of this detail with the killing of the Witnesses as an association of the fall of Jerusalem and the conquest of Spain in the context of the martyrdom of the Cordoban Christians (Williams 134).

Beatus' *Commentary* was copied many times and there survive twenty-six illuminated manuscripts with portrayals of Antichrist as human and beast. The popularity of Beatus's work suggests that the poet of *Beowulf* could have seen and consulted the illuminated Beatus Commentaries.[76]

Beowulf *and Islam*

There are some indications to Islam in *Beowulf.* (1) The most prominent one is the reference to Egypt, Cham's kin. Egypt, as we have noted before, was populated, according to the biblical tradition, by the descendants of Cham. Grendel's name is associated with the genealogy of Cham, and as a descendant of Cham, Grendel is associated with Islamic Egypt, which attacked Christian Spain. The second reference to Egypt is found in the first fight of Beowulf; the hero cuts off Grendel's arm and disables him. (2) It seems that the poet is applying Ezekiel 30:21 to this episode: "Son of man, I have broken the arm of Pharao, king of Egypt; behold, it is not bound up to be healed, to be tied with clothes and swathed with linen that it might recover strength and hold sword. The arm of Pharao shall fall, and I will disperse Egypt among the nations and will scatter them through countries" (30:25-6). (3) The mysterious passage in *Beowulf* that Grendel would not have peace with the Danes with the payment of tribute (146-63) can be interpreted in the context of Islam in occupied Spain. In accordance with the teaching of the Qur'an, non-Muslims are given protection on condition they pay tribute to the Islamic state. (4) According to the Qur'an, Christians, though being the people of the Book are protected, should still "be brought low" (sura ix); this means no public worship, ringing of bells, procession, and blaspheming of the Prophet. In *Beowulf,* we read that the creation song sung to the accompaniment of musical instruments angers Grendel and brings his wrath on the Danes (86-98).

Antichrist in Beowulf

The Eastern Apocalyptic association of Islam with Antichrist is not merely a Spanish phenomenon. It is also part of an earlier Byzantine tradition. The Eastern Christians, as McGinn points out, were very creative in their apocalypses, which the West later adopted and adapted for three reasons: (1) They did not have to endorse the Augustinian-Bedan allegorical theory and explain away historical apocalypticism. (2) The Eastern Christians still viewed their Rome (Byzantium) as the "Restraining Force" of 2 Thessalonians 2:6. (3) They had to contend with the irruption of the new power of Islam long before the West had to face it.[77]

The Byzantine apocalypses, in spite of their eschatological preoccupation, show a marked reluctance in the use of the term *Antichrist*; instead, they use a series of circumlocutions. In Pseudo-Ephrem's homily, *antichristus* appears only once, toward the end; he prefers terms like *malus, draco, nequissimus serpens, abominatio desolationis, adversarius serpens,* etc.; in *The Oracle of Baalbek,* Antichrist is a clever shape-shifter. Pseudo-Ephrem also dwells on Antichrist's cleverness, hypocrisy, lies, and wrath almost as in the case of the monsters of *Beowulf.* The homilist writes:

> The accursed destroyer of souls, rather than of bodies, a crafty serpent while he grows up, appears in the cloak of justice before he assumes power. For all men he will be cunningly gentle, unwilling to accept gifts or to place his own person first, lovable to everybody, peaceful to all, not striving after gifts of friendship, seemingly courteous among his entourage, so that people will bless him and say he is a just man—they do not realize that a wolf is hidden beneath the appearance of a lamb and that he is inwardly rapacious under the hide of a sheep.[78]

In the Oriental tradition, the devil-Antichrist receives more emphasis as a dragon monster than as a man. Pseudo-Ephrem begins with the announcement that he will speak "on the most shameless and terrible dragon that will bring disaster into the world."[79] The following description of Antichrist from Ephrem is not found in later Byzantine writings except in its adaptation in *Beowulf's* description of the depredations of the dragon:

> A great conflict, brethren, in those times amongst all men but especially amongst the faithful, when there shall be signs and wonders by the dragon in great abundance when he shall again manifest himself as God—in fearful phantasms, flying in the air, and all the demons in the form of angels flying in terror before the tyrant; for he crieth out loudly, changing his forms also, to strike infinite dread into all men. (Bousset 146)

The description of the ravages done by the dragon to the Geatish people found in *Beowulf* is very similar:

> Then this newcomer began to spew forth coals of fire and burn the brightest dwellings. The glow of burning rose up, bringing horror to men; the hateful creature that flew through the air meant to spare no living thing. From far and near could be seen the spiteful onslaught of the serpent, their cruel foe, showing how the warlike ravager hated the Geatish people and was humbling them. (2311-9)

In the Syriac version of Ephrem, Antichrist comes from the lower world (Syriac *abada*) (Bousset 152). Andreas, in his *Commentary on Apocalypse* 11:7, says: "Antichrist comes out of the dark and deep recesses of the ground, to which the devil had been condemned" (Bousset 152-3). The Antichrist-like Grendel and the dragon also ascend from underground: Grendel's lair is an underground cave and the dragon's abode is an underground barrow.

The early Eastern traditions also represent Antichrist as a human monster as the *Beowulf*-poet does. For example, the Apocalypse of Ezra says: "The form of the face of him is as of a field; his right eye as the morning star, and the other one that quaileth not; his mouth one cubit; his fingers like unto sickles, the imprint of his feet two spans, and on his brow the inscription *Antichrist*" (xxix) (Bousset 156).[80]

As we have seen in chapter three, Antichrist is not devil, pure and simple; he is also human with devil's features such as having horns and a tail as often found in iconography; he is also a monster, serpent, or dragon, especially in Eastern traditions. Remarkably, Antichrist's avatars in *Beowulf*— Grendel, Grendel's mother, and the dragon—are called human, devil, and serpent, as discussed earlier. That means the English poet follows the Eastern Antichrist-tradition closely by referring to Antichrist as dragon and monster.

Jewish Origin of Antichrist

One other feature of the Eastern Antichrist is his Jewish origin. Antichrist, according to the New Testament (2 Thess. 2:9-12; John 5:43; Apoc. 11; Matt. 14:15) appears in Jerusalem, as the abomination of desolation in the holy place, as Satan's emissary working wonders and telling lies, as a false messiah among the Jews. Hippolytus says that he will get circumcised: "Christ came into the world in the circumcision, and the other [Antichrist] shall come likewise." (ch. vi). Further Antichrist's Jewish origin from the tribe of Dan—as opposed to the notion of the gentile Antichrist as Nero redivivus, which is not found in Eastern apocalypses—occurs as early as in Ireneus. According to Pseudo-Methodius, "And immediately the son of perdition will be revealed.... He is a man of sin clothed in a body from the seed of man, and he will be born from a married woman from the tribe of Dan."[81] Antichrist's birth from the tribe of Dan also shifts his geographical location to Babylon whither the tribe of Dan was deported (Bousset 172). This notion of Antichrist's Jewish origin must be as old as the New Testament times, as the testimony of Ireneus, the disciple of Polycarp, who in turn was the disciple of Evangelist John, indicates: "And for this reason this tribe [Dan] is not numbered in the Apocalypse amongst those that are saved" (V.30.2). Jerome sums up the theory of the Oriental origin of Antichrist while commenting on Daniel 11:37: "But our [interpreters] explain in the above sense everything concerning Antichrist, who is to be born of the Jewish people and to come from Babylon" (Bousset 172).

The Jewish origin of Antichrist is relevant to *Beowulf* on three counts:

(1) The tribulations—Grendel, Grendel's mother, and the dragon—afflicting the Germanic people correspond to the three woes pronounced by Christ on the cities of Chorazin (Antichrist was born there), Bethsaida (Antichrist grew up there), and Capernaum (Antichrist ruled from there). Pseudo-Methodius says:

> And the Son of Perdition will be revealed, the false Christ: He will be conceived in Chorazin and will be brought up in Bethsaida and will rule in Capernaum. And Chorazin will glory in him that he was born there, and Bethsaida that he was raised there and Capernaum that he ruled there. And because of this Our Lord pronounced the *Woes* over the three of them in his gospel: Woe to thee, Chorazin, and woe to thee, Bethsaida, and thou, Capernaum that hast exalted thyself unto heaven, thou wilt descend to Hell [Matt. 11:20-24]. (Alexander 50)

It is possible that these three towns are cursed not necessarily because of their refusal to repent but also in view of their association with Antichrist in the theological framework of the gospel writers.

(2) Antichrist will issue his edict imposing universal circumcision "according to the rite of the ancient law (Old Testament)," as Pseudo-Ephrem says.[82] In this context Beowulf's apprehension that he might have sinned against the ancient law (*ofer ealde riht* in line 2330) makes good sense. According to the poem, the dragon's depredations brought much suffering to Beowulf, who imagined that he had bitterly offended the Eternal Lord and Ruler by sinning against some ancient law (2329-31). The implication of this passage seems to be that Beowulf had not circumcised himself and thus offended against the old law of circumcision. On the other hand, literally, if he had circumcised himself, he would have offended against the God of the New Testament, which discouraged the old law of circumcision in the case of converted pagans (Acts ch. 15). Beowulf's suspicion was well-founded: He had not had himself circumcised in accordance with the edict of Antichrist; therefore, he incurred the wrath of the Dragon-Antichrist.

(3) The reign of Grendel at Heorot for some twelve years (144-9) corresponds to Antichrist's rule from the Temple of Jerusalem. Ireneus says: "But when Antichrist shall have ravaged everything in this world...he shall seat himself in the Temple" (V.25). Antichrist will set himself up to be worshipped as God. Again, as Ireneus puts it, "And he shall indeed depose the idols that he may persuade the people that he is himself God, setting himself up as the one idol" (V.25.1).[83] In this context of Antichrist worship, the Beowulfian passage regarding the Danes' practice of idolatry (175-81) makes sense. It seems that many Danes, unlike Hrothgar, went too far and worshipped Antichrist, hoping for a respite from their sufferings: "They [the Danes] prayed that the destroyer of souls [the Devil-Antichrist] might ren-

der them aid against the calamities of their nation" (175-8).

The twelve-year-old rule of Grendel in Heorot is perplexing as far as the numerical symbolism is concerned. The number of twelve is not accounted for the reign of Antichrist in the Bible or for the reign of historical antichrists in Byzantine apocalypses. Of course, the symbolic number twelve may refer to the twelve tribes of Israel or to the twelve Apostles (Matthew 19:28) in view of the poet's reference to the throne of grace (*gifstol* of line 168) in the larger context of the Apocalypse's references to the throne of God surrounded by the elders. In the Antichrist-context of the poem, the number twelve may refer to the twelve sons of Ishmael (Gen. 19:20), whose offspring Islam is represented as Antichrist in medieval lore as mentioned above. The number symbolism also may refer to the twelve tribes of Apocalypse 17:4-8, which excludes Dan, the ancestral father of Antichrist, who is excluded from the list of Israel's twelve tribes in the Book of Apocalypse. However, there is one reference in the Eastern tradition for the length of the time of the residence of the Last Emperor in Jerusalem, which is twelve years in the Slavonic Daniel, which is derived ultimately from Pseudo-Methodius. Again, this intriguing point suggests that the English poet probably knew Eastern Antichrist traditions fairly well.[84]

The reference to the tribe of Dan raises an interesting issue. In medieval folklore, Denmark was considered to be the home of the tribe of Dan. The appearance of Antichrist Grendel in Denmark among the members of the tribe of Dan is quite appropriate in the apocalyptic imagery and symbolism of the poem. Similarly, through the use of Healfdenes, perhaps the poet may be alluding to the fact that some (half) of the Danes (Healfdenes), like Hrothgar, did not follow Antichrist!

Further, in the apocalyptic context, Grendel's ravages of Heorot correspond to Antichrist's profanation of the Jewish Temple and to Daniel's "abomination of desolation." According to the Greek Visions of Daniel, Antichrist will trample the Temple of God underfoot.[85] As Lactantius puts it, "He will attempt to overthrow [*eruere templum Dei conabitur*] (Alexander 206). Most importantly, Grendel's attempt to grab Beowulf has a very close parallel in Antichrist's attempt to capture God. According to the Erithrean Sibyl's prophecy, "Antichrist will extend his lips and palate to the heavens and will stretch out his hands to grab God the Highest; the people will say, 'Is this not the one the prophets had announced'" (Alexander 207). In *Beowulf*, first Grendel seeks to grasp the hero with his hand (745-8); later, Grendel's mother grabs him (1501).

Also, the breaking down of the doors of Heorot finds a significant parallel in the legends of the apocalyptic figure of Alexander, who became the focus of romance in Alexandria probably in the third century CE. The Alexander romance was popularized by Pseudo-Callisthenes, whose versions are found in some twenty-four languages. The Syriac versions of the Greek text was the first to fuse Alexander legends with classical apocalypticism; they were translated into Latin in the tenth century (McGinn 57). According to the romance, Alexander constructed a wall or gate in a mountain pass of the Caucasus to prevent the wild barbarian tribes from invading civilization.[86] In 395, the Huns overran the barriers and invaded the empire. What is important for *Beowulf* studies is the reference that the invaders were not allowed to enter Jerusalem just as Grendel was not allowed to touch the gift-throne (of Hrothgar), though the Danes had deserted Heorot because of all the havoc done by Grendel in Heorot:

> When night had come, Grendel went forth to seek out that lofty hall.... From that time on, whoever escaped the foe kept himself at a safe distance for the future. Thus did Grendel make himself master and wage a wrongful war against them all, single-handedly, until that finest of halls stood empty.... He took Heorot...to be his abode in the dark nights; yet, under Providence, he had never been permitted to come near the precious throne, the source of gifts. (115-168)

The *Beowulf*-poet's familiarity with this Eastern tradition can be seen in this passage if we compare it with a passage from the metrical homily ascribed to the Syrian writer Jacob of Serugh:

> On the day on which these people go forth over the earth at the end of times...mighty Rome from her greatness He shall throw down to the depths....They shall not, however, enter into Jerusalem, the city of the Lord. For the sign [of the cross] of the Lord shall drive them away from it, and they shall not enter it. All the saints shall fly away from them to Mount Sanir; all faithful true ones and the good and all the wise. They shall not be able to approach mount Sinai, for it is the dwelling place of the Lord, nor to the high mountains of Sinai with their shame.[87]

Antichrist is supposed to create apostasy among the believers. As there is apostasy during the reign of Antichrist, there are two cases of apostasy in *Beowulf.* In the first instance, during the raids of Grendel on Heorot many Danes abandoned the worship of the one God and resorted to idol worship. In the second instance, while Beowulf was engaged in the fight against Antichrist-dragon, his own hearth companions fled in terror to save their lives, abandoning their liege lord (2596-2601).

Double Antichrist and the Last Emperor

Two other related features of the Antichrist legend that bear on the Old English poem are the notion of the double Antichrist and the legend of the last emperor.

The basic idea behind the variants of the last-emperor motif is simply that as Christ came down to battle Satan first and then defeated Antichrist at his second coming, a noble king will appear to conquer God's enemies in the end times and surrender his crown to God, paving the way for the manifestation of Antichrist who will be vanquished by Christ and his angels. The earliest version of the last-emperor legend appears in the Pseudo-Ephrem homily and in the seventh-century Syriac Pseudo-Methodius apocalypse.

The Pseudo-Ephrem sermon (early seventh-century homily preached before the rise of Islam), after describing the sufferings and persecutions of the last times, especially the wars between the Romans and the Persians, announces that one sign predicted by St. Paul in 1 Cor. 15: 24—"Afterwards the end, when he shall have delivered up the kingdom to God and the Father, when he shall have brought to nought all principality and power and virtue [shall come]"—hasn't been fulfilled yet:

> And when the days of the times of those races have been completed, after they shall have corrupted the earth, the kingdom of the Romans will also rest and the empire of the Christians "will be taken from their midst and handed to God and the Father." Then will come the consummation, when the kingdom of the Romans will begin to be consumed and "every principality and power" will have ended.[88]

Pseudo-Methodius, composed later in the seventh century after the rise of Islam and written in Syria where Islam was dominant, describes the destruction of the Persian Empire and the irruption of Islam, the children of Ishmaelites. The emperor of the Greeks and his sons will go forth against the Ishmaelites and utterly destroy them. During the subsequent peaceful period, the unclean nations of Gog and Magog, earlier imprisoned by Alexander will sally forth to the plain of Joppa, where they will be destroyed by hosts of angels. After that the king of the Greeks will reign in Jerusalem for ten-and-a-half years until he surrenders his kingdom to Christ on Calvary and "gives up his soul to his Creator." The Son of Perdition will be revealed soon thereafter.

Paul Alexander's careful study of the legend of the last emperor lists the following apocalyptic stages—not necessarily in the same order—in different texts:

1. The appearance of warlike races.

2. The surrender of the last empire (1 Cor. 15:24).

3. The "first" manifestation of Antichrist in his adolescence and youth.

4. The "second" manifestation of Antichrist, as adult and ruler.

5. The description of the short reign (42 months) of Antichrist.

6. The coming of Elijah and Enoch who will resist Antichrist.

7. The second coming of Christ and the death of Antichrist.[89]

One interesting aspect of the last emperor legend has to do with the identity of the last emperor: in the Byzantine apocalypses the last emperor is the king of the Greeks; in the Latin versions the emperor is the king of both the Romans and the Greeks; in the Germanic version of Adso (tenth century), culled from Pseudo-Methodius, the Roman emperor becomes the Frankish king, successor to the Roman emperor.[90]

As we compare the Pseudo-Methodian Antichrist tradition with *Beowulf,* we find vestiges of it in the English poem. The poet uses elements of this tradition according to his will and pleasure, without slavishly adhering to it, as is his practice with all his subtexts. On the theme of the last emperor, the following observations are in order. After having accomplished the reconquest of his realm at the hands of the dragon by destroying him, at his death Beowulf ascends—metaphorically—the funeral pyre and surrenders his soul. He orders Wiglaf to build a burial mound on a hill (*hronesnaes*); the hero also renders thanks to God like the last emperor:

> To the Lord of All, the King of Glory, the Eternal Lord, will I utter my thanks…that I was able to acquire such things for my people before the day of my death…. Bid men…build a fair burial-mound on the headland by the sea…Beowulf's barrow. (2793-2808)

Later the poet would say about the giving up of his spirit: "These were the last words to reveal the thoughts in the aged man's breast before he chose the funeral pyre and the hot destroying flames; his soul passed away from his breast to seek the glory of the righteous" (2817-20).

Like the last emperor, Beowulf also triumphs over all his enemies and leaves no son as heir behind, which implies that the poet makes Beowulf the last emperor of the Germanic peoples:

> I would now wish to give my war-garb to my son, if it had been granted me that any heir of my body would remain after me. I have ruled this nation for fifty winters; there was no king among all neighboring peoples who dared attack me with trusty swords or threaten terror against me (2729-36).

Further, according to the testimony of the dying king himself and that of other men, Beowulf resembles the last emperor not only as a hero king but also as a holy king:

> I guarded well what was mine, I did not pursue crafty spites, I did not swear any oaths unjustly…when my life slips from my body, the Ruler of men will have no cause to accuse me of the murderous slaughter of any kinsmen.

(2736-42)

The king's retainers said that among all the kings in this world Beowulf had been "the gentlest of men, the most gracious, the most kindly to people, and the most eager to win renown" (3180-2).
Indeed, the apocalyptic king Beowulf wins renown as the legendary last Germanic emperor.

The apocalyptic idea of the double Antichrist or of the two comings of Antichrist has its reverberations in the poem. In the Eastern tradition, as noted above, Antichrist makes two appearances: as a young man and as an adult ruler. The English poem also refers to the two comings of Antichrist; first, during the youth of Beowulf and later during the old age of Beowulf, and we are all too familiar with Tolkien's own famous contrasting distinction between the youthful Beowulf and the aged Beowulf, between beginnings and ends. Indeed, the English poet develops the career of Beowulf in two stages, first as a young man, the thane of Hygelac, and later as the ruler of the Geats. During both these stages of his career, Beowulf encounters Antichrist, first Grendelkin and next the dragon; that is, Antichrist appears in the English poem in two stages as in Pseudo-Ephrem and Pseudo-Methodius.

Anglo-Saxons and Pseudo-Methodius

There is every reason to believe that the Anglo-Saxons knew the Oriental apocalyptic tradition as they were aware of Islam from the eighth century. For example, the Apocalypse of Pseudo-Methodius was very popular in Western Europe, second only to the canonical Bible and Church Fathers.[91] The key evidence that attests to the popularity of Pseudo-Methodius in England and Europe consists in the comparatively large number of surviving manuscripts of Pseudo-Methodius. There are over twenty-four short and long versions of Pseudo-Methodius, excluding fragments and extracts, in the various libraries of England. There are five manuscripts in the British Library, six at the Bodleian, and several more at the colleges in Oxford and Cambridge.[92] Further, the frequent citation of Methodius in various English works would also suggest a wide knowledge and use of his text (D'Evelyn 144-56). It is this popularity of Pseudo-Methodius in England that culminates in three independent Middle English versions, two in prose and one in metrical verse.[93] Indirectly, Pseudo-Methodius was known in England also through Adso's paraphrase of it in his famous work on Antichrist.

Anglo-Saxons and Islam

The association of Islam with the dragon of *Beowulf* inevitably raises the question of the Anglo-Saxons' knowledge and awareness of Islam. The answer is that the Anglo-Saxons knew much about Islam like their neighbors in Spain and elsewhere in Europe and the Middle East since they belonged not only to England but also to the larger world of Catholic Christianity.

From the time of Bede and Alcuin, Islam was a powerful force that Europe had to reckon with; in fact, it was the most potent power in the entire Middle East, including North Africa, the former Roman colony and the home of the immigrant Germanic tribes like the Vandals.

After the death of the Prophet in 632, a hundred years before Bede's death, or by the time of Bede's death, Islam expanded its sway from the Atlantic to the Indus. By 640, the Byzantines had lost Syria and Palestine to Islam; in 642 they lost Alexandria; between 673 and 677, an Islamic force laid siege to Constantinople, and Carthage fell in 698. In 710 the Arabs crossed to Spain from Mauritania, Africa, and overthrew the Visigothic kingdoms of Spain and moved into Provence. In 732 Charles Martel won a decisive victory over a probing expeditionary force of the Muslims at Poitiers. Bede refers to this particular victory in apocalyptic language in his *Ecclesiastical History*, which he just completed:

> In the year of the Lord's incarnation 729, two comets appeared by the sun.... One of them went before the rising sun in the morning, and the other followed him when he set at night, as it were presaging much destruction to the east and the west...to signify that mortals were threatened with calamities at both times. They carried their flaming tails towards the north, as it were to set the world on fire....At which time a dreadful plague of Saracens ravaged France with miserable slaughter; but they not long after in that country received the punishment due to their sins. (v.23)

What is remarkable here, as Wallace-Hadrill puts it, is, "A northern civilization [Frankish kingdom] was emerging as surely as an Arabic civilization of the Mediterranean."[94] Just as Byzantium took over the imperial role of Rome in the fourth century, now Germanic Western Europe would take it over from the declining Byzantium, while contenting with Islam which was emerging in the East as the political power that was slowly but surely edging out Byzantium. The crowning of Charlemagne on Christmas day in the year 800 symbolized a momentous historical change in the West. Henri Pirenne's seminar work, *Muhammed and Charlemagne*, best illustrates this historical polarity of the times.

How much did the West know about Islam even at the beginning of the eighth century? Very much, if Bede's own writings alone are an indication. *De locis sanctis*, a guide book for travelers to the Holy Places, based on Adamnan's earlier work, which Bede composed between 702 and 709, contains much valuable information. The information was supplied by Arculf, a Frankish bishop, who traveled between 679 and 682 to the Holy Land held by the Arabs. Though Bede was rather indifferent toward the Saracens in his earlier references in 711, after the Arab invasion of Spain in 711, he viewed them as enemies of the Church in his *Commentary* on I Samuel 25:1.[95] In 720, Bede went further and branded the Saracens, the children of Ishmael, who had much of Africa and parts of Asia and Europe under their power, as enemies of the entire world (Wallace-Hadrill 6). In 725, Bede's *de Temporum Ratione* refers to the Saracen attack on Sicily, to the capture of Carthage, and the great siege of Constantinople in 716 and 717. That Bede's knowledge of the events is factual can be seen in his change of *triennio* to *biennio* and *cum immenso exercitu* in Liber *Pontificalis*. He also appends the story of the pestilence among the besiegers as well as the story of the transfer of the bones of St. Augustine from Africa to Sardinia to Pavia (Wallace-Hadrill 7). It is perhaps coincidental that the regnal years of Bede's greatest hero Oswald (634-42) were almost the same as those of Caliph 'Umar (634-44).

Perhaps the most significant use of an Islamic source, the Qur'an, by Bede is found in Bede's story of Caedmon. As I had discussed extensively in a previous study, the closest parallel to the Caedmon story—the bestowal on Caedmon of poetic gift from heaven—is the Qur'anic testimony of the miraculous enlightenment of Prophet Muhammed by Archangel Jibril. Let me restate the fascinating parallels found in these two miracle stories:

> In both stories the protagonists are untutored, unlettered, and mature adults. Both receive the revelation in a dream or a trance. The angel commands Caedmon two times to sing; the angel orders Muhammed three times to proclaim from the book. The subject matter of the revelation in both cases is creation. Both of them sing a verse on creation and remember the words after they wake up. There is a woman behind the revelation in each case; Abbess Hilda in the case of Caedmon and Khadijah in Muhammed's case. The women refer the matter to a third party who confirms the authenticity of the revelation. All the main topics Bede says that Caedmon sang about such as the revelation of God on creation, the origin of the human race, the story of Genesis, Exodus, and the story of Jesus are found in the Qur'an and, of course, much more.[96]

Bede even seems to pattern Caedmon's death scene, in which Caedmon requests that he be taken to the Eucharist instead of having the Eucharist brought to him, after the story of the Prophet's night flight to Jerusalem, where the Prophet shows his humility to go to Mount Moriah instead of having Mt. Moriah brought to him. Bede's possible use of the Qur'an makes sense if only we recall the fact that we do not know the authority for it either from Bede or from any other historical sources.

By 732, Bede viewed the Saracen threat as "*gravissima Sarracenorum lues*' (the *gravissima lues* of Gregory of Tours v.34) after their move against Tours in 732, their campaign in Toulouse in 721, and after their capture of Carcassone and Nimes in 725. In 732, Boniface also referred to the Saracen threats to Europe in his letter to the English nun Bucga, advising her to delay her pilgrimage to Rome.[97] Henri Pirenne argues that the Muslims effectively cut off commercial sea-lanes in the Mediterranean from practical use both by the Western Empire and Byzantium. These dramatic changes weakened the Merovingian kings in north-west Europe and encouraged the gradual rise of the Carolingians, with whom the Pope allied himself in the latter part of the eighth century for political reasons, especially by crowning the Frankish Charlemagne as emperor in Rome in 800. Pirenne writes:

> It is therefore strictly correct to say that without Muhammed Charlemagne would have been inconceivable. In the seventh century the ancient Roman Empire had actually become an empire of the East; the Empire of Charles was an empire of the West.[98]

It often happens that armchair theologians and preachers as well as poets in their literary imagination, because they are removed from the theater of realpolitik, tend to exaggerate the confrontation of the forces of Islam and Christianity in apocalyptic terms. On the other hand, men like Emperor Charlemagne and Caliph Harun-al-Rashid respected each other and eschewed total war by making compromises and diplomatic overtures based on mutual understanding for mutual advantage. At one point Harun-al-Rashid even sent the gift of an elephant to Charlemagne, who in 799 wrote a letter to Alcuin for a copy of the *Disputatio cum Sarraceno* composed by a certain Felix. Alcuin wrote back saying that the treatise could be found with Liutprand of Lyons; Alcuin, however, added that information on that issue could also be obtained from the Pisan Peter who was at that time residing at Charlemagne's own court.[99] Indeed, at least some among the English and the French knew Islam and the Muslims fairly well.

The Spirit of Beowulfian Apocalypse

Unlike preachers and propagandists, the poet of *Beowulf* seems to have his own vision of the end times. He uses apocalyptic motifs and metaphors without falling into literalism and millenarism. As we have seen before, he uses allegory to avoid the scylla of literalism and interpretations of history to avoid the charybdis of Augustinian spiritualist view of the Apocalypse.

The final end, the end of the world, does not come about in the poem with the death of Antichrist-dragon. On the contrary, it seems that the death of the dragon is only the beginning after an end, the end of one cycle and the beginning of another, as in Indian apocalyptic mythology, where we find the constant passage of ages. The poet suggests this eschatological view by giving several indicators. First, King Beowulf anoints Wiglaf as his successor by bestowing on him royal insignia (2809-16). Similarly, the poet's other references to the succession of the kings Scyld and Beowulf I, Healfdene, Hrothgar, and so on seem to point toward the on-going process of history without end but not without hope. It is this note of hope that characterizes the spirit of the English poem, following on the heels of apocalyptic doom. The poet seems to say that tragedy should spell not necessarily despair but hope not only for victims of the tragedy but also for their heirs. As for the dead Beowulf, there is hope because he would long abide in his tomb, his final abode, "in the keeping of the God the Ruler," resting in peace (3105-9). As for Beowulf's followers, sinners and saints alike, his burial mound would presumably function as a beacon light for the safety of the sailors in the storm-tossed sea of life.

The poet adds caution as a safeguard against unbridled optimism by indirectly alluding to future attacks from Franks, Frisians, and Swedes (2910 ff). The poet's message seems to be this: prevent wars if you can in order to postpone the inevitable end. Though it was not possible to save Beowulf's life because he was fated to die, it is possible to postpone the inevitable end just as Beowulf did by triumphing over obstacles and enemies. Just as Beowulf lived to mature old age by leading a life of courage and virtue, it is possible for individuals to postpone the end by living a righteous life at least for the sake of a fuller, longer life, resonating the Deuteronomic theological view, "Honor thy father and mother, as the Lord thy God hath commanded thee; that thy days may be prolonged and that it may go well with thee in the land" (Deut. 5:16).

The Beowulfian apocalypse is not a simple replica of the final vision of the biblical apocalypse, where the visionary sees "a new heaven and a new earth...a new Jerusalem coming out of heaven as a bride adorned for her husband...[as a place] where God shall wipe away all tears and where death, mourning, crying, and sorrow shall be no more (21;1-4). The English poet would have nothing of such sentimental, maudlin, unrealistic dream vision in this world. On the contrary, in the Beowulfian universe, only those who have died in the Lord— Scyld, Beowulf I, and Beowulf II, to wit—have that privilege; the living have to live death, mourning, crying, and sorrow. This is the message the poet sends through the wailing of the Geatish woman, probably even Beowulf's own wife, literally or figurally: "She would know days of mourning, and a time of great slaughter and terror among the host, with humiliation and captivity" (3150-55)—which could be eschatological or merely futuristic troubles ahead, a sentiment expressed by the last survivor (2910-23), cited earlier.

This somber view seems to be imbued with the spirit of Germanic apocalypticism. The picture of the end is similar both in *Beowulf* and in the *Voluspa*. In *Beowulf* both hero Beowulf and the villainous dragon are killed as in *ragnarøk*, where both gods and demons meet their inevitable end just as in Hindu mythology. However, the sons of gods as well as two members of the human race survive the *ragnarøk* to start the reconstruction of heaven and earth. In *Beowulf*, Wiglaf and his companions survive the death of their lord and the dragon. In fact, Beowulf instructs Wiglaf to look after the needs of his people (2801-2). To repeat, "Make the best of both worlds" seems to be the parting message of the poet. In other words, life must go on because life is stronger than death. That is, though destruction casts its pale shadow on earth, the spirit of reconstruction will rise ever resplendent, flame-like, like the legendary phoenix of the East, from the fuzzy fire and grey smoke enveloping the burning pyre of Beowulf.

NOTES

1. S. J. Crawford, "Grendel's Descent from Cain," *MLR* 23 (1928): 208.

2. Zacharias P. Thundy, "*Beowulf* Date and Authorship," *NM*, 87 (1986): 102-116.; Kevin Kiernan, *Beowulf and Beowulf Manuscript* (New Brunswick, 1981); Kiernan, "The Eleventh-Century Origin of *Beowulf* and the *Beowulf* Manuscript," in Colin Chase, ed. *The Dating of Beowulf*, pp. 9-22.

3. On the Eastern dimension of *Beowulf*, see Zacharias P. Thundy, "*Beowulf*: Geats, Jutes, and Asiatic Huns," *Littcrit* 17 (1983): 1-8.

4. James Earl, *Thinking About Beowulf* (Stanford, 1994), p. 1.

5. Kemp Malone, "Grundtvig as Beowulf Critic," *Review of English Studies* 17 (1941): 129-138; George Clark, *Beowulf* (Boston, 1990), for a good survey of critical approaches to the study of *Beowulf*.

6. W. P. Ker, *Epic and Romance* (London, 1908), p. 158.

7. J. R. R. Tolkien, *Beowulf* The Monsters and Critics," in Lewis E. Nicholson, ed. *An Anthology of Beowulf Criticism* (Notre Dame, 1980), p. 54.

8. My apocalyptic interpretation of the poem accounts for the role of Grendel's mother rather well; see "*Beowulf*: Method, Meaning, and Monster," *Greyfriar* 24 (1983): 5-34.

9. F. A. Blackburn, "The Christian Coloring in *Beowulf*," *PMLA* 12 (1897

205-25; Marie P. Hamilton, "The Religious Principle in *Beowulf*," *PMLA* 61 (309-31; M.B.McNamee, "*Beowulf*—An Allegory of Salvation?" *JEGP* 59 (1960): 190-207; Margaret E. Goldsmith, "The Christian Perspective in *Beowulf*," *Comparative Literature* 14 (1962): 71-80; Edward B. Irving, Jr., "The Nature of Christianity in 'Beowulf'," *ASE* 13 (1984): 7-21, recently counted approximately 178 Christian references in Beowulf, consisting of words all could agree on such as epithets for God and references to sin, hell, and heaven: "These figures confirm our sense that we have in *Beowulf* as a poem narrated by an unquestionably Christian poet" (9).

10. Fr. Klaeber, *Beowulf and the Fight at Finnsburg* (Boston, 1950), xlviii.

11. Margaret E. Goldsmith, "The Christian Perspective in *Beowulf*," in Lewis Nicholson, *An Anthology of Beowulf Criticism*, p. 375.

12. Margaret Goldsmith, *The Mode and Meaning of "Beowulf"* (London, 1970), pp. 254-56, 72-73, 146.

13. Robert E. Kaske, "*Sapientia et Fortitudo* as the Controlling Theme of *Beowulf*," *Studies in Philology* 55 (1958): 423-56.

14. Charles Donahue, "*Beowulf* and Christian Tradition," *Traditio* 21 (1965): 55-116.

15. Beowulf and Christ are not contradiction in terms or contradiction *in adjecto*, but contraries like colors; for example, black and white do coexist and mix to give a new coloring. Contradictories, on the other hand, are incompatible like a square and a circle so much so we can't have square a circle.

16. Edward Risden, *Beasts of Time: Apocalyptic Beowulf* (New York, 1994), p. 83. I am indebted to this study for the exploration of some of the eschatological themes of *Beowulf*.

17. See Risden, pp. 89-109, for a good discussion of the theme of death in the poem.

18. The poet's reference to the flying hawk in lines 2263-64, indeed, reminds the readers of his probable acquaintance with Bede's *Ecclesiastical History*, where we find the colorful image of the sparrow flying through the hall.

19. See Risden, pp. 84-89 for additional references to the works of critics like Dronke, Irving, Lee, Gatch, and Earl.

20. Pseudo-Bede, *de quindecim signis*, PL 94:555.; Risden 62 ff. These signs are the following: 1) the sea rises, 2) mountains descend, 3) sea and land are even, 4) sea monsters growl, 5) sea monsters burn, 6) grass and trees become bloody, 7) buildings are destroyed, 8) stones battle one another, 9) earth quakes, 10) earth becomes a plain, 11) men run from their caves, 12) stars fall, 13) bones of the dead rise, 14) all men die, 15) and the earth burns.

21. Helen Damico, *Beowulf's Wealhtheow and the Valkyrie Tradition* (Madison, 1984), p. 84; Risden, 63.

22. The Geatish woman should also remind us of Virgin Mary, the sorrowful Mother, whose heart would be pierced by a sword with her son set up as a sign of contradiction and for the fall and rising of many (Luke 2:34-5).

23. I have no intention to enter into the fray on the oral-formulaic composi-

tion of *Beowulf,* which was first written and then recited.

24. For the discussion of apocalyptic literary devices, I am indebted to the studies of Bernard McGinn, "Revelation," in *The Literary Guide to the Bible,* ed. Robert Alter and Frank Kermode (Cambridge, 1987), pp. 523-41 and Edward Risden, *Beasts of Time,* pp. 70-77.

25. See Ward Parks, "The Traditional Narrator and the 'I Heard' Formulas in Old English Poetry," *ASE* 16 (1987): 45-66.

26. See Schüssler-Fiorenza, pp. 171-3.

27. Chaucer seems to use a similar method in *The Canterbury Tales.*

28. See Hugh Thomas Keenan, "The Apocalyptic Vision in Old English Poetry," Dissertation, University of Tennessee, 1968, pp. 208-13.

29. F. C. Burkitt, ed. *The book of Rules of Tyconius.* Text and Studies III, pt. 1 (Cambridge, 1894), p. xxi. It seems that Bede understands recapitulation as a retelling of events only and not as the simultaneous presence of type and antitype, as Tyconius uses the term (see Keenan 208-13). Bede uses recapitulation to explain Apoc. 4:1, 8:1, and 20:1

30. Keenan, pp. 122-4.

31. A thorough application of the principle of recapitulation is beyond the scope of this work. Fred Robinson's *Beowulf and Appositive Style* (Knoxville, 1985) is an excellent starting point for such an undertaking.

32. Thomas E. Hart, "Ellen: Some Tectonic Relationships in *Beowulf* and Their Formal Resemblance to Anglo-Saxon Art," *Papers on Language and Literature* 6 (1970): 263-90; "Tectonic Design, Formulaic, Craft, and Literary Execution: The Episodes of Fin and Ingeld in *Beowulf,*" *Amsterdamer Beiträge zur älteren Germanistik,* 2 (1972): 1-61; David R. Howlett, "Form and Genre in *Beowulf,*" *Studia Neophilologica* 46 (1974): 309-25.

33. Philo, *On the birth of Abel and the Sacrifices Offered by Him and by His Brother Cain,* in *Philo in Ten Volumes,* trans. F. H. Colson and G. H. Whitaker, II (Cambridge, 1958), pp. 95-7; cited by Gerald L. Bruns, "Midrash and Allegory: The Beginnings of Scriptural Interpretation," in *The Literary Guide to the Bible,* p. 639.

34. It is very likely that the poet is referring to the works of Philo in the Abel-Cain passage of the poem.

35. A. C. Bartlett, *The Larger Rhetorical Pattern in Anglo-Saxon Poetry* (New York, 1935), pp. 9-22; Constance B. Hieatt, "Envelope Patterns and the Structure of *Beowulf,*" *English Studies in Canada,* 1 (1975): 249-65; J. O Beaty, "The Echo-Word in *Beowulf* with a Note on the Finnsburg Fragment," *PMLA,* 49 (1934): 365-73; David R. Howlett, "Form and Genre in *Beowulf,*" *Studia Neophilologica,* 46 (1974): 309-25; H. Ward Tonsfeldt, "Ring Structure in *Beowulf,*" *Neophilologus,* 61 (1977): 443-52; John Niles, "Ring Composition and the Structure of *Beowulf,*" *PMLA* 94 (1979): 924-35.

36. See more on this below.

37. See endnote 34.

38. David R. Howlett, "Form and Genre in *Beowulf,*" *Studia Neophilologica*

46 (1974): 325.

39. Martin Green, "Man, Time, and Apocalypse in *The Wanderer, The Seafarer,* and *Beowulf," JEGP* 74 (1975): 515.

40. Literature on Grendel is rather voluminous. Wayne Hanley's article "Grendel's Humanity Again" *In Geardagum* XI (June 1990), 6-13, contains a current bibliography. I am grateful to Professor Raymond Tripp for calling my attention to his study.

41. "The Formulaic Expression of the Theme of 'Exile' in Anglo-Saxon Poetry," *Speculum* 30 (1955): 205. See also Fr. Klaeber, Die christlichen Elementen im *Beowulf," Anglia* 35: 252.

42. Gregory, *Moralia, PL* 56: 113.

43. R. W. Chambers, *Beowulf: An Introduction to the Study of the Poem* (Cambridge, 1967), p. 4.

44. For this section of the paper, see Adela Collins "Oppression from Without; the Symbolization of Rome as Evil in Early Christianity," *Concilium* 200 (1988): 66-74.

45. M. R. James, *Apocrypha Anecdota* II (Cambridge, 1893), p. 188.

46. *In Matthaei Evangelium Expositio* iv; *PL* 92: 103: "Vae praegnantibus etc. Hoc quoque secundum historiam dici potest quod in persecutione Antichristi seu Romanae captivitatis praegnantes...."

47. See Kenneth Baxter Wolf, "Christian View of Islam in Early Medieval Spain," in John V. Tolan, ed., *Medieval Christian Perceptions of Islam* (New York, 1996), p. 88.

48. It is interesting to note that, while the persecuted Christians viewed Islam as Antichrist and as dragon, the British viewed the Saxons almost in the same terms. Gildas (d. 570) writes in a style reminiscent of the style of the *Beowulf-* poet:

> Then a brood of whelps, breaking forth from the lair of barbaric lioness...borne in three ships...under favorable sails, with omen and divinations wherein it was being foretold...that for three hundred years [see *Beowulf* 2278-79] they should occupy the fatherland...first infixed their terrible claws in the eastern part of the island.... To whom the aforesaid mother (of the brood)...sends a second and larger jail-gang of accomplices and curs, who...attach themselves to their bastard comrades. Then the seed of iniquity...sprouts in our soil." (Wade-Evans 147-48)

49. In Middle English also *Kaymes kin* is the ordinary form of the name; see Oliver F. Emerson, "Legends of Cain, Especially in Old and Middle English," *PMLA* 21 (1906), p. 885.

50. Some medieval people mistakenly derived the origin of Muslim Saracens from Abraham's wife Sarah; the Muslims were also called "Hagarenes" from Abraham's wife/mistress Hagar, and also "Ishmaelites" from Ishmael.

51. Edmund Hoga, *The Irish Nennius from L. na Huidre,* Royal Irish Academy Todd Lecture Ser 6 (Dublin, 1895), pp. 7-8; cited by Ruth Mellinkoff, "Cain's Monstrous Progeny in *Beowulf* Part II, Post-Diluvian Survival," *Anglo-Saxon*

England, 9 (1980): 193: "And Cham was thus the first person that was cursed after the Deluge, and he was the heir of Cain after the Deluge, and from him sprang the Luchrupans, and Formorians, and Goatheads, and every unshapely form in general that there is on men. And it is therefore that overthrow was brought on the descendants of Cham and that their land was given to the sons of Israel in token of the same curse. And that is the origin of the Torothors, and they are not of the seed of Cain as the Gaels relate, for there lived not aught of his seed after the Deluge, for it was the purpose of the Deluge to drown the descendants of Cain, and all the descendants of Seth were also drowned along with them, but for Noah with his sons and with their four wives, as Moses, son of Amram, tells in Genesis of the Law."

52. For the mix-up of the Cain-Cham traditions, see Francis Lee Utley, "The Prose *Salomon and Saturn* and the Tree Called Chy," *MS* 19, (1957): 62.

53. Alcuin, *Interrogationes et Responsiones in Genesim* 96; *PL* 100:526. In the Muslim tradition, the daughters-in-law of Noah were all descended from Cain (Mellinkoff 196).

54. See C. M. Jones, "The conventional Saracen of the Songs of Geste," *Speculum* 17 (1942): 205 and n. 2, 218-9; W. W. Comfort, "The Literary Role of the Saracens in the French Epic," *PMLA* 55 (1940): 629, 652.

55. Charles Donahue, "Grendel and the *Clanna Cain,*" *Journal of Celtic Studies* 1 (1949-50): 167-75; see also Ruth Mellinkoff, "Cain's Monstrous Progeny in *Beowulf:* Part I, Noachic Tradition," *ASE* 8 (1979): 143-62.

56. It is because all the monsters, the descendants of Cain, perished in the Flood that Lewis E. Nicholson, "The Literal Meaning and Symbolic Structure of Beowulf," *Classica et Medaevalia* 15 (1964): 151-201, argues that the story takes place in pre-diluvian times.

57. D.W. Robertson, "The Doctrine of Charity in Mediaeval Literary Gardens: A Topical Approach through Symbolism and Allegory," *Speculum* 26 (1951): 33.

58. *Vita Guthlaci,* c. 19; Marie Padgett Hamilton, "The Religious Principle in *Beowulf,*" *PMLA* 61 (1946): 316.

59. *Venerabilis Bedae Commentaria in Scripturas Sacras,* ed. J. A. Giles, I, 67, 70-71, 74-75, 78-79.

60. This passage is reminiscent of the abduction of the Danes by Grendel and his mother.

61. *Adversus Haereses,* 1.31.1-2; cited by Birger A. Pearson, *Gnosticism, Judaism, and Egyptian Christianity* (Minneapolis, 1990), p. 97.

62. Cited by Pearson, p. 104.

63. Hamilton, p. 317.

64. *PL* 76:183.

65. *PL* 76:716.

66. See D. J. Sahas, *John of Damascus on Islam: the Heresy of Ishmaelites* (Leiden, 1972).

67. Eulogius, *Liber apologeticus martyrum,* 19; cited K. B. wolf, p. 97.

68. *Liber apologeticus martyrum,* 19; cited by K. B. Wolf, p. 99.

69. Cited by Edward P. Colbert, *Martyrs of Cordoba* (Washington, 1962), p. 70.

70. *PL* 115:766.

71. *Indiculus Luminosus*; *PL* 121:535-6.

72. *PL* 115:159-60; Colbert, pp. 334-8.

73. Gomez-Moreno, "Las primeras chronícas de la Reconquista: el ciclo de Alfonso III. *BRAH*, 100 (1932): 622-3; *Crónicas asturianas*, ed. J. Gil et al. (Oviedo, 1985); pp. 186-7, 261-2.

74. Elipandus, *Letter of the Bishops of Spain to the Bishops of Gaul* 5, ed. Joannes Gil in *Corpus Scriptorum Muzarabicorum* (Madrid, 1973), p. 92; see references in John Williams, *The Illustrated Beatus* (New York, 1994), pp. 115-7. The credibility of Elipandus' charges is equivocal because of the caricatural tone of the response.

75. *Mozarabes y asturianos* 151-2; cited by Harvey Williams, p. 134.

76. A project on *Beowulf* and iconography, using illustrated apocalypses is an undertaking well worth the effort of a PhD candidate, but it is beyond the scope of this paper. I have done some work in this regard; my webpage http://www.nmu.edu/staff/zthundy carries the article "*Beowulf,* Apocalypse, and Iconography" with images and sound.

77. Bernard McGinn, *Antichrist,* p. 88.

78. Pseudo-Ephrem, cited by Paul J. Alexander, *The Byzantine Apocalypse Tradition,* pp. 194-5.

79. The following citations and references are from W. Bousset's classical work *The Antichrist Legend* (London, 1896), p. 145.

80. See McGinn, *Antichrist,* pp. 70-4, for more on the physical descriptions of Antichrist as found in the Eastern tradition.

81. Cited by Alexander, p. 195; in Pseudo-Chrysostom and the Byzantine Visions of Daniel, Antichrist's mother is a whore.

82. Caspari, p. 277.13: "Proponent enim edictum ut circumcidantur homines secundum ritum legis antiquae. Tunc gratulabuntur et Iudaei eo quod eis reddiderit usum prioris testamenti."

83. See Bousset, pp. 160-2.

84. Alexander, p. 198.

85. Alexander, p. 206.

86. According to Josephus, the excluded tribes are the Scythians.

87. Cited by McGinn, *Visions of the End*, p. 58; the translation is from E. A. Wallis Budge, *History of Alexander the Great*, pp. 186-88.

88. Cited by McGinn, *Antichrist,* p. 90.

89. Alexander, pp. 218-9.

90. See Adso Dervensis, *De Ortu et Tempore Antichristi necnon et tractatus qui ab eo dependunt,* ed. D. Verhelst, *CC* 45 (Turnhout, 1976).

91. Ernst Sackur, *Sibyllinische Texte und Forschungen* (Halle, 1898), pp. 4 ff.

92. See Charlotte D'Evelyn, "The Middle English Metrical Version of the Revelation of Methodius; With a Study of the Influence of Methodius in Middle

English Writings," *PMLA* 33 (1918), pp. 139 ff.

93. See D'Evelyn, *passim.*

94. Wallace Hadrill, *Bede's Europe,* Jarrow lecture 1962, p. 2.

95. Cited by Wallace-Hadrill, p. 6: "Quae Saracenos specialiter adversarios ecclesiae generaliter describunt." Boniface, in a letter to King Aethelbald of Mercia, described the invasion of Spain as a punishment for sin, *Epistola* 73, MGH, *Epistolae Selectae,* I (1955): 151.

96. Zacharias P. Thundy, "The Qur'an: Source or Analogue of Bede's Caedmon Story?" *Islamic Culture* 63 (1989): 109.

97. See R. W. Southern, *Western Views of Islam in the Middle Ages* (Cambridge, 1962), p. 18.

98. Henri Pirenne, *Muhammed and Charlemagne,* pp. 234-5.; Richard Hodges and David Whitehouse, *Muhammed, Charlemagne, and the Origins of Europe* (Ithaca, 1983), p. 4. Recent historians and archeologists argue that even before the Muslim invasions, the empire was gradually declining; they claim that Muhammed and Charlemagne were both products of the collapse of Rome.

99. *Epistola* 172, *MGH, Epistolae* IV: 284-5.

CONCLUSION

Fuzzy Literature

So far as the laws of mathematics refer to reality, they are not certain. And so far as they are certain, they do not refer to reality. —Albert Einstein *Geometry and Experience*

Into every tidy scheme of arranging the pattern of human life, it is necessary to inject a certain dose of anarchism. —Bertrand Russell *Skeptical Essays*

Beauty is in the interval. —Henri Bergson

This chapter contains my final reflections on the subject as well as my theory of literature, which I call "fuzzy literature" after the path-breaking works in fuzzy logic by scientist-engineer-thinker Lotfi Asker Zadeh.[1] Increasingly I am becoming convinced that all literature is fuzzy and the closer you look at a text it gets fuzzier at the borders. It is somewhat like saying that the more you know the more you realize that you know less. Consequently, the overall purpose and expected effect of this book has been to call into question received cultural and literary assumptions on literature, especially on the New Testament and medieval Western literature, and show that past certainties are but today's uncertainties and skeptical roads to tomorrow's discoveries. As Christopher Fry would put it, "There may always be another reality to make fiction of the truth we think we've arrived at."

The great Indian novelist-poet Rudyard Kipling sang in his oft-quoted "The Ballad of East and West" (1899): "OH, EAST is East, and West is West, and never the twain shall meet." Here we have bivalancies transferred from mathematics to literature and two poles borrowed from directionalities to refer to two vague, gray, fuzzy metaphysical concepts.[2] Here geographical places merge into mental space and physical locations with fuzzy borders into boundless artistic realm. Confusion confounded.

A few years ago, I wrote a monograph, "Pre-Colonial Travelers to India"; in this paper writing from India—now I am writing from the upper Midwest—I had to refer to "that" side of the Mediterranean comprising Palestine, Israel, Syria, etc. as "Midwest" rather than "Middle East." Sounds very unconventional, but true, nevertheless, from the perspective of one viewing the rest of the world from the land of the rising sun.

Some readers may find the sounding of my phrase "the great Indian novelist-poet" jarring to their ears or offensive to their sensibility. They may ask: Is Rudyard Kipling, realistically speaking, an Indian writer as well as a great writer? Let me answer this question with another question: Are you British or American if you are born, raised, traveled, and worked in Britain or America even if you do not hold or have applied for a British or American passport? The obvious answer is "yes." The very words "British" and "American" are fuzzy because you can claim to be British even if you do not have a drop of Celtic blood and a single Celtic gene—if ever there is some thing called a Celtic gene—in your veins or in your body. The same goes with a Chinese or Russian child born in the United States. In India you are considered Indian if you were born in India or if your parents are Indian even if you were not born in India. As for Kipling, he was born and raised in India and worked for a time in India and the United States before settling down in England. He also wrote an incredible number of poems, novels, and essays on all kinds of topics, especially about his experiences in India, and his Indian novel *Kim* stands out as a great work of art. All these credentials of Kipling should naturally make him a great Indian writer; nevertheless, he is also a British writer, American writer, and so on. But many still would not give him his due because he is still considered, euphemistically speaking, an Anglo-Indian writer; hence he is not a *pukka sahib*; therefore, they are somewhat reluctant to attribute the sobriquet "great" to Kipling as though greatness like athletic skills is reserved to one ethnic group. In fact, *great* is also a fuzzy set or a generalized set to which participating objects can belong, like in analogy or metaphor, in various degrees and on various levels. Remarkably, it is the United States—or rather some folks from Michigan's Upper Peninsula—that immortalized him by naming two places—Rudyard and Kipling—after him in the Upper Peninsula of Michigan.

The point I am making is that the referential terms we constantly use and the definitions we give them are imprecise and fuzzy. Racial epithets, like *Caucasian, Black, Native American, Hispanic,* and *Asian* are good examples. If both your parents are "white" even though they may come from the racial melting pot of Sicily, Spain, or Italy with a lot of "Moorish" and

"Semitic" blood in your veins, you are "caucasian" or "white." On the other hand, if one of your parents or grandparents or great grandparents happens to be "black," you are racially classified as "black." In Louisiana, you were legally black up until recently if one of your great-great-great-great-grandparents was black. That is the one-drop rule of American racial identity. Take the case of the golf professional Tiger Woods. In public broadcasts and popular journals he is called "black," "the great black hope" of golf even though the "educated" broadcasters know very well that his color is brown, that his mother is from Thailand with Chinese and Indian (of India, and Indians are part Aryan) ancestry and that on his father's side he has a native American for a grandparent. As such, Tiger Woods is one-quarter black, one-quarter Chinese, one-eighth Native American, and one-eighth white (Aryan).[3] Though Woods sometimes describes himself "mathematically Asian," his father is skeptical: "In America there are only two colors—white and non-white." Obviously, race in the U.S. doesn't go by majority rules. The honest truth is that Tiger Woods is Native American, Aryan (white), Black, and Chinese—all in one. The affable guru of fuzzy logic is another example of the same racial or ethnic fuzzyism. Zadeh is an American born to Iranian parents in the former Soviet Union and educated in Russia, Persia, and America, holding an American passport. Like Woods and Zadeh, objectively speaking, all of us are of mixed ancestry and defy racial stereotypes though we continually ignore our own fuzzy ethnic origins and seek linguistic refuge in racial stereotypes and commit cultural suicide by refusing to recognize our mixed, fuzzy cultural and ethnic heritage.

East and *West*, similarly, are fuzzy words and mental landscapes with fuzzy borders. People underquote Kipling and use him to bolster up their own pet notion of the incompatibility of East and West. The entire first stanza of the ballad, in fact, celebrates the fuzzy sets of East and West:

> OH, EAST is East, and West is West, and never the twain shall meet,
> Till Earth and Sky stand presently at God's great Judgment Seat;
> But there is neither East nor West, Border, nor Breed, nor Birth,
> When two strong men stand face to face, though they come from the
> ends of the earth!

The Hindu Kamal who lifts the English Colonel's favorite mare and the Colonel's son who stands up to Kamal are equally brave, and they learn from each other and respect each other. Kamal admires the bravery of the English youth and returns the Colonel's mare. The Colonel's son admires the courage of Kamal who dares challenge the mighty British Empire by stealing the mare. Further, Kamal sends his own son into the service of the "White Queen" before he would be hanged in Peshawar, as he puts it, for

stealing a horse. Here is a case of the East sacrificing itself in the service of
the West after giving the West its very best. Kipling implies that in the final
analysis greatness and courage transcend the borders of race, region, and
religion. That statement is very true of literature as well. The New Testament is not just a Western text; its intertextuality is deeply embedded in the
Eastern literary tradition beyond that of the Hebrew Bible as I have tried to
demonstrate in my last book on Buddha and Christ.[4] Similarly, European
medieval literature, especially Old English literature which is the subject
matter of this study, is very Eastern while remaining in the ambiance of
Western Germanic Christendom.

   The introduction of fuzziness into literary studies is a departure from
the traditional models of literary research which emphasize the scientific
principles of universality and necessity, precision and certainty, the salient
features of modern empirical science, which arose in the seventeenth century under the aegis of Reformation humanism and Newtonian deter-
minism.

   It gives me much comfort when I make a statement like "2 + 2 = 4,
neither more nor less," is necessarily true everywhere in the universe, though
in fact I know only one world in the universe. I like to think that there is
precision, finality, and universality to such a statement. Similarly, the statements "I am young," "I am tall," and "I am saved" also give me a sense of
assurance. Descartes' famous starting point in metaphysics *Cogito, ergo
sum* is another classical statement of this position. Twentieth-century science and fuzzy logic take away that comfort zone from under our very
nose. In the late 1920s Werner Heisenberg stunned the scientific world
with the uncertainty principle of quantum mechanics. He showed that if
we know how fast an electron speeds along a line, then we do not know
with certainty where it is along the line, and vice versa. What Heisenberg
did was show that in quantum mechanics we shall never know some things
because they are unknowable in principle. He made Descartes' metaphysical
doubt and theologians' "unknowability of God" "scientific."

   And we were left with probability, the mathematical theory of chance.
Probability is a number given to an event, like 1 for rain and 0 for non-rain
as in "Probably it will rain today" and "Probably it will not rain today." The
larger the number, the more likely the event will occur. We hear this kind
of probable weather forecasts all the time on TV and radio. Pascal's famous
metaphysical wager is another fuzzy case in point: "If God doesn't exist, I
don't stand to lose anything even if I don't lead a good life," "but if God
does exist, I stand to lose everything if I don't lead a good life." Thus, in
Pascal's wager faith is a fuzzy noumenon bordering on God's positive exist-

ence (bright side) and God's negative existence (dark side).

When it comes to literature, we rely on the probability principle and then sublimate it to the certainty principle to live cozily in the comfort zone, whereas in reality certainty is the probability zone of common parlance. The late James E. Cross, the pre-eminent intertextual scholar of modern Old English studies, proposes the lofty, unreachable goal of the literary scholar-critic in his Gollancz Memorial Lecture of 1972 as follows:

> I said, perhaps provocatively, that a student of sources and their ideas could be the better half of a literary critic, certainly, if criticism...consists of two aspects, explication deriving from understanding and then evaluation. Perceiving what a poem says and what the poet is attempting to do from the ideas presented and identified within it is a necessity for good criticism. The perception of those ideas in their sequences within a poem written some thousand years ago is often available only to a critic who is immersed in the waves of current thought. Obviously certain ideas linked with the unchanging condition of man are received clearly by the alert modern reader; but in our Old English literature, as we already know, many allusions, references and attitudes need explication, many seemingly illogical sequences of thought need to be tested. Valid evaluation is based on full understanding of the ideas presented in the form and style which the poet has chosen.[5]

We know that it is impossible to turn the time-clock back to the first millennium and be reincarnated in the era of Bede, Alcuin, and Alfred. So we have to live in the world of probability as Cross himself confesses: "Most of our suggestions within the humanities are only probabilities at best and this should encourage us to continue" (5).

I prefer to apply "fuzzy" instead of "probability" to the world of literature and logic because "fuzziness" refers not only to subjectivity but also to objectivity, whereas "probability" refers only to one side of the equation and excludes the other and ignores the essential ambivalence of reality located between the two poles of bivalence, between 0 and 1. When I say "it will probably rain today," I exclude its opposite and ignore the excluded-middle between A and not-A. I can look at an inexact oval and say: "This drawing is probably a circle." My statement ignores that the drawing is also probably an oval. The following example of parking, probable parking, and fuzzy parking given by Bart Kosko is a better illustration of fuzzy sets:

> Say you park your car in a parking lot with 100 painted parking spaces. The probability approach assumes you park in one parking space and each space has some probability that you will park in it....The probability approach assumes parking in a space is a neat and bivalent affair. You park in the space or not, all or none, in or out. A walk through a real parking lot shows otherwise. Cars crowd into narrow spaces and at angles. One car hogs a space and a half and sets a precedent for the cars that follow. To apply the probabil-

ity model we round off and say one car per space.

> Up close things are fuzzy. Borders are inexact and things coexist with
> nonthings. You may park your car 90% in the thirty-fourth space and 10%
> in the space to the right of it, the thirty-fifth space. Then the statement "I
> parked in the thirty-fourth parking space" is not all true and the statement
> "I did not park in the thirty-fourth parking space" is not all false. To a large
> degree you parked in the thirty-fourth space and to a lesser degree you did
> not. To some degree you parked in *all* the spaces. But most of those were
> zero degrees. This claim is fuzzy and yet more accurate. It better approxi-
> mates the "fact" that you parked in the thirty-fourth parking space. (12-13)

Fuzzy logic recognizes the fuzziness of sets to which objects can belong
with various degrees or grades as in the case of the car parked in two spaces.
It is also the case of the part belonging to the whole and the whole in part.
The part cannot contain the whole unless the part is equal to the whole,
but the part contains the whole in direct proportion to its size or mass. In
other words, containment is not whole or none; things are white and black;
East is also West. The real world is fuzzy, so are the concepts we create and
use to deal with fuzzy reality. This means that we cannot precisely describe
objects or processes because they are not amenable to precise definition or
measurement. That means systems are fuzzy and their boundaries are fuzzy,
contrary to the standard set theory which states that an object does or does
not belong in a set. Fuzzy set has objects that belong to several sets to a
degree. All complex systems such as social systems, economic systems,
management systems, decision processes, ethical determinations, human
perception, and linguistic constructs are all fuzzy systems.

In mathematics the fuzzy set theory translates the human thinking process into a mathematical framework for developing computer algorithms
for computerized decision-making processes for process control, medical
diagnosis, engineering design, and so on. Fuzzy theory is increasingly used
with significant results in the world of industry more so in Japan, Europe,
and China than in the United States.[6] Perhaps the most important application of the theory developed in the United States is AT&T's expert system
on a chip by Hiroyuki Watanabe and Masaki Togai who argue that manipu-
lation of information is easier with fuzzy logic because it takes less engineering time to develop applications.[7] Daniel McNeill and Paul Freiberger,
in their book *Fuzzy Logic*, sum up the contribution of fuzzy logic to modern society:

> Fuzzy logic is practical in the highest sense: direct, inexpensive, bountiful. It
> forsakes not precision, but pointless precision. It abandons an either/or hair-
> line that never existed and brightens technology at the cost of a tiny blur. It
> is neither a dream like AI [artificial intelligence] nor a dead end, a little trick

for washers and cameras. It is here today, and no matter what the brand name on the label, it will be here tomorrow.[8]

As for linguistic constructs, take, for example, the word *house*. You can point to certain structures and call them houses without batting an eye. But when it comes to certain dwellings such as castles, trailers, mobile homes, duplexes, condos, teepees, caves, tents, lean-tos, and cardboard boxes, it is a matter of degree. Some are more "houses" than others. "They are to some degree a house and not a house.... So fuzziness holds: The noun *house* stands for a fuzzy set of houses" (122).

As *house* is a fuzzy set, so are terms like *East* and *West* in literary works such as the Bible and *Beowulf*. The uncertainty and fuzziness of these terms result from the very nature of their referents, which are themselves fuzzy. For example, where do we draw the line between East and West, geographically speaking? At the Ural Mountains, the traditional border between Asia and Europe? On the Italian border excluding Greece on whose cultural foundation is the Western civilization supposedly founded? Is Russia in the West? Exclude Turkey from the West because in religion the Turks are Muslims even if it is the homeland of the original Indo-Europeans according to Colin Renfrew? Note that during the cold war period it was fashionable to exclude Russia from the Western world.

As for the people of East and West, the situation is more complex. I live in the Midwest in the heartland of America, the torch-bearer of Western culture. But present-day America is made up of people not only from Europe but from Mexico, South America, Japan, China, Africa, India, Pakistan, Malaysia, and the rest of the East. America is becoming ethnically more diverse than ever. For example, ninety percent of the student population of Baruch College of the City University of New York today is ethnic, namely, of non-European ancestry, as my colleague Wayne Fincke of Baruch College tells me. Where in America can I draw the line between Western and Eastern? In myself? No. In the world of business? No. In the world of letters? No. In the world of entertainment? No. Yes, East is an integral part of America just as much as is West.

In the ancient and medieval world there did not exist such a distinction or dichotomy between East and West. The distinction gradually emerged during Roman times especially after the Empire was divided by Constantine's successors and with the establishment of Byzantium in the fourth century. Political division subsequently caused the division between Eastern Christendom and Western Christendom. East and West were literally one till the fourth century, and the borders continued to be porous even after, as people moved to and fro effortlessly.

From a historical perspective, however, there exists in our culture this contrived artificial dichotomy of bivalence: A and not-A, one excluding the other; either this or not-this. The sky is blue or not blue. Bart Kosko thinks that our opposition to fuzzy logic is derived from Aristotelian logic, which is not true. Aristotelian logic makes a clear distinction between contradictories and contraries, and fuzzy logic deals primarily with the latter. It is rather Reformation logic that opposes fuzzy logic. When Martin Luther and his defiant followers proclaimed the three tenets of Protestantism—*sola scriptura* (faith comes from the Bible alone), *sola fide* (we are saved by faith alone), and *sola gratia* (grace alone, and not works, saves us)—they rejected compromise, the gray area, and fuzzy logic. Traditional Catholic theology, on the other hand, makes distinctions between venial sins and mortal sins and human imperfections; Protestantism rejects such distinctions and proclaims that a human being is either a sinner or a saint. While the medieval church argued for the authority of tradition alongside the authority of the Scripture, Protestantism rejected the authority of tradition. It is this kind of uncompromising but pragmatic and powerful dichotomization that gave birth to modern science and the triumph of capitalism and the colonization of the Eastern world by the West. It was also the Reformation logic that gave rise to the unabashed opposition between East and West in the political imagination of the West rather than the logic of Aristotle.

The truth is that East and West are not contradictories like the notorious square circle, but rather they are like an oval circle, which is not quite an oval nor quite a circle, but both. East and West are fuzzy sets or the contraries of Aristotelian logic. As contraries or fuzzy sets, they embody opposition as well as complementarity. In other words, *contraria sunt complementaria*. We can illustrate this relationship between East and West by comparing it to the phenomenon of light. Does light consist of particles or waves? Although it may appear that the two descriptions of light as particle and wave are mutually exclusive, the fact is that light behaves both as particle and as wave when observed and measured experimentally. Niels Bohr showed that these two contrary forms of behavior are not mutually exclusive but complementing contraries.

Similarly and subsequently, theoretically speaking, there are no two disparate standard sets called Western literature and Eastern literature, Western classics and Eastern classics, Western Christendom and Eastern Christendom, which are but convenient political divisions inspired by ambitions of empowerment at the price of enslavement. But, practically speaking, there do exist two fuzzy sets called Eastern and Western, amenable to each other and permeating each other, then as now in varying degrees and proportions.

NOTES

1. L. A. Zadeh, "Fuzzy Sets," *Information and Control* 8 (1965): 338-53; *Fuzzy Sets and Applications: Selected Papers*, edited by Yager, Ovchnikov, et al. (New York, 1987); Bart Kosko, *Fuzzy Thinking: The New Science of Fuzzy Logic* (New York, 1993), *passim*—an excellent, clearly written book with a good bibliography; I am indebted to some of the ideas expressed in this book. I am grateful to my brilliant colleague R. Bharath for bringing this work to my attention as well as for the many discussions we have had on fuzzy logic.

2. In bivalent logic, every statement is true or false or has the truth value 1 or 0. Alfred N. Whitehead and Bertrand Russell have shown that most mathematics relies on bivalent logic, and it is this logic that we use in computer technology.

3. The issue of defining Indians as Caucasians has an interesting history. In two cases, U.S. v. Balsara in 1910 and re Ajhoy Kumar Mazumdar in 1913, the lower Federal courts had held that Indians were Caucasians and qualified under naturalization legislation of 1790 and 1875 as "white persons." In 1923, however, the Supreme Court ruled in U.S. v. Bhagat Singh Thind, that East Indians were not Caucasian. It argued that in the "understanding of the common man" East Indians were not Caucasians. The unanimous decision was that "white" be determined according to the "common understanding" of the term and not the anthropological or other definition, and white would include only people of European descent. Nonetheless, U. S. census seemed to have included Indians as part of the Caucasian group right up to 1980. Since then, because some Indians preferred a minority status category for the purpose of securing special quotas in the Small Business Administration contracts etc., INS and other bodies have a new category "Asian or Pacific Islander." But the dictionary definition based on anthropolgy still includes Indians, Europeans, Neareasterners, and North Africans in the category of "Caucasoids" (*Webster's New World Dictionary*, Second College Edition). The old category of "mulatto" (part white and part black) disappeared from the census in 1920 but is now making a comeback under a new name , the "multi-racial." With the gradual disappearance of affirmative action programs, it is likely that some minorities are likely to give up their minority status since minority status no longer holds any distinctive political or economic advantages.

4. Zacharias P. Thundy, *Buddha and Christ: Nativity Stories and Indian Traditions* (Leiden, 1993).

5. J. E. Cross, *The Literate Anglo-Saxon—on Sources and Disseminations* (London, 1972), pp. 10-11.

6. See Kosko, *passim.*

7. See "Lotfi Asker Zadeh," in *Notable Twentieth Century Scientists* (New York, 1996), p. 2286; I agree with this assessment because my own study of medieval Western literature in the context of the East is more enlightening and more fruitful than a narrow close reading of the so-called Western text.

8. Cited by *Notable Twentieth-Century Scientists*, p. 2286.

Wulfstan: "Apocalypse Now! Antichrist Is Here Among Us!"

Archbishop Wulfstan preached the following three sermons on the end of the world, on Antichrist, and ON Antichrist's times around the year 1000.[1]

1. Sermo Lupi ad Anglos

Know this for a truth, my dear people: This world is moving fast toward to its preordained end. The longer we live, the worse it gets on earth. It is all on account of our sins, and it shall get still worse before Antichrist's coming, when there shall indeed be a grim and terrible time all over the world.

It is important to know that the devil has led this nation astray for years on end to the point that there remains little trust among the people as they engage in deceptive speech; indeed, too many lies run rampant on the land. Alas, there aren't many among them who have sought for a cure for the nation's ills. Instead, they themselves have added more guilt to the nation's guilt, committed many sins and crimes throughout the entire land. On that account, we have endured many sufferings and insults. Therefore, if we expect any respite at all, then we have to earn it, more deservedly than we have done before now. In fact, we deserve all the miseries that beset us on account of our own evil deeds; now if our situation is to improve at all, we must request the remedy from God by our performance of many more good deeds. Of course, we know very well that a wide breach needs much repair work, and a great fire requires much water to be put out. Therefore, henceforth it is the bounden duty of every human being to observe God's law earnestly and fulfill His ordinances faithfully.

Among heathen nations one dare not disregard not only the greater laws but also the lesser ones that pertain to the worship of false gods, but we too frequently disregard the greater laws of the true God. Among the heathen peoples, no one may dare take away any part of anything brought to the idols or offered in sacrifice to them, but we have despoiled God's house inside and out. God's servants are everywhere deprived of honor and protection. Among pagans no one may dare ill-treat the priests of idols in any manner, as one treats the servants of God widely, whereas Christians ought to uphold God's laws and protect God's ministers.

I tell you the truth: It is imperative to find a remedy inasmuch as God's laws have been flouted too long in the midst of this nation in every direction ; civil and ecclesiastical laws have been broken all too often; sanctuaries have been violated everywhere; the houses of God have been deprived of their possessions and stripped inside of all valuables. Widows have been forced into unlawful marriages and many reduced to poverty and greatly humiliated. The poor are sorely deceived and cruelly defrauded and sold unjustly into slavery far away from this land to foreign masters; children in the cradle also are turned into slaves for petty theft through the harshness of unjust laws throughout the land. Freemen are deprived of their rights, the rights of slaves are curtailed, and charitable obligations are restricted. In short, God's laws are detested and His teachings despised. On account of all this, through God's wrath we suffer the present disgrace. Let him understand who can: this calamity will infect the entire nation, no matter what one may think, unless God protect us.

Therefore, it is plain and clear to us all that we have committed more transgressions than we have amended for; that is why this people suffer so much. Hard times have befallen us for so long at home and abroad, and thus there have been wars and famine, arson and bloodshed in every region over and again; thefts and murders, pestilence and strifes, plague and disease, hatred and malice; raiders' depredations have injured us immensely; unjust taxes have hurt us much; bad weather has hurt our crops. Thus it seems that for a number of years there has been on this land and among its people much crime and uncertain loyalty. Now kinsmen do not protect kinsmen any more than a foreigner, nor father his son, nor the son his own father, nor brother his own brother, nor do we lead our lives as we should, nor do the monks live according to their rules, nor the lay folk in accordance with the civil law. The pursuit of pleasure has become a law unto us all too often that we have followed neither the laws and precepts of God nor of man as we should. One does not hold honest intentions toward the other as one should, and almost everyone has deceived and injured the other in word and deed. Indeed, most people stab one another in the back in shameful attacks and would do more if only they could.

Here in this country there lurk many plots against God and the state, and there are traitors of many hues and colors in this country. The worst form of treachery is that one should betray his lord's soul by persuading him to commit sin. Indeed, it is the greatest treason in this world that one should slay his master or banish his living lord from his country. In fact, both these crimes have been committed in this country. Some plotted against Edward, then murdered him, and afterwards burned his body; they also banished Aethelred from his home. They have massacred far too many godparents and godchildren of this nation. Too many holy houses perished because of certain unworthy men who were put in charge of them and who should never have been if we are to honor God's sanctuaries. Too many Christian people are still being exiled from this country. All this is hateful to God. You must believe it.

Scandalous it is to repeat what is only known too well, and horrifying it is to hear about what many still do often—the crimes people commit. Several men contribute money and buy a woman together as common property and perform foul deeds with her one after another and each on the other, just like dogs which don't care about filth, and then sell overseas to the enemies this creature of God, whom God had bought at a great price. We also know too well where the following crimes were committed: a father sold his son, a son his mother, a man his brother into the power of strangers. These are horrible crimes! Understand whoso will.

And yet there are many more manifold crimes that undermine this nation. Many are forsworn and perjured; pledges are broken all too often, and it is manifest among this people that God's anger is upon us. Understand this whoso can.

Lo and behold, is it possible that greater shame befall this nation through God's wrath than has already happened to us on account of our evil deeds? It happens all too often that a slave runs away from his master and away from Christian territory and become a Viking, and after that it happens that there takes place an armed conflict between the thane and the thrall, and if the slave slays the thane, no wergild is paid to his kinsmen. But if the thane slays his former slave, he is bound to pay thanegild. Such foul laws and shameful forced payments are found among us because God's just anger permits them to happen. Understand whoso can.

Many misfortunes have befallen this nation often and again. It has not gone well now with us for a long while, here or abroad, but malicious destruction has been inflicted on us in every district over and again. And the English have been without victory and in utter despair through God's anger. Vikings are so strong with God's permission that in battle one Viking puts to flight ten of us, sometimes fewer but other times even more, all again on account of our sins. Often ten or twelve of them, one after another, violate the honor and virtue of a thane's wife, sometimes that of his daughter, and sometimes that of his nearest kinswoman, while he, who considered himself brave, strong, and mighty before that happened looks on helplessly. Often a thrall binds fast the thane who was his master before and makes him a slave, again because of God's ire. Often two Vikings, or sometimes three, chase droves of Christians in fetters from sea to sea, then through this land, to the public shame of all of us, as though we had really any sense of shame left at all. We return worship for insults as they continue to dishonor us. We honor them without ceasing while they humiliate us on a daily basis. They ravage and burn; they steal and rob us and load their ships with their booty. Lo, in the midst of all these calamities what else other than God's anger is clear and visible over this nation?

It is no wonder then that misfortune is our lot because we know very well that for many years people have paid little attention to what they did in word and deed, but these people, as it appears, have become corrupt through sins of all kinds and through many evil deeds: through murders, through assaults, through covetousness, through greed, through theft, through robbery, through slave trade, through dealings with heathens, through betrayals, through deceptions, through the breaches of law, through deceits, through assaults on kinsmen, through manslaughter, through attacks on the clergy, through oath-breaking, through adultery, through incest, and through many falsehoods. We have often failed to observe fasts and feasts of saints. Also here in this country there are many abominable apostates and fierce persecutors of the Church, too many terrible tyrants, arrogant scoffers of God's law and Christian customs. Everywhere in this country there are fools who ridicule the admonitions of God's ministers, especially those that are commanded by God's law. Now the evil custom is in vogue far and wide that people are more ashamed of good deeds than are proud of them, for very often people scorn good deeds derisively and blame godfearing folks without restraint, and they treat with contempt especially those who happen to love righteousness and entertain fear of God. Because some people behave thus, it happens that they scorn what they should praise and loathe much what they should love; thus they reduce many things to bad intentions and wrong deeds so that they do not feel guilty even though they sin grievously and offend God seriously in all this; but because of the inane fear of slander, they are ashamed to atone for their misdeeds, as the books teach, like those fools who for pride refuse to guard themselves against harm, against their own will, until they become totally helpless.

Here in this country too many suffer from too much guilt. Here there are man-slayers and kinslayers, slayers of priests and haters of convents; here there are perjurers and murderers; here there are whores and infanticides; here there are wizards witches; here there are plunderers, robbers, and burglars; in short, we suffer from too many evil deeds and countless crimes. And, worst of all, we don't feel guilty about them either.

We are greatly ashamed even to begin to make amends for our sins, as the books teach us, and that appears to be the real problem with this wretched, sinful people. Alas, many may be able to call to mind easily, besides what one man could not quickly recall, how wretchedly has this nation fared all this while. Let us, therefore, examine ourselves sincerely and avoid procrastinating. But lo, in God's name, let us do what is necessary and save ourselves as earnestly as we can lest we all perish together.

During British times there lived a historian called Gildas who wrote about the misdeeds of the Britons, how on account of their sins they had made God so angry that at long last He permitted the English army to conquer their land and destroy the British army completely. That happened, as he says, through the depredations of the British rulers, through their jealous possessiveness of wrongly acquired treasures, through the lawlessness of the British nation, through the abuses of justice, through the sloth of the bishops, through the cowardice of God's ministers who remained silent too often and mumbled with their jaws instead of speaking aloud. Through the foul corruption of the British people, through gluttony, and through their many sins, they destroyed their country and perished themselves. But let us do what is needful and be forewarned by their example.

I tell you truly: we see more grievous sins among the English people than we have heard about existed in the British nation. Therefore, it is urgent that we examine our conscience and intercede earnestly with God. Let us do what is necessary for ourselves and turn to the path of righteousness and in full measure avoid evil and atone zealously for our sins. Let us love God and follow God's laws; let us fulfill earnestly the promises we have made at baptism or those promises our godparents have made for us. Let us choose our words and do our deeds correctly, purify our thoughts assiduously, fulfill oaths and pledges faithfully, and uphold trust among us truthfully. Let us often call to mind the great Day of Judgment that we will be called to and protect ourselves against the raging fire of hell and earn for ourselves the glories and joys which God has prepared for those who do His will on earth. God help us. Amen.

2. The Times of Antichrist

My dear people, it is very important that we come aware of the dangerous days that are at hand. Now Antichrist's time is fast approaching; we
must understand and realize well that it is the most frightening time that
ever will be since the creation of the world. Antichrist is devil incarnate
even though he may appear as a member of the human race. Christ, on the
contrary, is true God and true man, but Antichrist is true devil and true
man. Through Christ came help and healing for all on earth; through Antichrist comes the greatest terror and the most dreadful danger that will
ever happen on earth. And all mankind would perish forthwith had not
God shortened his days. But God had shortened Antichrist's days for the
sake of those whom He had elected and whom He wants to keep as His
own. During the period of his reign, Antichrist will commit more crimes
than have been committed ever before. He will tempt every one to aban-
don the Christian faith, and he will lure the faithful into his heresy if he can.
God will allow him to try to do so for a brief period of time for two reasons.
One is that, since all humans seem to be in the state of sin, it is only fitting
that the devil should openly test them to find out the bad ones who will
follow him. The second reason is that God wills that those who are truly
faithful may persevere in the true religion and resolutely withstand the devil.
He wills that they be promptly tested and purified from their sins by means
of the great persecution and subsequent martyrdom they shall undergo.
Consequently, all sinners shall receive as their due the severe punishment
which their sins deserve either here or elsewhere. Since persecution will
be very hard on the elect, they have to be quickly cleansed and purified
before the coming of the great Judgment. Those who have been dead a
hundred years or more, may already have been purified. We, on out part,
need to suffer very much if we should come clean before Doomsday because we do not have the same advantages that those who were before us
had. Let one and all take heed if they will; not one of us will enter the
kingdom of God before we are cleansed of every vestige of sin just as gold
becomes bright and clear only after purification.

My dear people, God permits the devil Antichrist to persecute good
people in order that they be purified through persecution and then be ushered into the heavenly kingdom. Of course, Antichrist will spare here on
earth those who trust in his lies and worship him, but soon after they will
be damned forever and dwell with him in the depths of dark hell. The
incarnate cunning devil will perform many wonders and will claim that he
is God himself and by his shifting shapes he will deceive many people. He
will force, if he can, those whom he is unable to persuade to reject God to

worship him. If they refuse to follow his behests, they will have to endure
much persecution and suffer a wretched death as well. Blessed, however,
are those who resolutely persevere to the end without slackening; indeed,
by God's grace Antichrist will not be able to deceive them either through
his cunning artifices or through the horrors he besieges mankind with.

Our Lord Jesus Christ healed many who were sick; Antichrist will bring
harm and injury on many who were whole before. Antichrist will be able
to heal only those whom he himself has injured. After he has hurt people,
then he can offer them his healing provided he has been able to deceive
them by leading them to commit sins. He is full of all kinds of evil designs.
After he has deceived too many people thus, he will secretly injure them so
that he may heal them in sight of the public as they watch. The public will
see what he does without realizing what he has done before. Every imag-
inable sin he can commit he will. He will call down fire from above as
though from heaven. With that he will burn down many things as he had
done earlier within the household of Job. Those who for fear of this fire
will turn to him will abide in hell fire for ever. Neither I nor anyone else
can describe the terror that the devil will afflict the earth with. Therefore,
we must beseech God that He shield us against the terror and strengthen us
with His grace.

It is the devil from hell who will appear as the wretched Antichrist, and
truly he is devil and man. He will oppress all mankind openly and deceive
many more than ever before. It is, therefore, imperative that we become
acutely aware of this crisis and admonish those who are ignorant of what is
at hand because that end time which the ignorant are unwilling pay attention to is very near. It is all too evident that in this world things are going
from bad to worse day by day. I can also assert truthfully that the devil, if he
can, will hinder our mind from understanding what we have heard from
and what we have been warned against by the Lord. Thus most people will
be so badly deceived that they will become foolish and unprepared.

Human beings will not be able to survive these days unless God watches
over them and unless they, forewarned, change their ways for the better so
that they may not fall into the snares of the devil. Let us admonish one
another. Pray God to protect us. Let us have steadfast hope and firm faith
in God. Indeed, we deserve to endure much persecution and suffer much
hardship unless we wake up; then, if we persevere in the practice of true
faith and reject heathen worship, God will grant us eternal rest. In God's
name I pray that each Christian think earnestly on God, eagerly turn toward Him, turn away from all heathenism and sins, and become privileged
to enjoy the fellowship of saints in the heavenly kingdom with Him who

lives and reigns world without end. Amen.

3. Antichrist

Everyone who does not live according to the dictates of the Christian religion or teaches contrary to the Christian doctrines is Antichrist by virtue of the meaning of the name. He is called Antichrist because he is opposed to Christ. Of course, many will not witness the times of Antichrist, but yet they are often members of the body of Antichrist, as we read in the Gospel, for false christs and false prophets will arise and perform great signs so that they may lead even the elect into error if it be feasible.

When the Lord said "if it be feasible" as if expressing doubts, understand that He who knows past and future has no doubts about any thing at all; rather it is not feasible in the case of the elect. In the case of those who are not the elect, it is possible and feasible to seduce them. The Lord says it is feasible because people will tremble on account of the numerous signs of the times; if they do not falter and waver in their faith, they are indeed the elect. For then there shall be troubles and suffering such as had never been from the creation of the human race till that time. Unless those days are shortened, no one will be saved; but those days will be shortened on account of the elect so that they may not be led astray.

The time of Antichrist will last three-and-a-half years, as attested by the Scriptures. Antichrist and his minions will walk roughshod all over the Holy City, that is, the Holy Church. At that time Enoch and Elijah will appear, as it is written: "I will give unto my two witnesses etc." (Apoc. 11:3). And the Beast that will ascend from the abyss will overcome them and slay them, and their bodies will lie unburied in the streets of the City, which in the spiritual sense is called Sodom and Egypt, where the Lord was crucified; that is, that Jerusalem which was formerly the Holy City but afterwards called Sodom and Egypt on account its sins and heresy.

Everyone, therefore, who is a teacher in the Church, should admonish the people about those times, for, as it is written, the last days will be menacing times. When those dangerous days come, may He find the faithful people ready and may they, always instructed enlightened against that enemy, the ancient serpent and Satan, be prepared to resist him. Terrible persecution will there be in the Church in those days that, as the Lord had predicted, brother will betray brother unto death and father will betray his own son, and children will rise up against their own parents and they will harbor hatred against one another. Then many will become prey to scandals and become infidels on account of the great signs and on account of the severity of punishments and torments which will be inflicted on Christians by Antichrist and his hosts who will persecute them throughout the whole wide world. However, as it is written, those who persevere till the end will find salvation. The wise will then shine like stars in the sky and those who instruct the many faithful will also shine like the well-lit sky for all eternity.

It is necessary, therefore, that priests and all those who study the Sacred Scriptures instruct those who are unaware of this grave danger so that they may deserve a double reward for themselves and their audience and that none may perish due to ignorance. It is quite possible that many may not be immediate witnesses to this danger; however, because the preachers instruct all the faithful, may Antichrist, the Son of Perdition, when he comes, find Christians capable of resisting him and his minions. Amen.

May God shield us against that terror and lead us into eternal bliss which has been prepared for those who do His will. And that bliss will last world without end. Amen.

NOTES

1. The following three eschatological sermons by Archbishop Wulfstan are illustrative of the popular views on the end times and Antichrist, the precursor of the last days. The first sermon called *Sermo Lupi ad Anglos* was preached in the year 1013; the second and third sermon were preached about the beginning of the second millennium. The translations are mine. See Dorothy Bethuram, *Homilies of Wulfstan* (Oxford, 1957).

Bibliography

Alcuin. *Commentaria in Apocalipsin. PL 100* cols. 1085-1164.

Alexander, Paul J. *The Byzantine Apocalyptic Tradition*. Berkeley: University of California Press, 1985.

————."Byzantium and the Migration of Literary Works and Motifs: The Legend of the last Roman Emperor." *Medievalia et Humanistica* 2 (1971): 47-82.

————."Medieval Apocalypses as historical Sources," American Historical Review 73 (1968): 1997-2018.

————. *The Oracle of Baalbek: The Tiburtine Sibyl in Greek Dress.* Washington, DC: Dumbarton Oaks, 1967.

Alter, Robert and Frank Kermode. *The Literary Guide to the Bible*. Cambridge: Cambridge University Press, 1987.

The Anglo-Saxon Chronicle. Trans. G. N. Garrnonsway. 2nd ed., rev. Everyman's Library 624. London: Dent, 1960.

Asin-Palacios, *Islam and the Divine Comedy*, trans. Harold Sutherland. London: Frank Cass, 1968.

Aznar, Jose Carnon. "Art in the Beatos and the Codex of Gerona. *Beati in Apocalypsin Libri Duodecim*. Madrid: Editoria Internacional de Libros Antiguous, Edilan, S.A., 1975.

Babcock, William S., trans. *Tyconius: The Book of Rules*. Society of Bible Literature. Texts and Translations 31. Early Christian Literature Series 7. Atlanta, GA: Scholars Press, 1989.

Bailey, Richard N. *Viking Age Sculpture in Northern England*. London: Collins, 1980.

Baldwin, Edward C. *The Prophets*. New York: Thomas Nelson & Sons, 1927.

Barclay, William. "Great Themes of the new Testament." *Expository Times*, 70 (1958-9): 260-5.

Barnstone, William. *The Other Bible*. San Francisco: Harper, 1984.

Bately, Janet. "Linguistic Evidence as a Guide to the Authorship of Old English Verse: A Reappraisal, With Special Reference to *Beowulf*." Lapidge and Gneuss, 409-31.

Bede. *Bede's Ecclesiastical History of the English Church and People*. Eds. Bertram Colgrave and R.A.B. Mynors. Oxford Medieval Texts. Oxford: Clarendon, 1969.

——. *De Quindecem signis* (col. 555). PL 94 cols. 539-60.

——. *Explanatio Apocalypsis. PL* 93 cols 129-206. Trans. Edward Marshall. *The Explanation of the Apocalypse.* Oxford: James Parkes, 1959.

Benson, Larry D. The Pagan Coloring of *Beowulf. Old English Poetry: Fifteen Essays.* Ed. Robert P. Creed. Providence, RI: Brown University Press, 1967. 193-213.

Beowulf and the Fight at Finnsburg. 3rd ed. Ed. C. L. Wrenn, rev. W. F. Bolton. London: Harrap, 1973.

Berg, Knut. "The Gosforth Cross. *Journal of the Warburg and Courtald Institutes* 21 (1958): 27-43.

Berger, Harry, Jr., and H. Marshall Leicester, Jr. "Social Structure as Doom: The Limits of Heroism in *Beowulf*." Old *English Studies in Honor of John C. Pope.* Eds. R. B. Burlin and Edward B. Irving Jr. Toronto and Buffalo: University of Toronto Press, 1974: 37-79.

Bethuram, Dorothy. *The Homilies of Wulfstan.* Oxford: Clarendon, 1957.

Bestul, Thomas H. "Continental Sources of Anglo-Saxon Devotional Writing." Szarmach 103-26.

——. "Ephraim the Syrian and old English Poetry." *Anglia* 99 (1981): 1-24.

Biblia Sacra: Iuxta Vulgatam Versionem. Ed. Bonifatio Fischer *et al.* Stuttgart: Wurttembergishche Bibelanstalt, 1969.

Birnbaum, Henrik and Jaan Puhvel. *Ancient Indo-European Dialects.* Berkeley: University of California Press, 1966.

Blackburn, F. A. "The Christian Coloring of *Beowulf*." *PMLA* 12 (1897): 205-25. Rpt. in Nicholson 1-21.

Blair, Peter Hunter. *An Introduction to Anglo-Saxon England.* 2nd ed. Cambridge: Cambridge University Press, 1977.

Bodden, Mary Catherine. "The Preservation and Transmission of Greek in Early England." Szarmach 53-64.

Bousset, Wilhelm. *The Antichrist Legend.* London: Hutchinson, 1896.

Boyce, Mary. *A History of Zoroastrianism* I: The Early Period. Leyden: E. J. Brill, 1975.

Breeze, Andrew. "The Transmission of Aldhelm's Writings in Early Medieval Spain." *Anglo-Saxon England* 21 (1992): 5-22.

Brock, Sebastian. "The Syriac Background." pp. 30-52. In *Archbishop Theodore,* ed. M. Lapidge. Cambridge: Cambridge University Press, 1995.

Burkitt, F. C., ed. *The Book of Rules of Tyconius.* Cambridge, 1894.

Butt, Wolfgang. "Zur Herkunfft der Voluspá." *Beitrage zur Geschichte der deutschen Sprache und Literatur Tübingen. 91 (1969):* 82-103.

Cabaniss. Allen. *"Beowulf* and the Liturgy." *JEGP* 54 (1955): 195-201. Rpt. in Nicholson 221-32.

Caie, Graham D. *The Judgment Day Theme in Old English Poetry.* Publications of the Department of English, University of Copenhagen 2. Copenhagen: Nova, 1976.

Calder, D. G. ed. *Sources and Analogues of Old English Poetry: 11 The Major Germanic and Celtic Texts in Translation.* Cambridge: D. S Brewer; Totowa, NJ: Barnes and Noble, 1983.

Caspari, C. P. *Briefe, Abhandlungen, und Predigten aus dem zwei letzten Jahrhunderten des kirclicher Altertums und dem Anfang des Mittelalters.* 1890; rept. Brussels: Culture and Civilisation, 1964.

Chambers, R.W. *Beowulf: An Introduction.* Cambridge: University Press, 1967.

———. *Widsith: A Study in Old English Heroic Legend.* New York: Oxford University Press, 1965.

Chance, Jane. *Woman as Hero in Old English Literature.* Syracuse: Syracuse University Press, 1986.

Chase, Colin, ed. *The Dating of Beowulf.* Toronto Old English series 6. Toronto: The Centre for Medieval Studies, University of Toronto Press, 1981.

Clark, George. *Beowulf.* Twayne's English Authors Series 477. Ed. George D. Economou. Boston: Twayne, 1990.

Cohn, Norman. *The Pursuit of the Millenium.* 3rd. ed. New York: Oxford University Press, 1970.

Collingwood, R. G. and J. N. L. Myers. *Roman Britain and English Settlements.* London: Oxford University Press, 1936.

Collins, Adela Y. "The Early Christian Apocalypses." *Semeia* 14 (1979): 61-121.

———. "Oppression from Without: The Symbolization of Rome as Evil in Early Christianity." *Concilium* 200 (1988): 66-74.

Collins, John J. "Apocalypse." *The Encyclopedia of Religion.* Vol. 1. Ed. Mircea Eliade. New York: Macmillan; London: Collier Macmillan, 1987. 334-6.

———. "Introduction: Toward the Morphology of a Genre." *Apocalypse: The Morphology of a Genre. Semeia* 14 (1979). 1-20.

Crawford, S. J. "Grendel's Descent from Cain." *Modern Language Review* 23 (1928): 207-08.

Cróinin, O. "Rath Melsigi, Willibrord, and the Earliest Echternach Manuscripts." *Peritia* 3 (1984): 1-36.

Cross, James E. *The Literate Anglo-Saxon—On sources and Disseminations.* Proceedings of the British Academy. London: Oxford University Press, 1972.

Damico, Helen. *Beowulf's Wealhtheow and the Valkyrie Tradition.* Madison: University of Wisconsin Press, 1984.

Daniélou, Jean. *The Origin of Latin Christianity.* Chicago: Regnery, 1977.

Dark, K. R. *Civitas to Kingdom: British Political Continuity 300-800.* Leicester: Leicester University Press, 1994.

Donahue, Charles. "*Beowulf* and Christian Tradition." *Traditio* 21 (1965): 55-116.

Dresher, Bezalel. *Old English and Theory of Phonology.* New York: Garland, 1985.

Dronke, Ursula. "*Beowulf* and Ragnarök." *Saga Book of the Viking Society* 17 (1969): 302-25.

Earl, James W. (1982): "Apocalypticism and Mourning in *Beowulf.*" *Thought* 57 (1982): 362-70.

———. *Thinking About Beowulf.* Stanford: Stanford University Press, 1994.

Edda Snorra Sturlusonar undivet efter handshrifterne. Ed. Finnur Jonsson. Copenhagen: Gyldendal, 1931.

Emmerson, Richard K. *Antichrist in the Middle Ages: A Study of Medieval*

Apocalypticism, Art, and Literature. Seattle: University of Washington Press, 1981.

———. "The Prophetic, the Apocalyptic, and the Study of Medieval Literature. Wojcik and Frontain 40-54, 190-94.

Emmerson, Richard K., and Ronald Henman. *The Apocalyptic Imagination in Medieval Literature.* University of Pennsylvania Press, 1992.

Emmerson, Richard K and Bernard McGinn. eds. The *Apocalypse in the Middle Ages.* Ithaca: Cornell, 1992.

Enslin, Morton S. "The Apocalyptic Literature." Laymon 1106-9.

Fernandez-Armesto, Félipe. *Millennium: A History of the Last Thousand years.* New York: Scribner's, 1995.

Focillon, Henri. *The year 1000.* Trans. Fred D. Wieck. New York: Frederick Ungar, 1969.

Ford, Josephine. Trans. The Revelation of John. Anchor Bible. New York, 1975.

Fredriksen, Paula. "Tyconius and Augustine on the Apocalypse." In Emmerson and McGinn 20-37.

Gang, T. M. "Approaches *to Beowulf.*" *Review of English Studies n.s. 3* (1952): 1-12.

Garmonsway, G. N. and Jacqueline Simpson. *Beowulf and Its Analogues.* New York: E. P. Dutton, 1971.

Gatch, Milton McC. "Eschatology in the Anonymous Old English Homilies." *Trad- tio* 21 (1965): 117-65.

———. *Loyalties and Traditions: Man and His World in Old English Literature.* Pegasus Backgrounds in English Literature. New York: Bobbs-Merrill, 1971.

———. "Perceptions of Eternity." *The Cambridge Companion to Old English Literature.* Ed. Malcolm Godden and Michael Lapidge. Cambridge: Cambridge University Press, 1991. 190-205.

———. *Preaching and Theology in Anglo-Saxon England: Aelfric and Wulfstan.* Toronto and Buffalo: University of Toronto Press, 1977.

Gilmour, S. MacLean. "The Revelation to John." Laymon 945-68.

Gneuss, Helmut. "A Preliminary List of Manuscripts Written or Owned in England up to 1100." *Anglo-Saxon England* 9 (1981): 1-60.

Godden, Malcolm and Michael Lapidge. ed. *Cambridge Companion to Old English Literature.* Cambridge: Cambridge University Press, 1991.

Goldsmith, Margaret E. "The Christian Perspective in *Beowulf.*" *Comparative Literature* 14 (1962): 71-80.

———. *The Mode and Meaning of Beowulf.* London: Athlone Press, 1970.

Green, Martin. "Man, Time, and Apocalypse in *The Wanderer, The Seafarer,* and *Beowulf. JEGP* 74 (1975): 502-18.

Greenfield, Stanley. "Beowulf and the Judgment of the Righteous." Lapidge and Gneuss 393-407.

Hamilton, Marie Padgett. "The Religious Principle in Beowulf." *PMLA 61* (1946): 309-31.

Hanson, Paul D. "Prolegomena to the Study of Ewish Apocalyptic." In *Magnalia Dei: The Mighty Acts of God,* ed. F. M. Cross et al. Philadelphia: Fortress, 1976.

———. Introduction. *Visionaries and Their Apocalypses.* Ed. Paul D. Hanson. Issues in Religion and Theology 2. Philadelphia, PA: Fortress Press, 1983.

Healey, Antonette di Paolo, ed. *The Old English Vision of St. Paul.* Speculum Anniversary Monographs 2. Cambridge, MA: The Medieval Academy of America, 1978.

Hennecke, E. and W. Schneemelcher. *New Testament Apocrypha.* Philadelphia: Westminster, 1964.

Hieatt, Constance B. "Envelope Patterns and the Structure of *Beowulf.*" *English Studies in Canada* 1 (1975): 249-65.

Higham, N.J. *The English Conquest: Gildas and Britain in the Fifth Century.* Manchester: Manchester University Press, 1994.

Hillgarth, J. N. "The East, Visigothic Spain, and the Irish." *Studia Patristica* 4 (1959): 442-56.

Hodges, Richard. *The Anglo-Saxon Achievement.* Ithaca: Cornell University Press, 1989.

Hodges, Richard and David Whitehouse. *Mohammed, Charlemagne, and the Origins of Europe.* Ithaca: Cornell University Press, 1983.

Holder-Egger, O. "Italienische Prophetieen des 13 Jahrhunderts." *Neues Archiv der Gesellschaft für ältere Deutsche Geschichtskunde* (1890), 15: 143-78; (1905), 30: 322-86; (1908), 33: 96-187.

Hollander, Lee M., trans. *The Poetic Edda.* 2nd ed. Austin: University of Texas Press, 1962.

The Holy Bible. Douay Version, 1609. New York: P.J. Kennedy & Sons, 1914.

Hopper, Vincent F. *Beowulf Together with Widsith and the Fight at Finnsburh.* New York: Barron's Educational Series, 1962.

Howlett, David R. "Biblical Style in Early Insular Latin," in *Sources of Anglo-Saxon Culture.* ed. Paul E. Szarmach. Kalamazoo: Western Michigan University Press, 1986.

———. "Form and Genre in *Beowulf.*" *Studia Neophilologica* 46 (1974): 309-25.

Hughes, Shaun F. D. "Voluspa." *Dictionary of the Middle Ages.* Ed: in-chief Joseph R. Strayer. 12 vols. New York: Scribner's, 1982-89. 12 (1989): 491 -92.

Hume, Kathryn. "The Theme and Structure of *Beowulf.*" *Studies in Philology* 72 (1975): 1-27.

Huppé, Bernard. *Doctrine and Poetry: Augustine's Influence on Old English Poetry.* Albany, SUNY Press, 1959.

Irving, Edward. B. *A Reading of Beowulf.* New Haven: Yale University Press, 1968.

Irving, Edward B. Jr. "The Nature of Christianity in Beowulf." *Anglo-Saxon England* 13 (1984): 7-21.

James, M. R. *Apocryphal New Testament.* London: Oxford University Press, 1924.

James, Montague R. *Apocrypha Anecdotal.* Texts and Studies 2, No. 3. Cambridge: 1893. 11-42.

Jonsson, Finnur. *Edda Snorra Sturlusonar.* Copenhagen, 1931.

Jordan, Louis. Demonic Elements in Anglo-Saxon Art," in Szarmach 261-82.

Kaske, Robert E. "*Sapientia et fortitudo* as the Controlling Theme of *Beowulf.*" *Studies in Philology* 55 (1958): 423-57.

Kasemann, Ernst. "The Beginnings of Christian Theology." Apocalypticism. *Journal for Theology and the Church 6*. Ed. R. W. Funk. [n.p.]: Herder and Herder, 1969

Keenan, Hugh T. *The Apocalyptic Vision in Old English Poetry.* Diss. University of Tennessee 1968. Ann Arbor, University of Michigan Press, 1969.

Kerrigan, William. *The Prophetic Milton.* Charlottesville, VA: University of Virginia Press, 1974.

Kermode, Frank. *The Sense of an Ending: Studies in the Theory of Fiction.* New York: Oxford University Press, 1966.

Kiessling, Nicolas K. New *Aspects of the Monsters in Beowulf.* Diss. University of Wisconsin 1967. 67-12, 439. Ann Arbor, University of Michigan, 1968.

Kiernan, Kevin. *Beowulf and Beowulf Manuscript.* New Brunswick: Rutgers University Press, 1981.

———. "The Eleventh-Century Origin of *Beowulf* and the *Beowulf* Manuscript." Chase, *Dating* 9-22.

Kirby, W. F. "The Voluspa, the Sybil's Lay in the Edda of Saemund." *Saga-book of the Viking Society* 8 (1912-13): 44-52.

Klaeber, Fr., ed. *Beowulf and the Fight at Finnsburg.* 3rd ed. Boston: D. C. Heath, 1950.

Klaeber, Fr. "Die Christlichen Elemente in *Beowulf.*" *Anglia* 35 (1911-12): 111-36, 249-70, 453-82: (1912): 169-99.

Klein, Peter. "Introduction: The Apocalypse in Art." In Emmerson and McGinn 159-99.

Klimkeit, Hans-Joachim. *Gnosis on the Silk Road: Gnostic Texts from Central Asia.* San Francisco: Harper, 1992.

Koch, Klaus. *The Prophets.* Philadelphia, PA: Fortress, 1982.

———. *The Rediscovery of the Apocalyptic.* Studies in Biblical theology, 2nd ser., vol. 22. Naperville: Allenson, 1970.

Kosko, Bart. *Fuzzy Thinking: The New Science of Fuzzy Logic.* New York: Hyperion, 1993.

Krapp, G. P., and E. V. D. Dobbie. *The Anglo-Saron Poetic Records.* 6 vols. New York: Columbia University Press, 1931-53.

Kurfess, Alfons. "Christian Sibyllines." In E. Hennecke and W. Schneemelcher, 2: 703-45.

Laing, Lloyd. *Celtic Britain.* Britain Before the Conquest [Series]. A Paladin Book. London: Granada, 1981.

Lapidge, Michael. ed. *Archbishop Theodore.* Cambridge: Cambridge University Press, 1995.

Lapidge, Michael. *Irish Books and Learning in Mediaeval Europe.* Cambridge: Cambridge University Press, 1991.

Lasater, Alice. *Spain to England: A Comparative Study of Arabic, European, and English Literature of the Middle Ages.* Jackson, MI: University of Mississippi Press, 1974.

Lerner, Robert E. "The Medieval Return to the Thousand-Year Sabbath." In Emmerson and McGinn 51-71.

Leyerle, John. "The Interlace Structure of *Beowulf.*" *University of Toronto Quarterly* 3 (1967-68): 1-17.

Malone, Kemp. "*Beowulf.*" *English Studies* 29 (1948): 161-72.

Martin, John Stanley. *Ragnarök: An Investigation into the Old Norse Concepts of the Fate of the Gods.* Assen: Van Gorcum, 1972.

Matter, F. Ann. "The Apocalypse in Early Medieval Exegesis." In Emmerson and McGinn, 38-50.

McDonald, William J., ed. *New Catholic Encyclopedia.* 17 vols. New York: McGraw Hill, 1967-79.

McGinn, Bernard. *Apocalyptic Spirituality.* New York: Orbis, 1979.

———. *Apocalypticism in the Western Tradition.* Norfolk: Scholars Press, 1994.

———. "Early Apocalypticism: The Ongoing Debate." Patrides and Wittreich 2-39.

———. "Revelation." *The Literary Guide to the Bible.* Ed. Robert Alter and Frank Kermode. Cambridge, MA: Harvard University Press, 1987. 523-41.

———. *Visions of the End: Apocalyptic Traditions in the Middle Ages.* New York: Columbia University Press, 1979.

———. *Antichrist. Two Thousand Years of the Human Fascination with Evil.* San Francisco: Harper, 1994.

———. "Apocalypticism in the Middle ages: An Historiographical Sketch," *Mediaeval Studies* 37 (1975): 252-86.

McNamee, M. B. "*Beowulf:* An Allegory of Salvation?" *Journal of English and Germanic Philology (JEGP)* 59 (1960): 190-207.

Mellinkoff, Ruth. "Cain's Monstrous Progeny in *Beowulf:* Part I, Noachic Tradition." *Anglo-Saxon England* 8 (1979): 143-62.

Migne, J. P., ed. *Patrologiae Cursus Completus.* Series Latina. (*PL*).

Migne, J. P., ed. *Patrologiae Cursus Completus.* Series Graeca. (*PG*).

Morris, R., ed. and trans. *The Blickling Homilies of the tenth Century.* EETS S8, 63, 73. London: Trubner, 1874-80.

Newman, John K. *The Classical Epic Tradition.* Madison: University of Wisconsin Press, 1986.

Nicholson, L. E., ed. *An Anthology of Beowulf Criticism.* Notre Dame, IN: University of Notre Dame Press, 1963.

Nicholson, Lewis E. "The Literal meaning and Symbolic Structure of *Beowulf.*" *Classica et Medaevalia* 15 (1964): 151-201.

Niedner, Felix. "Ragnarok in der Voluspa." *Zeitschrift für deutsches Altertum* 43 (1899): 101-12.

Niles, John D. *Beowulf: The Poem and Its Tradition.* Cambridge, MA: Harvard University Press, 1983.

Niles, John D. "Ring Composition and the Structure of *Beowulf.*" *PMLA* 94 (1979): 924-35.

The Old English Vision of St. Paul. Ed. Antonette DiPaolo Healey. Speculum Anniversary Monographs 2. Cambridge, MA: The Medieval Academy of America, 1978.

Ogilvy, J. D. A. *Books Known to the English, 597-1066.* Medieval Academy of America

Publication No. 76. Cambridge, MA: Medieval Academy of America, 1967.

Ohlgren, Thomas H. "Some New Light on the Old English Caedmonian Genesis." *Studies in Iconography 1 (1975)*: 38-73.

———. "The Crucifixion Panel on the Gosforth Cross: A Janusian Image?" *Old English Newsletter* 20/2 (1987): 50-51.

Parker, Mary A. *Beowulf and Christianity.* New York: Peter Lang, 1987.

Parks, Ward. "The Traditional Narrator and the 'I Heard' formulas in Old English Poetry." *Anglo-Saxon England* (ASE) 16 (1987): 45-66.

Paschoud, François. "La doctrine chrétienne et l'idéologie impériale romaine." In Yves Christe, L'Apocalypse de Jean: Traditions exégétiques et iconographiques. Geneva, 1979.

Patrides, C. A. and Joseph Wittreich, eds. *The Apocalypse in English Renaissance Thought and Literature.* Ithaca, NY: Cornell University Press, 1984.

Puhvel, Martin. *Beowulf and the Celtic Tradition.* Waterloo, Ontario: Wilfrid Laurier University Press, 1979.

von Rad, Gerhard. *The Message of the Prophets.* Trans. D. M. G. Stalker. New York: Harper & Row, 1967.

Reeves, Margorie. "The Development of Apocalyptic Thought: Medieval Attitudes." Patrides and Wittreich 40-72.

Renfrew, Colin. *Archeology and Language: The Puzzle of Indo-Europeans.* New York: Cambridge University Press, 1987.

Riche, Pierr. Education and Culture in the Barbarian West: Sixthe through Eighth Centuries, trans. J.J. Contreni. New York: Columbia University Press, 1976

Risden, Edward. *Beasts of Time: Apocalyptic Beowulf.* New York: Peter Lang, 1994.

Robertson, D. W. "The Doctrine of Charity in Mediaeval Literary Gardens: A Topical Approach Through Symbolism and Allegory." *Speculum 27* (1951): 24-49. Rpt. in Nicholson 165-88.

Robertson, Orrin. *Old English and Its Closest Relatives.* Stanford: Stanford University Press, 1992.

Robinson, Douglas. *American Apocalypses: The Image of the End of the World in American Literature.* Baltimore: Johns Hopkins University Press, 1985.

Robinson, Fred C. *Beowulf and the Appositive Style.* Knoxville: University of Tennessee Press, 1985.

Rushdie, Salman. *Haroun and the Sea of Stories.* New York: Penguin, 1990.

Russell, James C. The Germanicization of Early Medieval Christianity. New York: Oxford University Press, 1994.

Sackur, Ernst. *Sibyllinische Texte und Forschungen.* Halle: Niemeyer, 1898.

Sage, C. M. *Paul Albar of Cordova.* Washington, DC: Catholic University Press, 1943.

Schimmel, Annemarie. *Mystical Dimensions of Islam.* Chapel Hill: University of North Carolina Press, 1975.

Schüssler-Fiorenza, Elisabeth. *The Book of Revelation: Justice and Judgment.* Philadelphia: Fortress, 1985.

Shippey, T. A. "Winchester in the Anglo-Saxon Period and After." In *Winchester: History and Literature.* Ed. Simon Barker and Colin Haydon. Winchester, 1992.

Smith, James I and Yvonne Y. Haddad. *The Islamic Understanding of Death and Resurrection.* Albany: State University of New York Press, 1981.

Smyth, Marina. *Understanding the Universe in Seventh-Century Ireland.* Woodbridge: Brewer and Boydell, 1996.

Strousma, R. "Aspects de l'eschatologie manicheenne." *Revue de l'histoire des religions* 198 (1981): 163-81.

Szarmach, Paul. ed. *Sources of Anglo-Saxon Culture.* Kalamazoo: Western Michigan University Press, 1986.

Thomas, Charles. *The Early Christian Archaeology of North Britain.* London: Oxford University Press, 1971.

Thompson, A Hamilton. ed., *Bede: His Life, Times, and Writings.* London: Oxford University Press, 1935.

Thorpe, Benjamin. ed. *The Homilies of the Anglo-Saxon Church: The First part, containing the Sermones Catholici or Homilies of Aelfric.* London: Oxford University Press, 1844.

Thundy, Zacharias P. "*Beowulf:* Date and Authorship." *Neuphilologische Mitteilungen* 87 (1986): 102-16.

———. "*Beowulf:* Meaning, Method, and Monsters." *Greyfriar* 24 (1983): 5-34.

———. "*Beowulf:* Geats, Jutes, and Asiatic Huns." *Littcrit* 17 (1983): 1-8.

———. *Buddha and Christ: Nativity Stories and Indian Traditions.* Leiden: E. J. Brill, 1993.

———. "The Qur'an: Source or Analogue of Bede's Caedmon Story?" *Islamic Culture* 63 (1989): 105-10.

Tietjen, Mary C. Wilson. "God, Fate, and the Hero of *Beowulf.*" *JEGP* 74 (1975): 159-71.

Tolan, John V. ed. *Medieval Christian Perceptions of Islam.* New York: Garland. 1996.

Tolkien, J. R. R. "*Beowulf:* The Monsters and the Critics." *Proceedings of the British Academy* 22 (1936): 245-95; reprinted in Nicholson.

Tonsfeldt, H Ward. "Ring Structure in *Beowulf.*" *Neophilologus* 61 (1977): 443-52.

Trawick, Buckner. *The Bible as Literature: The New Testament.* New York: Barnes & Noble, 1964.

Trawick, Buckner. *The Bible as Literature: The Old Testament and the Apocryphal* New York: Barnes & Noble, 1963.

Tripp, R. P. *More About the Fight with the Dragon: Beowulf, 2208b-3182, Commentary, Edition, and Translation.* Lanham, MD: University Press of America, 1983.

Turville-Petre, E. A. G. *Myth and Religion of the North: The Religion of Ancient Scandanavia.* New York: Holt, Rhinehart and Winston, 1964.

Vannemann, Theo. "Hochgermanisch und Niedergermanisch: Die Verzweigungstheorie der germanisch-deutschen Lautverschiebungen." *Beiträge zur Geschichte der deutschen Sprache und Literatur*, 106 (1964): 1-45.

Vasiliev, A. "Medieval Ideas of the End of the World: West and East." Byzantion 2 (1942/3): 462-502.

Vercelli Homilies IX-XXIII. Ed. Paul E. Szarmach. Toronto Old English Series 5.

Toronto: P, 1981.

Die Vercelli-Homilien: I- VIII. Ed. Max Forster. Bibliothek der angelsachsischen prose 12. 1932. Rpt. Darmstadt: Wissenschaftliche Buchgesellschaft, 1964.

Verdier, P. "Iconography of Apocalypse." McDonald 659-63.

Vielhauer, Philipp. "Apocalypses and Related Subjects: Introduction." In E. Hennecke and W. Schneemelcher, eds., *New Testament Apocrypha*, 2: 581-607. Philadelphia: Westminster, 1964.

Voluspa. Ed. Sigurour Nordal. Trans. B. S. Benedikz and John McKinnell Durham and St. Andrews Medieval Texts 1. Durham: Department of English Language and Medieval Literature, 1978.

Whitelock, Dorothy. *The Audience of Beowulf.* Oxford: Clarendon, 1951.

Whitelock, Dorothy. *English Historical Documents.* Vol. 1. New York: Oxford University Press. 1955.

Whitelock, Dorothy. ed. *Sermo Lupi ad Anglos.* Methuen's Old English Library. New York Appleton-Century-Crofts, 1966.

Williams, David. *Cain and Beowulf: A Study in Secular Allegory.* Toronto, Buffalo and London: University of Toronto Press, 1982.

Williams, Gerhild. *The Vision of Death: A Study of the "Momento Mori" Expressions in Some Latin, German, and French Didactic Texts of the 11th and 12th Centuries.* Goppinger Arbeiten zur Germantistik 191. Goppinger: Verlag Alfred Kummerle, 1976.

Wittreich, Joseph A. "'A Poet Amongst Poets': Milton and the Tradition of Prophecy." *Milton and the Line of Vision.* Ed. Joseph Wittreich. Madison, WI: University of Wisconsin Press, 1975. 97-142.

Wojcik, Jan, and Raymond-Jean Frontain, eds. *Poetic Prophecy in Western Literature.* Rutherford, NJ: Fairleigh, Dickinson University Press: London and Toronto: Associated University Presses, 1984.

Wormwald, Patrick. ed., *Ideal and Reality in Frankish and Anglo-Saxon Society.* Oxford: Oxford University Press, 1983.

Wormald, Patrick. "Bede, *Beowulf* and the Conversion of the Anglo-Saxon Aristocracy." *Bede and Anglo-Saxon England: Papers in Honor of the 1300th Anniversary of the Birth of Bede, Given at Cornell University in 1973 and 1974.* Ed. Robert T. Farrell. London: British Archaeological Reports 46, 1978. 32-90.

Wrenn, C. L. *A Study of Old English Literature.* New York: Norton, 1967.

Yorke, Barbara. "The Jutes of Hampshire and Wight and the Origins of Wessex." in Steven Bassett, ed. *The Origins of Anglo-Saxon Kingdoms.* Leicester: Leicester University Press, 1989.

Zadeh, Lotfi. "Fuzzy Sets." *Information and Control* 8 (1965): 338-53.

———. *Fuzzy Sets and Applications: Selected papers.* Edited by Yager, Ovchnikov, Tong, and Nguyen. New York: Wiley, 1987.

Index